Wrestling
with Our
Faith
Tradition

COLLECTED PUBLIC WITNESS, 1995–2004

Lloyd Lee Wilson

Quaker Press
  of Friends General Conference
Philadelphia, Pennsylvania

ISBN-13: 978-1-888305-36-4

Library of Congress Cataloging-in-Publication Data
Wilson, Lloyd Lee, 1947–
  Wrestling with our faith tradition : collected public witness, 1995/2004 / Lloyd Lee
Wilson. — 1st ed.
    p. cm.
  ISBN-13: 978-1-888305-36-4
  1. Society of Friends—Doctrines.   2. Christian life—Quaker authors.   I. Title.
BX7732.W499   2005
289.6—dc22
                                        2005013008

Cover art, *Jacob Wrestling with the Angel*, pen and ink drawing by Marianne Elliott.

Design and composition by David Budmen.

For further information about this publication
and other Quaker resources, please contact:

  Friends General Conference
  1216 Arch Street, 2B
  Philadelphia, PA 19107
  215-561-1700
  Or find us at www.fgcquaker.org

To order this or other publications call 800-966-4556
E-mail: bookstore@fgcquaker.org

You can order from us on the web at www.quakerbooks.org

*with deep appreciation to
my mother, and her generation*

To the Reader

Lloyd Lee Wilson, a recorded minister of the gospel and member of Rich Square Monthly Meeting, North Carolina Yearly Meeting (Conservative), submitted these texts of his spoken messages to the yearly meeting seeking clearness for him to publish them. Some members of the yearly meeting were present when these messages were first delivered; others have read these texts since, and have found them to be useful expositions of traditional Conservative Quaker faith and practice in the light of one contemporary Conservative Quaker's understanding.

Approved by the Representative Body
of North Carolina Yearly Meeting (Conservative)
in session at Cedar Grove Meetinghouse,
Woodland, North Carolina, Tenth Month 30, 2004

Table of Contents

Foreword

In 1993 a slim volume was published which continues to have an enormous impact within the spectrum of the Religious Society of Friends. This volume, *Essays on the Quaker Vision of Gospel Order*, by Lloyd Lee Wilson, explored aspects of the Quaker message, spiritual gifts and the faith community, and witness and testimonies. The combination of Lloyd Lee Wilson's knowledge of Quaker history, both deep and broad, and his ability to clearly articulate the contemporary Quaker experience makes this early volume accessible, useful, and encouraging to Quaker readers who have been longing for this expression of faith grounded within an historical context.

On the strength of the response to this earlier volume, and the known quality of Lloyd Lee Wilson's gift of speaking "to the condition" of Friends across the spectrum, many invitations followed the publication for Lloyd Lee Wilson to speak at various yearly meetings and Friends gatherings. It is these messages that have made their way into this new collection, *Wrestling with Our Faith Tradition*, which takes its title from one of the lectures. Divided into two sections, "Faith" and "Practice," the book spans ten years of Lloyd Lee Wilson's personal search for the fine balance between faithfulness to the tradition out of which our peculiar walk arises and living faithfully in our contemporary culture.

A strong central theme heard throughout the book is introduced in the first essay, "He Must Increase. . . ." We are invited to participate in the countercultural action of putting God at the center of our stories, rather than ourselves. The practice of "subtracting from our lives everything that interferes with our ability to listen, and allowing to remain only those things which enhance our ability to hear what God has to say to us" is offered as antidote to the powerful pull of the culture in which we are imbedded. As we can have a sense of ourselves in the cosmic story that begins with God, we may also come to see the meaning of our lives as being expressed in God's infinite love for us.

Listening, both individually and together, is a refrain throughout the essays. The importance of faith community to help one another hear and feel the guidance of the Holy Spirit is a critical element in realizing the kingdom of God on earth. In this realization, Quakers must concern themselves today to "address all the systemic evil that prevents the inbreaking of the kingdom of God in the present day, and that evil includes a great deal of nonviolent oppression." In seeking to find where the seeds of war and oppression are planted in our own lives, we are led into ever more integrated lives—kingdom lives. In this engagement we know, experientially, the truth of the following: "Our testimonies as Quakers are in their essence an attempt to communicate by direct action what we have witnessed about the truth of God and God's creation."

Unashamedly Christian, Lloyd Lee Wilson shares openly of his lifelong process of being born again, of his being shown early on by a mentoring Friend that everything he, new to Quakerism, liked about this particular faith walk stemmed from the fact that it is a Christian faith. In "A Confession of Faith" Lloyd Lee Wilson carefully defines the specificity of a Quaker Christian with gem-like phrases that speak of the often elusive distinctives. He is reminding the reader that our worship celebrates the loving presence of God rather than our devotion to God. His speaking of Friends as the "inheritors of a faith tradition that is pointed directly toward discovering that relationship (with the Divine) and preparing ourselves to participate in it," is an invitation into the Presence. That Friends have held two things to be true about capital-T truth—the first that truth is both complete in itself and unchanging over eternity—Christ the Son of God—the second that truth is incomplete and constantly unfolding—does much to illuminate how Quakerism has been called a third kind of Christianity.

The chorus of "changed lives" rings in and through these powerful essays. Many of us are resistant to change, and we are told that not only will our inner work be fierce and lifelong; the world around us will actively oppose our efforts. But within our loving community we can ask ourselves, "What does it mean for us to be children of God, God's agents in the world, at this particular time, this place, these people?" As we help one another recognize the gifts that God is sending through us, as we discern together what God is calling us to do, we can also address the question of why the world is the way that it is and how we can incarnate the kingdom of God in this world. Lloyd Lee Wilson, echoing the Inward Teacher, calls us to our higher purpose of bringing the kingdom of God into existence, by our life's work and witness.

— *Deborah Shaw, Greensboro, North Carolina, Third Month, 2005*

A Note about Bibles and Bible Translations

Some of the early readers of this book have asked about my use of a variety of translations of the Bible throughout, wondering if there is in my mind either a "default" Bible or some other discernible pattern about the use of a particular translation. I use a variety of translations in my study and in my personal devotions, and could not say that any one translation is always my preference. The good news contained in Scripture is bigger and fuller than can be expressed by any one translation, no matter how skilled the translators. Many passages of Scripture have multiple meanings or implications, beyond the capability of full expression by any one translation. One excellent translation of a particular verse may lift up some of these meanings, and another others.

When studying a passage of Scripture, I will typically look at the passage in a number of translations, trying to uncover the essence of its meaning by seeing how a number of English-speaking translators have expressed it. It is a great aid to study of this type to have use of a set of CD-based Bible translations, so one can compare multiple translations side-by-side on the computer screen, together with commentary and even reference to the underlying Greek or Hebrew words. The translation that best expresses the underlying thought I want to emphasize in a verse or passage is the one I will use in any given situation.

In explorations of how early Friends used and understood Scripture, I have preferred to use the King James Version, as that was the translation available to George Fox and his contemporaries. The King James Version is the Bible I grew up with in the church of the rural South, and its cadences still resonate in my heart in a very powerful way. The New English Bible, though, is the translation that opened the scriptures to me as an adult; encountering that translation for the first time was like looking into Chapman's *Homer*. In recent years, I have been using the New Jerusalem Bible for devotional reading, as it combines a poetic style with a slightly different perspective on familiar verses that keeps them fresh and helps me avoid reading without hearing the real message of the passage.

Part One
Faith

"He Must Increase . . ."

This talk was given at the opening sessions of Philadelphia Yearly Meeting in Third Month, 1998. I had been advised to "keep it short," as the yearly meeting had a considerable amount of business to accomplish that evening. It came to me to repeat one of the greatest, and shortest, sermons on record, and then to make a few comments on the same subject. The experience of standing in front of so many Friends in the historic Arch Street Meetinghouse, where so much North American Quaker history has transpired, made a never-to-be-forgotten impact upon me.

John the Baptist gave the greatest sermon on spiritual growth in Christian history—a sermon whose message rings through the ages, and has as much wisdom for you and me today as it did for his original audience some two thousand years ago. John said:

He must increase, and I must decrease.[1]

Among them that are born of women there has not risen a greater than John the Baptist,[2] but his encounter with Jesus of Nazareth can have but one conclusion: Jesus must increase, and John must decrease.

Two thousand years later, our own encounter with the risen Christ, the one who has come to teach his people himself, is no less real and no less dramatic than John's encounter with his cousin on the banks of the Jordan. And if we are to open ourselves to the reality of that encounter and all it promises us, there can be only one conclusion for us, as well: Christ must increase, and we must decrease.

Here is the gospel, the good news that God extends to every human being: "There is one, even Christ Jesus, who can speak to thy condition;" who not only can speak, but does speak, for "Christ has come to teach his people himself." When Christ speaks

[1] John 3:30.
[2] Matthew 5:19.

to you and me as individuals and to us as His gathered people, we better listen. What He has to say to us calls for one response: "He must increase, and we must decrease."

To make that response is to put God at the center of our story rather than ourselves. This is crucial to any understanding of Christian spiritual growth, and as such it is resisted at every moment and at every level. As infants and young children, through adolescence and into the first years of adulthood, our main task in life is to find out who we are as a unique individual and to develop that individual self to its highest potential. At this time of life, we are rightly at the center of our story—we are all rightly on the journey of ascent: the long climb up, to discover and live into who we are as precious personalities that have never been duplicated in the long history of humankind. From the first steps of the toddler and the youngster who demands, "Let me do it myself, Daddy!" to the self-confident young man who believes himself to be "Ten feet tall and bulletproof," we are striving to discover who we could be, and to make that potential self a reality. This is important work, and cannot be neglected or short-circuited. Part of our social troubles today stems from our failure to provide adequate means for young people to make this journey of ascent properly.

Beyond that time, the dominant culture of our day constantly presses home the message that we should continue to be at the center of our own stories, and that the dominant culture's lifestyle is the only way to treat ourselves properly. "Buy Pepsi, get stuff!" You and I live in the midst of a society that has raised the aggrandizement of self to the highest level, and that has unparalleled ability to cater to that exaltation of the individual.

Whether because of the dominant culture or human nature or some combination of the two, for some the journey of ascent never ends. They trade the games of youth for the corporate ladder, the social pyramid, or the alluring world of politics, with their power, prestige, and possessions. There is a hook for each of us, to pull us back into the center of the story, back onto the never-ending climb. But it is only when I give up the journey of ascent and begin the journey of descent that meaningful change happens, and deep spiritual growth can begin.

We make this transition by becoming broken: by realizing, often as a result of some painful experience, that we are fundamentally flawed and never going to reach the top of whatever pyramid we've been climbing. Then we remember that we depend on God for our continuation moment to moment, breath to breath, and spiritual growth can occur.

As we increase, as we make this journey of personal ascent, it becomes more and more important to protect the self at the center of our own story and to control our surroundings on its behalf. We work to control our outward appearance, our physical surroundings, our career development, our personal prestige and image, in order to protect the self we have worked so hard to discover and develop. We desire even to be in control of our spiritual growth— to keep the pace slow enough to be comfortable, to choose what we will incorporate into our sense of self, and when that will happen.

Jesus Christ our prophet sounds a counter-claim in the clearest of terms: that's not it. As we climb feverishly upward in the quest to find our true selves, to be nice to ourselves, to liberate the self within, to take care of our self, to give our self the luxuries it has earned and deserves, et cetera, et cetera, Jesus stands below and to one side, calling quietly but persistently: "I'm not up there, Lloyd Lee!"

Everything the society around us tells us about personal growth is about being in control, being in charge, being the one who makes the choices. The goal, after all, is to actualize the self—to make me the best person I can possibly be, to maximize my potential and enhance my performance as employee, spouse, parent, entrepreneur or whatever. It is all about the journey of ascent, and Jesus is standing below and to one side, saying "That's not it, folks!"

At some point, some of us realize that He's right: that's not it— it doesn't work. Putting one's self at the center doesn't work, because it ultimately must fail. No matter what attention I give to my personal development, my individual rights, my physical and emotional and mental health, my financial security and my estate planning, ultimately the me at the center of this story dies. Whatever we build on and around, other than God, ultimately dies—it lets us down.

When that realization hits it is devastating—no softer word will do. George Fox spent three and a half years looking for something to put at the center of his story: the liturgy of the established church, the wisdom of educated Christian pastors, the stability of married life, the discoveries of the Dissenters. Nothing was satisfactory, and George reported:

> I fasted much, walked abroad in solitary places many days, and often took my Bible, and sat in hollow trees and lonesome places till night came on; and frequently in the night walked mournfully about by myself; for I was a man of sorrows in the time of the first workings of the Lord in me.[3]

> I cannot declare the misery I was in, it was so great and heavy upon me.[4]

Finally, Fox experienced the truth that only God could satisfy his hunger:

> When all my hopes in [priests and separatist preachers] and in all men were gone, so that I had nothing outwardly to help me, nor could I tell what to do, then, oh, then, I heard a voice which said, "There is one, even Christ Jesus, that can speak to thy condition" and when I heard it, my heart did leap for joy.[5]

We cannot truly put God at the center of our story unless and until we have experienced that no one and no thing other than God at the center can give us satisfaction. Only the journey of ascent can teach us that the journey we should be on—must be on—is the journey of descent.

When our pride is broken and we are willing to exchange the journey of ascent and increase for the journey of descent and decrease, the tender mercies of God surround us and we find that balm in Gilead told of in the old spiritual. But healing, the end of sorrow, and even the joy of the presence of the Lord are only the start of the story. God has a much larger purpose in mind than simply putting an end to our despair and helping us feel good. We are being called to bring the kingdom of God into existence, by our life's work and witness.

[3] George Fox, *Journal*, 1647, Rufus Jones edition, p. 79.
[4] *Ibid.*, p. 80.
[5] *Ibid.*, p. 82.

This is the great purpose God sets before you and me today—to play our part in enfleshing the kingdom of God. We are called to an Abrahamic journey, leaving the familiar to walk with God as a stranger in a strange land, always inviting and invoking a kingdom that is now and not yet, about to become and already here.

How do we learn of this purpose and our tasks within the scheme of this great journey? By listening to Christ our Teacher, our Prophet and our Guide. By the *via negativa*: the path of subtracting from our lives everything that interferes with our ability to listen, and allowing to remain only those things which enhance our ability to hear what God has to say to us. For nearly everyone, sooner or later and usually sooner, the most important interference is ourselves. Our own ego, our own willfulness, our own creatureliness—whatever name we give it—it is our self that most blocks our ability to hear Christ's voice. The solution: He must increase, and we must decrease.

Now this is a peculiar vision of the nature of spiritual growth, and bears looking at directly. I am saying that spiritual growth is not an increase in one's placid nature, or improvement in vegan diet; it is not great devotion to a program of social reform or an increase in simplicity, or any other form of personal piety. Spiritual growth is no more and no less than an increase in one's ability to hear and respond to Jesus Christ the Teacher, Prophet, and Guide—an increase in spiritual discernment.

Discernment is the spiritual gift we all share, and the gift that we experience in its fullness only when we exercise it together. Discernment is nothing more or less than the ability to hear what it is that Christ is saying to us at this moment in time, in this very place. Some Friends have described it as another sense, like sight, hearing or touch. I like that metaphor, because these other senses are inherent in all of us, yet we can learn to use them to their fullest potential only through long years of patient effort. The help of more experienced teachers can help us appreciate a fine painting or symphony, but cannot actually show us the colors as the teacher sees them, or the harmonies as she hears them. We must learn for ourselves to see, and hear, and understand.

To grow spiritually we must learn to hear and understand and open ourselves to what it is that Christ the Teacher has come to teach us, the truth that Christ the Prophet has come to reveal to us, the path that Christ the Guide has come to make clear to us. But how can I tell what Christ has to say to me? How can I tell whether the voice I hear is truly Christ's? These are questions I hear over and over again as I travel among Friends.

To learn to hear, one must devote oneself to learning to listen—and spend time listening. This is discernment in its most fundamental meaning: to discern the voice of God, in the sense of being able to hear it at all, and to discern the voice of God in the sense of being able to distinguish that Voice from all the other voices clamoring for our attention. It is a cornerstone of our existence as a faith people that God is speaking to you and to me, and that we can hear that Voice. When George Fox heard that voice say there is one who can speak to thy condition, even Christ Jesus, he was putting into words what has since been the experience of a cloud of witnesses stretching through the generations from seventeenth-century England to you and me in this room tonight, and to other Friends in other meeting rooms all over the world.

Spiritual growth involves a kind of pruning like that spoken of by Jesus in John 15:2: not only the barren branches must be cut away from our life, but the fruitful ones must be pruned as well, to make them more fruitful still. This is the paradox of the orchardist, who makes apple trees more fruitful by cutting away their branches, and the paradox of our spiritual life, which becomes more full and more fruitful as we remove things from it, by means of the *via negativa*.

So one starts with the assumption that we have the ability to hear God's voice speaking to you and me individually. How do we hear that still, small voice in the midst of the cacophony of the modern world? Like trying to hear our mother's voice over a bad telephone connection, we either ask God to speak up, or we strive to surround ourselves with silence so we can concentrate on what's being said (or both).

With a few notable exceptions—the incident on the road to Damascus comes to mind—God seems not to shout at us very much—it is just not God's style. As the prophet learned, God is not in the earthquake or the tornado, but in the still, small voice that persists in the silence afterward. So while it is always useful to pray that God will speak up, it is good policy to be enfolding ourselves in silence at the same time. This is the *via negativa*. I may not be able to tell which voice is God's in my life today, but I can pick out one that is not God, and silence it or eliminate it from my life. Then I can pick out another one that is not God, and quiet that voice as well. If I keep on with this process, God's voice will come to stand out more and more, as there is less and less competition for my attention and loyalty.

To know which of these voices to silence and to which we should give our attention, one must test the spirit(s). Again, we know from Scripture and from the testimony of those who have gone before us that this is possible, but we mostly don't know how to do it, and distrust anyone who claims that they do. Remember that ours is an experiential faith, not a dogmatic one—so if we are to be about the business of testing the spirits, the test will be one of experience, not one of doctrine or dogma.

We must put what we have heard to the test of critical reflection and then apply the fruit of that reflection to our common life. In that process we will be able to discern what is of God and what is not. In short, to know the word at all we must be doers of the word, and not hearers only.

This is a new way of knowing for most of us, because it does not depend on *a priori* principles which can be applied to our experience, but relies on our experience to unveil principles which can then guide future experience. Luke's account of the two disciples on the road to Emmaus the afternoon of the resurrection is an excellent teaching example of how we can use this cycle of reflection and action, sometimes called the cycle of praxis, to bring about spiritual growth.

At the beginning of Luke's story the two disciples are asking each other, "What is going on here?" This is the first point of the story. The two disciples are not trying to construct a theory or theology into which they can fit the events of the crucifixion and resurrection; they are recounting the events themselves—reviewing what actually happened. As they walk along, they meet a stranger on the road—apparently a rabbi, because he is certainly familiar with the law and the prophets. He makes the second point: to understand the present, you have to know and understand what has gone on before. He shows them the connection between Jesus' life and the great story. As they reflect together on recent events in the light of Jewish history, they come to a new understanding of the messiah and the meaning of redemption. This is intellectually stimulating, but things don't really fall into place until they put their new understanding into action by a redeeming act: they invite this stranger to a meal with them—they make him their companion. This action catalyzes their understanding, as they recognize Jesus in his action—they know him in the breaking of the bread of their meal.

Now Luke makes his final point: in the instant of their recognition, Jesus disappears! As educated North Americans on the edge of the next millennium, you and I may have difficulty with the physics of that report: in our experience, people don't just disappear into thin air. The theology of the story at this moment should be clear nonetheless: as soon as the moment of insight is reached around the table, the action is no longer around the table. The disciples do not take time to relax and bask in the afterglow of this miraculous experience, but get up immediately and head back to Jerusalem—which is where the action is, after all. They left as dispirited, frightened, bewildered men who had just had their fondest hopes crushed and were afraid for their lives; they returned as part of a small band of believers who were about to turn the world upside down.

When we put aspects of our own life to this test of praxis, to determine what should be broken off and what pruned to become more fruitful, we are engaging in discernment—in spiritual growth. We grow by decreasing: by subtracting from our life all that is manifestly not of God, and by putting what remains to the test of praxis, of action and critical reflection, and discarding all that does not meet the test. Both steps—subtraction and praxis—require that we give up control, familiarity, and even stability for a new life with God at the center.

The Friend who invited me to speak this evening said that this session would be considering "Change as an Opportunity for Spiritual Growth." What I am saying about change is that it is not an opportunity among others for spiritual growth. I am saying that change is the only condition under which spiritual growth occurs. By change I don't mean what happens when I choose to change jobs, or decide to change apartments, or make a New Year's resolution to change my diet. Change is what happens when I am no longer in control, no longer making the choices, and no longer able to maintain the illusion that I am at the center of the story. Stability is the fruit of the journey of ascent: an increasing desire and ability to protect oneself from meaningful change. Stability can be defined as that state in which we are able to buy our way out of change, to protect ourselves from the necessity to grow spiritually. Change is the fruit of the journey of descent, the blessed state of inner poverty in which we no longer have the choice or option of staying as we are. The risen Christ sent word to the first disciples that they should get up and leave where they were, for he had gone before them, into Galilee. Christ is always telling us to get up and leave, to get up and change, to get up and grow.

We often forget this, in the individual age in which we live, but the task to which we are called is corporate, not individual. We are not being called to lives of individual piety or righteousness, we are being called to establish the kingdom of God, and that by its very nature is a corporate undertaking. Over against the individualism of the current age, Christ calls us to be a kingdom people. Our call— our vocation—is not to build up our personal righteousness, and not to build up the Religious Society of Friends as an institutional church full of saints. Our call is to establish the kingdom of God here and now, at this place and time, with the materials at hand. The question is not "How can I be saved?" and certainly not "Have you been saved, sister?" The question is "Why is the world this way, and how can we incarnate the kingdom of God in this world?"

The kingdom of God is a term that troubles some sensitive souls, because it smells of patriarchy and submission. I know of no other term, however, that carries so many of the subversive nuances of meaning that are included in this vision of how the world is to become. For early Friends, and for early Christians, the kingdom of God was subversive of economic life as well as political institutions; it deconstructed patriarchy and other social organizations and reorganized all of creation, people included, into a new harmony.

The sign of spiritual growth is that the individual has moved more fully into the kingdom of God, and that is a corporate experience. God's plan involves bringing groups of individuals into a new order, a new harmony, in order to establish the kingdom, and this can happen only to the extent that those individuals and those groups are willing to place God at the center of their story.

While our structures and patterns are intended to provide continuity and stability, the real effort needed is to embrace necessary change—which is never our first reaction to the new and unexpected. Even the disciples of Christ, who knew first hand the fresh gospel in all its power, were constantly trying to fit this new experience into old patterns and familiar ways of understanding. At the Transfiguration, Peter wanted to build three shelters—to understand this brand new experience in terms of what was familiar—when what was needed was an appreciation that God was doing something new in the world. Not unconnected with what had gone before—in fact deeply rooted in it—but something new, nevertheless, which must be understood in new ways.

Our call, both individually and corporately, is to enflesh the kingdom of God, and to do that we must get up from where we have been and move into new space, made sacred by our faithfulness. Like Abram, we are called to change our familiar surroundings and move into a strange, new world. Like Abram, we may never see the fulfillment of the new kingdom, though we may be allowed a glimpse, as he was given a view of the night sky and understood that his descendants, heirs of the covenant, would be even more numerous than the stars. You and I can even begin this journey only because we understand, on some deep level, that God must be at the center of our story, and not ourselves. The journey itself is no more and no less than the realization that He must increase, and I must decrease—and working that truth into the warp and woof of our daily life. That journey ends with Christ in eternity.

A Confession of Faith

The annual J. M. Ward Lectures have been a part of the Guilford College experience since at least the 1950s. As a 2004–2005 Distinguished Quaker Visitor at Guilford, I was asked to deliver the lecture for 2004. My struggles to discern the right topic are documented below; the satisfying part was the number of young people who attended, listened to the lecture, and asked such good questions afterward.

Those of you who know me know that I do not accept pre-assigned topics when I am invited to speak to a group; in fact, over the years my own ability to predict what my subject might be has been proven to be quite modest. It is my practice to enter into the Divine Conversation, seeking some guidance there about what I should say. That guidance is often quite different from what I would have chosen had it been my decision to make.

A few weeks ago I went to our regular First Day morning worship while I was engaged in this discernment. In the course of worship, several possible topics came to mind, but none with the power that would identify them as the right one. The meeting had been silent for about forty-five minutes when I asked God whether I should simply share my own faith with you all. Immediately, the patriarch of our yearly meeting spoke up in his usual strong voice:

> I've been thinking this morning of the words of Paul, who said, "I am not ashamed of the gospel, because it is the power of God for the salvation of everyone who believes: first for the Jew, then for the Gentile."[6] Like Paul, I am not ashamed of the gospel; I am not ashamed to be called a Christian, and not ashamed to be called a Quaker.

All I could do at that point was to look heavenward and think to myself, "Thanks, God—I heard that one. I'll get right on it!"

6 Romans 1:16.

So tonight I want to make a confession of faith. I want to give an account of the joy that is in me, and why it survives and thrives and sustains me through the often dark times of life, and why what I have found to be true is cause for celebration when I rise, in my goings out and comings in, and when I reflect on each day at day's end.

Though I was born in a very rural section of Maryland's Eastern Shore, I was raised and educated in the great tradition of the modern mind. I have two degrees from the Massachusetts Institute of Technology, and the entire progress of my early life was a testament to the faith that the intellect and reason of human beings could and would solve all our problems, leading humanity ever forward in a steady progress toward a better and better world. More technology would solve all our problems. In that gestalt, or worldview, the real world was what could be measured and touched and understood; God's involvement was primarily to monitor behavior along a limited number of moral prohibitions.

It has become increasingly clear over several decades, even to people like me, that there is another world—or another way of seeing and understanding this world—and in that different gestalt, God is reaching out to be in relationship with each one of us, to be our companion and guide and healer and teacher and many more things beside. As Hamlet might have observed, "There are more things in heaven and earth, Lloyd Lee, than are dreamt of in your philosophy."[7]

It has not been an easy journey. Before I could see the world in this new way, and experience God reaching out for me, my old world had to be broken and my confidence that I was in charge of my own life had to be overcome. Before that happened, I had some painful times and caused other persons considerable pain as well. Perhaps the most excruciating time was immediately after receiving my undergraduate degree, when I realized I was now an Air Force officer headed off to help fight the war in Viet Nam—a war that no longer made sense to me.

It was my great fortune, and a blessed bit of divine intervention, that at the moment I was broken open and able to see just a little

[7] William Shakespeare, *Hamlet*, Act I, Scene V.

bit of this different paradigm, I encountered Friends. It was a further blessing that in the meeting I was led to, all unwitting, there were a number of seasoned Friends who understood the faith tradition and were clear in articulating that tradition to brash youngsters like myself who were likely to jump to all the wrong conclusions about who and what Quakers were and are. When I remarked to Tim Nicholson, soon after I started attending meeting, that Quakers were the most radical people I had ever encountered, he quietly replied that Quakers weren't radical at all; they were conservative, trying to re-establish the first century Christian church. That set the wheels in my mind spinning, to be sure!

Because these Friends were faithful, because God did not abandon me even when I tried to abandon God, I have come to know the Holy Spirit of Christ, and to become in a small way a learner in the school of Christ. Against all my expectations, and to some extent against my intention, I have become a Christian.

Specifically, I have become a Quaker Christian. Christianity is a large tent, as I am increasingly becoming aware, and it seems to me practically impossible to say simply "I am a Christian" in any more than the most general of terms. I am a Quaker Christian, because I encounter and am guided by and wait upon Christ in the context of that tributary of the great stream of Christianity called Quakerism.

Now some may say that Quakerism is post-Christian, or no longer Christian, or any number of similar things; but I testify to you all that the root and nurture and sustenance of Quakerism is Jesus Christ the risen and returned Lord of Creation. Whether you are personally Christian or not, my word to you is the same word that was given to me some thirty-five years ago: "You can believe anything you want, Lloyd Lee, but you have to remember that everything you like about Quakerism stems from the fact that it is a Christian faith."[8]

Well now immediately some folks are going to want to pick apart those words, and discuss what I mean by them, and whether they mean the same things, and whether or not that is so, whether they can agree with them. That's a good thing, and it is vitally necessary to keep our faith a living faith, and not a dead hand of

[8] Elmer Brown, personal communication, c. 1969.

past tradition. In fact, I'd like to do exactly that for a little bit tonight, because the vocabulary of Christianity is so diverse, as I alluded to earlier, that we don't know what either one of us means unless we do a little work together.

The context for my exploration and explanation is what I've come to call the classic Quaker tradition. Classic Quakerism is not the Quakerism of George Fox or Elizabeth Hooten, who preached the original vision, but it is the current manifestation of that vision. Some rough edges have been smoothed over the centuries, and some new insights have been incorporated in an incremental process of continuing revelation. We can't recreate the Quakerism of two hundred or three hundred years ago, and should not try. What we can and must do, if we are to be faithful to our own roots, is to ask how that earlier vision has been sustained and nurtured over the centuries, and where and how it survives in the present day.

The best one-sentence description of classic Quakerism I have encountered comes from the historical sketch in the current Discipline of North Carolina Yearly Meeting (Conservative), to which I belong. The Discipline speaks of Friends who sought

> to maintain the doctrines of the immediate and perceptible guid-
> ance of the Holy Spirit, of the headship of Christ over all things to
> his Church, and of the waiting worship and inspirational ministry
> which are, and must ever be, the outgrowth of these doctrines.

I have come to know, in my experience, in the daily activities of my life, the immediate and perceptible guidance of the Holy Spirit. I have come to recognize that my Guide is Christ, who bridges the divide between human and divine and reassures me, by precept and example, that the love of God for me, for my fellow humans, and indeed for all of creation, cannot be broken. No matter how badly we treat God, no matter how much we try to run from God, God will not run from us nor abandon us, nor cease to love us utterly. This for me is one of the deepest meanings of the Incarnation—an ever-loving God. It is an awesome thing to fall into the arms of an ever-loving God.

I know from experience, or as George Fox would have said, experimentally, that God who loves me offers guidance continually, and that this guidance is perceptible. From experience, I have put my faith in the fact that this guidance is aimed at my deepest happiness. What loving parent would not want to guide her children toward the good and away from the hurtful? What parent would guide his child in ways imperceptible or unintelligible to the child? God's help and instruction, God's guidance, is not out there where we cannot feel it, and it is not given in code or language and symbols we cannot understand. God's guidance is real and perceptible, offered in ways we can feel and understand, once we commit ourselves to listening and waiting for it.

God's loving guidance is perceptible, and it is immediate. Immediate guidance, to Friends, means guidance without a mediator, whether human or scriptural. The Holy Spirit's immediate guidance to me has taken a wonderfully wide variety of forms: there have been visions and voices, nudges, once the sight of a wooden light fixture in a Kentucky retreat house, and there is that indescribable moment in meeting for worship when I realize that I have been given a message to share. As I shared earlier, the Holy Spirit's guidance has at times included vocal ministry that seems directly aimed at my inner thoughts!

What is the content of this guidance? One's initial response might say it is to guide us toward the good and away from evil. My sense is, however, that if this is all we hear from the Inward Guide we are to some extent selling it short. There are many guides that will take us that far, if no farther: the rule of law, or any of numerous systems of ethics, such as the consideration of the greatest good for the greatest number, will help us differentiate between good and evil. No, my sense is that the most important guidance we receive is that which helps us choose between the good and the Gospel.

The relationship into which God is calling us and toward which the Holy Spirit guides us is more than an ethical life, more than living in accordance with any standards of morality, more than being a good person. God is not badgering us into some moral achievement, some sort of divine merit badge. God is offering us abundant life—the life for which we were intended and designed and which is the ground of true happiness—life in intimate relationship with our Creator who loves us. The question that divine guidance answers best, in my experience, is not "What is the right thing to do in this situation?" but "What does it mean for me to live in relationship with the all-loving God, Creator and Sustainer of the universe, in this moment and in this place?" The answers to that question transcend questions of what is ethical behavior or good behavior; they begin to establish the kingdom of God here on earth.

The headship of Jesus Christ over all things to his church, in my own experience, refers not to the buildings of the institutional church or the institutions themselves, but to that invisible church that is the Body of Christ. As a part of that invisible church, I acknowledge that I am not my own, but Christ's, and I seek to allow Christ's will to rule in me in all things. It is not so much that I squash my own will, but that I seek always to be such a person that God's will is my own. I fail utterly in this effort, but I continue to make the effort.

It has been my experience, over and over again, that the things and activities valued by this world are ultimately unsatisfying, ultimately hollow. When I step out of the flow and try to separate myself from the noise and chatter, I discover that there is One there already, who knows me and has been waiting for me. It is the Creator, who made all things and who sustains them from moment to moment by the will that the universe should continue.

But it is more than that. The One I meet in the silence did not simply wind up the universe and let it go, like a seven-day clock. God cares about and is present in the world you and I inhabit today, intervening in the affairs of human and beast to relieve our suffering and to keep us from going irretrievably astray. The great themes of Exodus move me to the deep precisely because I see and feel them acted out in me and all around me time after time after time. God hears the cry of those who suffer, even when they are not calling to God; God cares that they suffer, and God intervenes in the world on their behalf.

This divine intervention is not God as Lone Ranger, appearing from nowhere to punish the bad guys and make sure the good folks get the rewards they deserve. As Quoheleth, the Preacher, wrote thousands of years ago in the book we know as Ecclesiastes, a quick look around will demonstrate that the world does not work like that. God doesn't give everybody what I think they deserve all the time. And for that we can all be thankful: that God is not bound by what I think or know or understand—or, for that matter, by what you think or know or understand.

God is far beyond my understanding. There's a wonderful passage in Job when Yahweh responds to Job's demand for an explanation of why Yahweh has not, in Job's eyes, acted justly. "Where were you," Yahweh says, "when I set the foundations of the world? I don't remember you holding the plumb line when I lined up the heavens! Where were you standing when I separated the seas from the land?" In other words, we mortal finite beings can't hope to fully comprehend God or God's actions—we're just too limited.

What was true for Job is true for you and me also. My response to God's presence is Job's response—to cover my mouth with my hands, to listen and worship more than to talk. And yet, when I do feel that I have learned some little bit of truth about God, it gives me a joy beyond description. Robert Barclay was right when he wrote in his first Proposition that "the height of all happiness is placed in the true knowledge of God."[9]

I cannot comprehend God, but it is a certainty in my heart that God comprehends me. The demonstration that this is so is the life, death, and resurrection of Jesus of Nazareth, who was clearly a human being yet also possessed the Spirit of God to an unprecedented degree. I cannot say how Jesus came to have such a gift of the Spirit, and it is not of much importance to me to discuss exactly when the gift was given; but that he had that Spirit is to me beyond doubt.

I say this because my soul shivers when I hear and reflect on the stories of Jesus' life and of his followers. I say this also because it is in the form of the Spirit that was in Jesus that my connection with God is established, strengthened, and sustained.

For this reason, the precept and example of Jesus are especially important to me. Both his teachings and the example of his actions inform and guide me. When they seem to agree on a particular point, that carries a double strength.

9 Robert Barclay, *Apology for the True Christian Divinity*, Proposition I.

I am a born-again Christian. In this, I am in unity with the advices of my yearly meeting, which state clearly:

> let the words of our Holy Redeemer have due place with us all, "Ye must be born again."[10]

Friends have understood this experience of being born again somewhat differently from other Christian traditions. While some groups and individuals are filled with joy to be able to point to a specific place and time at which they were born again and their salvation was accomplished, Friends have understood the analogous event in their own lives to be only a starting point for a long process of growth into holiness. I can readily describe the time period in which I was convicted, to use the old Quaker phrase, that my old life was wrongly ordered, and I can remember vividly that meeting for worship in which I was convinced, to use another Quaker phrase, that the life of Friends was rightly ordered. But it seems to me, in my experience and in the writings of Friends, that this birth event, if that is what it was, was only the beginning of a new life. What counts is not when or where one was re-born, but how one lives the subsequent life.

I have tried to be, in Quaker terminology, a humble learner in the school of Christ for about thirty-five years now. Graduation day, though still uncertain, is getting closer. Have I learned anything? Have I put what I've learned into practice? Have I been a blessing to my fellow students, and indeed to all of creation? These questions form an *examen* each of us can ponder.

Graduation day is coming: graduation into what? Although I have increasingly come to understand and resonate with my father's conclusion that you make your heaven or hell here on earth, I also have come to believe that there is some continued life beyond death. William Penn wrote of "the reality of eternal rewards and punishments"[11] as one of three principle doctrines of the Religious Society of Friends. Otherwise, Penn said, Quakers would be the most miserable of people, having suffered terribly for forty years for

---

10 Discipline, North Carolina Yearly Meeting (Conservative), 1983.

11 William Penn, *The Rise and Progress of the People Called Quakers*, in *Twenty-First Century Penn*, edited by Paul Buckley, ESR, 2003, p. 363.

their beliefs. Some of our Christian brothers and sisters preach a sort of fire escape theology, emphasizing the eternal punishments that await those who do not believe and act rightly in this life. On the other hand, Friends like Philip Gulley[12] have recently written that God's grace means everyone will be "saved" and receive eternal rewards.

For myself, it seems most likely that life in some new form continues after the death which is familiar to us all—but it seems unlikely that any of us have a clear handle on what that life will be like. I like to say, "When we get to heaven, *everybody* is going to be surprised!" As for rewards and punishments, it seems to me that if Robert Barclay is right in saying that the height of all happiness results from the true knowledge of God—and I think he is—then the depth of all unhappiness must be the result of ignorance of God. My experience is that God is continually seeking to reveal the Divine nature to each one of us, and that the Divine nature is love in all its fullness. To remain ignorant of that love takes an act of will—which God, in infinite respect for our free will, allows to continue throughout our human lives and even beyond. "Hell," if one cares to use that name, consists precisely in the self-willed alienation from God, in this life or the next, and lasts just as long as a human being continues to will that alienation. No additional punishment is necessary—the sense of separateness from God is sufficient.

But that alienation, that separation, is always self-inflicted. God is indeed a God of love, a God of relationship, a God who yearns deeply and passionately to be in a loving, harmonious relationship with all of creation—humans, other creatures, and the inanimate parts of the universe as well. In my experience, God is always revealing to humans how to live in that harmony, and enabling us to do that. So in that seemingly endless debate about who is saved and who isn't, my understanding is that everyone can be saved—but when and where is up to the individual.

God's continuing effort to reveal the divine will and enable us to live in harmony with it is the substance of the "immediate and

12 Philip Gulley and James Mulholland, *If Grace Is True: Why God Will Save Every Person*, HarperSanFrancisco, 2003.

perceptible guidance" of which I spoke earlier. Because God is engaged in this great work of self-revelation and communion, we can indeed come to know God and live in relationship with God directly.

For this reason, we can settle into meeting for business and seek to find unity with the mind of Christ, to use an old term. Our decisions come not by majority vote, not by general agreement, not by human reason alone, but by seeking out and being receptive to the divine will for this group of Friends at this time.

For similar reasons, our worship celebrates the loving presence of God rather than our devotion to God. We gather in expectant waiting, with faith in the experience that if we turn our hearts and minds to God, we will once again discover that God is with us, among us, in us personally and corporately. We need not make a mighty noise to get God's attention, or make our petitions with eloquent words, or declare our loyalty and devotion to God. God is with us already, God knows our deepest needs, longings, and loyalties. All we need to do is to sit quietly, making space in our selves for the presence of God to become known.

It so happens, from time to time, that God decides to offer some explicit guidance to the corporate worship, and then we experience inspirational ministry. Our vocal offerings in worship are not our insights, or our human assessment of what the gathered body ought to hear or to learn, but God's offering to us all, through a human instrument. Our ability to hear God, even in this favorable setting, depends on our willingness not to clutter up the air with our own human messages, and to open our hearts to the messages of others, seeking to discern the voice of God in each one.

The joy that comes when Friends are truly gathered in worship, when they allow themselves to be covered, in the old phrase, by the Holy Presence, is another piece of that happiness from knowing God, and from doing what it means to be in relationship with the Lord of All in this moment and time.

So I stand before you all this evening—a work in progress. Not yet what I hope in time to become, yet no longer that person I once was, either. I am filled with joy that in the midst of a world that seems often about to overwhelm us all with grief and pain, sorrow and suffering, a Divine Friend has come to me in my human need to console and heal, to teach and guide, to offer and sustain a relationship that brings me great happiness no matter what darkness may surround me.

You and I, Friends, are inheritors of a faith tradition that is pointed directly toward discovering that relationship and preparing ourselves to participate in it. It requires of us that we quiet ourselves to hear the Divine conversation; that we open our eyes to the reality that God, not our own egos, is at the center of the universe; and that we humble ourselves to learn what God yearns to teach us. Let us honor that inheritance by living lives worthy of the love God has for each of us. Let us nurture and sustain that inheritance so that the generations following us may also drink of the same living water.

Wrestling with Our Faith Tradition

Southern Appalachian Yearly Meeting and Association (SAYMA) is a relatively young yearly meeting, spread over a very large territory, including part of North Carolina, where I make my home. I was honored to be able to accept their invitation to speak at yearly meeting sessions in Sixth Month 2003, and quite surprised to discover, some months later, that the invitation was to speak on two nights, not the usual one! As way opened, I was given material for two presentations, one focused mostly on faith and one on the implications that faith has for our common practice. These lectures eventually were published as an issue of the Journal of North Carolina Yearly Meeting (Conservative).

Part 1: Faith . . .

Dear Friends. We gather for these yearly meeting sessions in disheartening times. The broader North American culture in which we live appears in many ways to be falling apart at the seams. The "big ideas" that gave our culture a sense of order, stability, and meaning seem to be crumbling before our eyes, and the world is rapidly changing all around us—and seemingly not for the better.

The idea that humankind is inevitably progressing, evolving to a higher state, is denied daily by our inhumanity to one another. The moral authority of our institutions of religion and government and their ability to give order and meaning to our lives are undermined by the tragic flaws and blatant inconsistencies of those very institutions and the people who sustain them. The enlightenment project to develop a coherent secular, humanistic moral code has collapsed into a simple me-first code of the jungle. At the same time we are semi-intentionally continuing an environmental catastrophe covering the entire planet. All of this is accompanied by the soundtrack of the Twenty-first century—an unceasing cacophony of images, sounds, and data which overwhelms our ability to make any sense of it all, or even to take it all in.

There are several Quaker responses possible to our circumstances. The hopeless sort of Quaker develops a kind of siege mentality: we can't win against these overpowering forces, but we'll hold out heroically till the bitter end. Similar to this is the "faithful remnant" mentality: we can't win, but we'll hold out heroically until God intervenes on our behalf and shows all those other folks we were right all along.

Other Quakers still hope to redeem the world around us, and some seek for a way to adapt the faith tradition to what they perceive as a changed world: to make Quakerism more palatable to non-Quakers, often by making it more familiar in various ways. If one considers membership as a measure of success in ministering to the hurts of the world, these Friends have enjoyed a certain measure of success.

It is my sense, however, that what is needed—what we need as a people of faith and what the world needs—is not to change our faith and practice to fit modern times and circumstances. What we need is to understand more clearly the ways in which our faith tradition speaks directly to our needs and the needs and desires of the people all around us. I suggest this because the faith tradition as it exists already offers healing and transformation in each of these areas. To paraphrase G. K. Chesterton's famous comment, "The problem with classic Quakerism is not that it has been tried and found wanting, but that it has been found difficult and therefore left untried."[13]

I believe that classic Quaker spirituality and Quaker practice have particular relevance to the post-modern world in which we North Americans live. All around us are people whose old structures of values and meaning for life are to a greater or lesser extent inoperable. As a culture we no longer believe in absolute truth or

13 G. K. Chesterton said, "The Christian ideal has not been tried and found wanting; it has been found difficult and left untried." *What's Wrong with the World*, 1910, chapter 5.

ultimate meaning; we are suspicious of any central authority or institutional hierarchy that attempts to instruct us as to what is real or what we should believe. At the same time our hunger for God and our yearning to feel meaning and purpose in life is as strong as at any point in history.

Where there are no acceptable larger structures to which one can turn to find meaning, one will create meaning around oneself. This is happening to an unprecedented extent all around us, and the result is the rampant individualism that is so characteristic of our place and time. Even so, human beings understand at a very deep level that they need some larger truth, that putting themselves at the center of the story is ultimately dissatisfying. It is dissatisfying because eventually, no matter how important I consider myself to be or how many toys I accumulate, I die.

To these individuals seeking a larger truth, yet suspicious of institutional hierarchy or authority, Quakerism offers a spirituality that honors the unique worth and value of the individual as one in direct communion with the largest truth of all: God. In place of the authority of the institutional church, or of Holy Scripture, or human reason, Quakerism offers the interpretive community as the place where truth is discerned, tested, and acted out. In place of the incessant cacophony of modern Western culture, Quakerism offers a spirituality of subtraction: a cultivation of the Great Silence in which the dialogue with our Creator can be heard and attended to. Like all great spiritual paths, Quakerism requires commitment and discipline—but it is a commitment to practices whose value has been discerned locally, by the individual in conjunction with the monthly meeting community, and a commitment to disciplines not enforced by outside authority, but inspired by one's Inner Guide.

I believe that if we can communicate the true nature of the Quaker path to seekers and others, and if we can educate them in the true nature of the Quaker spiritual life, we will find a great many persons attracted to our meetings for worship. Some of them will taste and move on, but many of them will stay. Far from being an outmoded relic, our classic Quakerism is wonderfully constructed to speak to the condition of a great people yet to be gathered in the present day. The challenge facing us is not to modernize our faith tradition to meet a changing society, but to embody our faith tradition more fully so that we can be leavening and seasoning in that society.

Quakers have faced the challenges of a rapidly changing world before, and have had similar reactions. Friends gathered in North Carolina Yearly Meeting sessions some 130 years ago assessed the situation this way in an epistle to Dublin Yearly Meeting:

> We have no new truths to offer, no new way to point out. We would advocate, rather, a very close and prayerful examination of the ground before we would give up the established landmarks as to Doctrine, Discipline, and Practice, living and acting under which our predecessors, those sons of the morning, were enabled to faithfully bear testimony not only to the outward coming of the Lord Jesus . . . but that this same Jesus was the Word with God in the beginning, by whom the world was made, and that the same was the light and life of men. . . .
>
> While we wish not to fold our arms, sitting at ease in our ceiled houses, we feel assured that we are not to improve or leaven the world by assimilating our principles or practices to those of it.[14]

I agree. Let us therefore undertake a close and prayerful examination of the ground of classic Quakerism. The doctrine, discipline, and practice of Friends, not to mention their faith, is grounded in a corporate spirituality markedly different in nature from that of nearly all other Western Christians. This Quaker spirituality is the confluence of three great themes: an *apophatic* approach to God, an unmediated relationship with Jesus Christ that goes far beyond the traditional understanding of the priesthood of all believers, and an understanding that these experiences are grounded in the faith community, not merely the individual.

Quakers have claimed *apophatic* spirituality—the path of spiritual subtraction—as their own. This is the first great theme. The great epiphany of George Fox, that Jesus Christ has come to teach

---

[14] Extract from an epistle of North Carolina Yearly Meeting to Dublin Yearly Meeting, 1873, as quoted in *Rules of Discipline of the Yearly Meeting of Friends of North Carolina*, 1908 edition, printed by William H. Pile's Sons, Philadelphia, 1910, p. 18.

his people himself, embodies the other two themes: that we each have a direct, unmediated relationship with the Divine in our present life, and that this relationship is grounded in our life together as God's people. Weavers know the warp and the woof of a cloth are the threads that run through the cloth, and that the strength of the cloth depends on the strength of individual threads, how closely they are woven together, and the ways they are interwoven with threads running in a different direction. The spirituality of subtraction, the unmediated relationship with the living Christ, and the centrality of the faith community rather than the individual: these three great themes, and the interplay among them, make up the warp and woof of the whole cloth of the Quaker faith tradition.

I want to sketch each of these themes briefly and then consider how they work together to produce the integral whole that we know as Quakerism.

ONE: *APOPHATIC* SPIRITUALITY

The two great ways of knowing God are sometimes called *apophatic* theology and *kataphatic* theology. *Apophatic* theology can be described as knowing God by all the statements that can be made beginning "God is not ___." This is also called the negative road, or the spirituality of subtraction. One approaches God by subtracting from one's consciousness, from one's entire life, everything that is not God. Classic Quaker spirituality is heavily *apophatic*.

Kataphatic theology, by far the most prevalent among Christians in the West, can be described as knowing God by all the statements that can be made beginning "God is ___." On this spiritual path, one seeks a deeper understanding of and relationship with God through positive images, symbols, and ideas: singing a hymn, preaching and hearing messages about God and God's works in the world, responsive readings and vocal prayer in unison, and similar activities. It is the most common form of spirituality throughout the Christian church (Roman, Orthodox, and Protestant). Younger people typically start with a *kataphatic* spirituality, even if later in life they are drawn to an *apophatic* path. It is easier to learn about what and who God is, how God acts in the world, etc., than to start out by trying to grasp God by considering what God is not.

As Andrew Pritchard observes, *kataphatic* spirituality is a spirituality of immanence, of the Word made flesh, of God with us. It emphasizes God's dominion in this world. Success, progress, overcoming and victory are highly valued.[15]

Andrew Pritchard describes *apophatic* spirituality as placing emphasis on the values of self-emptying or denial—on suffering, sacrifice, and serving.[16] This sounds very much like the stories we've read of Quakers who speak of taking up the cross, of denying self, or overcoming their own will in order to be faithful, and for good reason. This is the signature Quaker spirituality. Scripture passages that illuminate this spirituality are familiar to us all: the suffering servant passage in Isaiah,[17] the humility of Christ in Philippians,[18] and those folks in Hebrews who are praised for acting in faith contrary to their own self-interest.[19]

Two: Unmediated Relationship with Christ

In his search for a true knowledge of God and God's desires for his own life, George Fox tried a series of paths to understanding, each of which he eventually rejected. He attended church services, but found them unsatisfying. He inquired of the priestly class, and found them unhelpful. He looked in the Scriptures, but found them not sufficient by themselves. As he records in his *Journal*:

> And when all my hopes in them and in all men were gone, so that I had nothing outwardly to help me, nor could tell what to do, then, Oh then, I heard a voice which said, "There is one, even Christ Jesus, that can speak to thy condition," and when I heard it my heart did leap for joy.[20]

The second great theme of Quaker spirituality is that it is Jesus Christ who has come to teach us. Christ is here, with us in the present moment and our present circumstances; and Christ is here to teach us directly everything that it is important for us to know

---

[15] Andrew Pritchard, "Your Church's Personality," *Reality Magazine*, Issue 45, www.reality.org.nz/articles/45/45-pritchard.html.

[16] *Ibid.*

[17] Isaiah 53.

[18] Philippians 2:5–11.

[19] Hebrews 11:35–19.

[20] George Fox, *Journal*, Nickalls edition, p. 11.

about God and God's desires for us and God's love for us. Our path
to understanding these things does not lead only through the Holy
Scriptures, and does not lead primarily through the accumulated
teachings of the institutional church or through holy sacraments
administered by a priestly class. Our path to understanding is not
human reason, either. Our primary path to understanding is a
direct, unfiltered and unmediated relationship with the risen
Christ who is here with each of us and with all of us in community.
Of course, we do value Scriptures and the accumulated wisdom of
our yearly meetings and the rational thought processes that help us
understand the consequences of our actions—it is simply that all
these are of secondary value in the Quaker tradition.

It is the experienced reality of the inward encounter with the
Divine that is the foundation stone and building block for everything else. In that encounter I discover the One who yearns to
abide with me, and in me, to be my Companion, Comforter,
Healer, and Guide. Others have had that experience, and have
written and spoken about it eloquently. Because the One we
encounter is the very nature of truth, what these other people have
said and written about their encounter with truth gets my great
respect, and is useful to me to help me understand my own relationship with Christ—but it can never be more important than the
relationship itself.

THREE: COMMUNITY

The third theme is that of community. George Fox did not see
a great crowd of individuals to be reached and taught individually.
Fox knew that Jesus Christ had not come to teach him in isolation.
His call was always to a people. He understood that Christ had
come to teach his *people*—a great people yet to be gathered but
whose gathering was beginning. It seems obvious in some ways:
Christ was always talking about how we should relate to one
another, and said that the way we treat one another is the true
measure of how we feel about and treat God. There is something
about the human condition, though, that keeps persuading us that
we can be right with God by thinking primarily about ourselves.
This is particularly seductive today, when the dominant culture all

around us seeks to convince you and me that we are in fact at the center of our story—rampant individualism. Quakerism has always understood this to be untrue, and its emphasis on community is a great theme of the Quaker faith tradition.

The Dance of the Three

Let us explore the ways these themes dance together. George Fox, of course, was practicing an *apophatic* spirituality when he had his epiphany. He tried all the conventional sources of spiritual wisdom and insight, but many of his signature insights came in times of retirement and solitude. He was walking in a field on a First Day morning when the Lord opened to him "that being bred at Oxford or Cambridge was not enough to fit and qualify men to be ministers of Christ,"[21] and again when "at another time it was opened in me that God, who made the world, did not dwell in temples made with hands."[22] His *Journal* reports many times that he spent entire days and sometimes nights as well in solitary contemplation, often with his Bible but not always.

The outgrowth of this practice of solitude and negation was a direct experience of God and the clear instruction and guidance of God, independent of Scriptures, church teachers, or human reason. As Fox described it:

> Now the Lord God hath opened to me by his invisible power how that every man was enlightened by the divine Light of Christ; and I saw it shine through all, and that they that believed in it came out of condemnation to the Light of life, and became the children of it. . . . This I saw in the pure openings of the Light without the help of any man; neither did I then know where to find it in the Scriptures; though afterwards, searching the Scriptures, I found it. For I saw, in that Light and Spirit that was before the Scriptures were given forth, and which led the holy men of God to give them forth, that all, if they were to know God or Christ, or the Scriptures aright, must come to that spirit by which they that gave them forth were led and taught.[23]

21 George Fox, *Journal*, Nickalls edition, p. 7.
22 *Ibid.*, p. 8.
23 *Autobiography of George Fox*, Rufus Jones edition, electronic version, chapter 2.

This is a deeply packed statement. Fox is claiming direct inspired revelation, independent of human help or Scriptural guidance, which is in itself a remarkable claim. "God told me to ___" is a claim secular culture often associates with mental illness, not spiritual health. But Fox doesn't stop there. He claims that the content of his revelation is that the same experience is available to everyone— not only is available, but must be availed of if any person is to understand Scripture rightly or to know God truly. (Remember, Barclay starts out the *Apology* with the proposition that "the height of all happiness is the true knowledge of God.") Finally, he claims that Scripture itself supports these claims, though it was not the source of them. He came to these understandings not by adding to his rational knowledge or by formal religious study, but by subtracting from his life whatever proved itself not to be God.

This spirituality of subtraction is a spiritual gift, a charism, which Friends offer to the entire Christian church: modeling *apophatic* spirituality in all of life, and especially in worship. To follow this spirituality of subtraction with heart, one must be consistent in one's practice. One removes from the meeting room decorations that might distract, and refrains from looking out the window to other possible sources of distraction. Some, like me, even keep our eyes closed to further protect. We do not speak unless directly moved to do so, and are careful even about our inward prayer. I try to take care of urgent prayer concerns early, while I am still "centering down" to worship. Later in meeting, if I find myself thinking, my practice is to repeat the Jesus Prayer a few times, until thought falls away again: "Lord Jesus Christ, Son of God, have mercy on me, a sinner." If some distraction does intrude upon my consciousness, my desire is to treat it as a pebble falling into a still pond: the ripples expand and the pond returns to stillness.

This is a slow path to God. I can't speak about other paths, but I know personally that this is a slow path. After more than three decades as a Friend, I still feel myself to be a beginner on this path. I am somewhat in awe of those more seasoned folks in my meeting who have incorporated this spirituality into every aspect of their lives so much more completely and apparently effortlessly than I have. It is a slow path, and paradoxically, anything one might do to help speed one's way has just the opposite effect. There is nothing I can add to my practice that will help me make progress on the path of subtraction. I can understand why patience is a proverbial Quaker virtue—it takes great patience to devote oneself to this path, and to stick to it for years and years.

On the other hand, there is a temptation among some Friends, who are impatient with the process of subtraction or who do not fully understand Quaker spirituality, to fill in the empty spaces with some thing or activity: Scripture readings, or sweat lodges, or hymn singing or whatever. All these things have their value, and all can be helpful, but they are not in their essence part of Quaker spirituality. Quaker worship is something different—not sacrifice, not praise, not petition nor contrition, but "simple" receptivity. As one Friend I know said recently to an attender considering membership, "it is fine to continue participating in Indian sweat lodge experiences after becoming a member, but thee cannot re-define Quakerism to include sweat lodges."

Understand that I am not saying that these other types of spirituality are wrong, or not helpful—they can be exactly right, and can be quite helpful to one's spiritual growth in the right contexts. They are not, however, part of that distinctive Quaker spirituality which is at the heart of our tradition. Nor am I praising silence in worship *per se.* To quote Job Scott:

> I know of nothing more acceptable to God, nor more useful, instructive, and strengthening to the souls of men, than true silent worship, and waiting on God for help immediately from his holy presence; nor of scarcely any thing more formal and lifeless, than that dull, unfeeling silence, which too many of our society are satisfying themselves with the year round, and from year to year.[24]

Perhaps the most common practice among other Christians that is similar to Quaker spirituality is contemplative prayer. Quaker practice is very similar, yet distinct from contemplative prayer. It is not so much that we Quakers choose to contemplate the Divine as that we choose to receive—to hear and accept—what the Divine has to impart to us.

[24] Job Scott, *op. cit.*, p. 76.

The spirituality of subtraction makes room in our lives for the type of direct interaction with the Divine that George Fox reported and that we wait for, expectantly, in meeting for worship. As it is hard to hear one another in a noisy room, it is hard to hear God in a noisy life. As our heart-longing for God grows, it is only natural that we should be continually simplifying our life, subtracting whatever is not God or not of God so that our awareness is single-pointed and competition for our attention is minimized. A noisy life not only competes with the Divine message, it distorts what it cannot drown out completely.

This admittedly large effort is worth our while because the dialogue it readies us for is in fact continuous. It may wax and wane, but seasoned Friends over the centuries have reported that God's presence is an ongoing personal conversation, not the intermittent and infrequent reception of a general broadcast. It is as if whenever we stop to listen, we discover that God is already speaking with us. As Carole Treadway of the School of the Spirit reports, an apt description of a Conservative Friend is one who seeks to live every moment under the immediate guidance of the Holy Spirit.[25]

So far this seems to be a good system—a spirituality that enables direct revelation from God, some of which undoubtedly concerns how to adjust one's life—how to use subtraction—to enable more and clearer revelation. The danger is that there is no anchor here. It does not take much imagination to visualize how this might lead to insanity. The faith community provides the stability and groundedness needed but not supplied by either the spirituality of subtraction or the direct experience of divine communion.

The faith community makes several needed—I would say necessary—contributions to this interplay between spirituality and revelation. Four of these are important to our conversation today.

First of all, there is a qualitative difference between corporate worship and individual worship. However sweet and authentic and powerful, and whatever other adjective one might correctly apply to individual retirement, corporate worship is something else—a different kind of encounter with the Divine, for which there is no

[25] Carole Treadway, personal communication, c. 2000.

substitute. Christ made a specific promise, recorded in the Scripture, to be with two or three gathered in his name; that promise is kept when we gather for corporate worship. In corporate worship we hear God differently, and I suggest more clearly, than in times of individual retirement.

An important example of this difference is the process of answering the queries and, in the larger community, responding to the answers. The queries are a unique form of *interrogatory theology*,[26] developed to facilitate spiritual formation in the context of a spirituality of subtraction and the reality of immediate divine guidance. The classic use of the queries, still followed in my yearly meeting, is that they will be answered by the meeting community in a single voice.[27] The answer to any given query is not a summary of the insights and observations of various individual Friends, but something larger and more true: the discernment of the community, as a body, of its spiritual condition. The queries are so important that the second issue of North Carolina Yearly Meeting (Conservative)'s *Journal* is devoted entirely to them.

The plan for the third issue of the *Journal* is that it will be devoted to the advices. Many of us have a watered-down view of the advices. Yearly meetings often quote a sentence of the famous letter from the Elders at Balby somewhere in their book of discipline or faith and practice:

> Dearly beloved Friends, these things we do not lay upon you as a rule or form to walk by; but that all, with a measure of the Light which is pure and holy, may be guided; and so in the Light walking and abiding, these things may be fulfilled in the Spirit, not in the letter; for the letter killeth, but the Spirit giveth life.[28]

True enough; but what we forget, if we ever knew, is that this sentence comes at the end of a list of twenty specific directions, or advices, on how Friends are to conduct their lives, ranging from where and how often to hold meetings for worship to relations between masters and servants, youth and their elders, and between

---

26 Ched Myers, private communication, July 1998.

27 Ched Myers, *Who Will Roll Away the Stone*, Orbis Books, 1995, pp. 37–38.

28 *Advices from a general meeting held at Balby*, Yorkshire (1656), published by Licia Kuenning and Quaker Heritage Press.

husband and wife. All of which is given forth, as the sentence preceding our familiar quotation, "that all in order may be kept in obedience, that he may be glorified, who is worthy over all, God blessed for ever."

A second contribution of the emphasis on community involves the Quaker insistence on a changed life as the consequence of a changed spirit. One is not justified or sanctified by works, but the changed person will live a changed life, and the community is the first place we live out those changes. The faith community is the place we practice (in both senses of the word) the acts of mercy, the qualities of love, and the testimonies of a Christian life. We learn how to live up to the light we have been given by practicing on one another and with one another. What mounds of forgiveness we need to pour out to one another in the process—but what joy to experience the Holy Spirit changing one another's lives, and knitting us together in Divine Love!

Thirdly, to the extent we are all faithful in that practice, the faith community becomes a witness to the world about how it should be ordered, and an instrument for God's use in beginning that re-ordering process. Our belief is that the risen Christ makes it possible for ordinary humans to live in the kingdom of God today. The faith community is the means by which we work to heal the world and model the present and coming kingdom. Beyond work on social concerns, the faith community can model social order— the present possibility that individuals can experience a unity beyond words that leads to harmony and social justice.

The fourth contribution of the faith community involves discernment and interpretation. Paradoxically, our emphasis on the importance of the direct unmediated relationship of the individual with the risen Christ leads to an increased importance of the faith community as the means of interpreting that relationship and its guidance for the individual. We believe, and know by experience, that the Holy Spirit with whom we commune inwardly is the infallible God of the universe. We know also that we are very fallible human beings. God may not be in error in instructing us, but we may very well be in error in understanding those directions. Hence the importance of the faith community as a locus of discernment and interpretation, balancing the insight of the individual with that of the group.

Community discernment is not the same thing as community decision making on behalf of the individual. It is not making decisions for the individual. To borrow a phrase from Marty Grundy, "discernment is the way we tell what is from God from what is not."[29] Discernment is a prime task of the Religious Society of Friends—as a society, not as an assembly of individuals. To the extent that I am committed to this spiritual path and that I trust the discernment of the community, the community should never be in a position of making my decisions for me—only helping me tell what is from God from what is not.

To practice discernment, the members of a faith community must truly know each other—must be aware of, and in some ways participate in the important aspects and developments in one another's lives. This takes much more time and effort than the average members of the typical monthly meeting are accustomed to investing in their fellow Quakers. If we are to be agents of discernment for one another, our lives must be transparent to one another, and that can happen only when we spend time together. One or two hours together each week at meeting for business or meeting for worship won't do it.

Be involved with one another economically: if there is a dentist in the meeting, that dentist should be the dentist of choice for the entire meeting. If there is an auto mechanic, everybody's car should get serviced at that Friend's shop. If I need to hire a babysitter, it should be a young Friend. We need to break bread with one another in our own homes, not just at the meetinghouse for monthly potluck. When we know one another deeply, our discernment will be easy and true. When I am with those persons who know me deeply, I often receive their discernment without saying a word.

For all this to work, of course, the individual must submit to the discernment of the community. How hard it is for us to deal with submission! Our individualistic culture fills us with thoughts about our independent rights, and our faith tradition wants us to submit to these folks who don't even know us? Well, no. As I've

---

[29] Marty Grundy, Traveling Ministries retreat, November 2002, Sixth Day evening.

been saying, our faith tradition wants us to submit to folks who know us very well, and love us, and have our best interests at heart.

When we practice submission, several things happen. One, we often learn that the community was right, for reasons we did not or could not see at the time. Second, we learn a lesson of humility that the larger secular culture is unlikely to teach us at any time. Thirdly, we give the community, of which we are a part, an opportunity to see what the implications and outcomes associated with its discernment are. By reflecting on these events, the community gets better at discernment, and we all become more faithful servants of the One Lord.

When we let go of ego and focus instead on God, we are (as one old Quaker said) gathered as in a net and drawn together as we are drawn closer to God, so that we look at one another and say "What?! Is the kingdom of heaven come among men?"[30] (and women!).

GROWING THE FAITH TRADITION

A word may be appropriate here about how all this affects the faith tradition itself. A faith tradition is not unchanging through time. Like all living things, it must grow and change if it is to continue to be healthy. A faith community is the only place a faith tradition grows legs and walks around on this earth. When such a community sees the effects of its discernment and advices and reflects on them, it is inevitably changed, if even just a little bit.

So when I talk about the individual submitting to the community, and the community seriously caring about what the individual does, that is all true—but it is only part of the story. On another level, the individual and community—prophet and priest—are engaged in a spiritual wrestling match that will leave both participants changed. The faith tradition is much larger than the individual, in many ways, so it will not change very dramatically from any one encounter. Over time, however, the ongoing wrestling matches between individuals and the tradition embodied by the community change the tradition itself, strengthening some parts and modifying others.

30 Francis Howgill's "Testimony" in the preface of Edward Burrough's *Works*, 1672. Quoted in New England Yearly Meeting's *Faith and Practice*, 1966, p. 44.

So no wonder we come back again and again to the same knotty problems—that's how the tradition stays alive and grows into new understandings of truth. John Woolman had to come back to his yearly meeting again and again to raise his concern about slavery (he was not alone of course)—but each year he was a little changed, and each year the yearly meeting was a little changed, until finally a tipping point was reached and the tradition began to interpret its own testimonies differently.

It is precisely that we have continued to submit our personal discernment to the guidance of the faith community that keeps the tradition alive and growing and relevant to our issues and concerns and discernments. When we decide the tradition is irrelevant, that the queries can be left unanswered and the advices ignored, when we don't make the effort to test our discernment with the larger faith community, our actions themselves are self-fulfilling. When we don't wrestle with the faith tradition, we rob it of the very thing it most needs to remain vital, alive and relevant: our deepest engagement.

The Quaker faith tradition is a body of experience and practice, and reflection on that practice and experience that interprets the cosmic big story of God and creation for those of us who commit ourselves to walk inside it. It is not the only authentic or true tradition, but it is authentic and true. One need not be a Quaker to reach the happiness of a true knowledge of God, but one needs some tradition greater than the individual, and the Quaker tradition is indeed greater than any one of us.

We need the faith tradition if we are to have individual spiritual growth. Otherwise, we are in the position of a swimmer dropped into the water at night, out of sight of land: we have no idea where land might be, no way to judge whether we're swimming in a straight line, no voice of encouragement when we get tired, and no advice on how to improve our stroke, so we can cover more ground with less effort. We have no guide, and no discipline to measure our strength against.

Beyond the importance of faith traditions in general, I believe that it is very important for an individual to choose a particular faith tradition to embrace and with which to wrestle. Eclectic and syncretic spiritualities, I believe, are dangerous because they encourage the individual to dodge the more challenging aspects of one tradition for an easier part of another—and by so doing, to avoid that hard spiritual work which may be necessary for spiritual growth. How can one truly embrace any tradition, if one gives it only half-hearted allegiance? To God-wrestle, we must be fully committed—for our sake and for the sake of the faith tradition, which must wrestle with us and be changed by that wrestling, if it is to survive.

Brian Drayton, among others, has spoken of the Quaker faith tradition as a "whole cloth." Just as warp and woof are interwoven to give a physical cloth its strength and durability, and removing threads from either warp or woof weakens the entire cloth and makes it less useful, so these themes discussed tonight are so interwoven that removing any one of them threatens the integrity and strength of the whole tradition. Before we discard any single aspect of the tradition, therefore, one should carefully examine the ways it is interwoven with and supports other aspects of the tradition that appear more useful or valuable.

Our challenge in the twenty-first century is to learn our own faith tradition in its fullness, and to find a way somehow to practice this tradition in the midst of a surrounding culture which honors very different values and activities. Our tradition requires our whole-hearted embrace, our single-minded commitment, and our faithful wrestling to grow and help us grow into a true knowledge of God. If we do these things, our meeting communities will indeed be a blessing and sweet savor to those who see us and interact with us, and our meetings for worship will see a steady increase in the numbers participating.

Part 2: . . . and Practice

Quakerism is eminently a path of praxis, of practice, not merely an intellectual paradigm for understanding the world. So how does one put the principles we discussed last night into practice? Can we put legs on the spirituality of subtraction, on the deep communion with Jesus Christ, and on the central place of the faith community and see how they walk around on the ground? Yogi

Berra is reported to have said that "In theory there's no difference between theory and practice. In practice there's a lot of difference." If the practice won't support our theology, the theology will have to change. If it does support it, we'll have a starting point for a continuing cycle of practice and reflection that will keep our personal faith and our faith tradition alive and growing indefinitely.

Now these three principles interact with one another to produce something greater than their sum: a synergy that opens up a new way of looking at and being in the world. This is a new gestalt, a new vision of what might be called gospel order: how the kingdom of God is even this moment breaking into and becoming real in our world. So as we talk tonight it will not be possible to take each principle and discuss it separately. Wherever we start the conversation, the other principles will inevitably involve themselves in the discussion.

Nevertheless, let's start with the spirituality of subtraction, also known as *apophatic* spirituality. There is a story, perhaps apocryphal, that a group or groups of Seekers in England, dissatisfied with the established public worship of the day, began to meet privately to worship among themselves. They began to delete from their worship everything that seemed to them not to be directly of God. Soon enough they were gathering in complete silence, having subtracted everything they knew how to subtract. Along came George Fox, the story goes, and showed them what was waiting for them in the silence: a deep and direct relationship with the Holy Spirit in many roles, or "offices:" healer, comforter, priest, king, guide, companion and others.

If there were no one waiting for us at the end of our journey, the spirituality of subtraction would leave Friends worship no different than numerous other meditation or mindfulness techniques: calming and simplifying our lives and minds so we can better deal with the stresses of the contemporary world. That in itself would be a good thing. But there is a Divine Other in the silence, and because of that we practice our subtraction in order to draw closer to that Other, to engage in an ongoing dialogue and communion.

Our experience is that the dialogue is indeed ongoing; that the Holy Spirit is speaking to us whenever we turn our attention to the conversation. Naturally, we want to order all our lives to be open to that conversation, not just the time we spend in meeting for worship. An attention to the spirituality of subtraction affects how we live each moment of each day. Our lives become simple—single-pointed—not because of economic doctrine, not so we can live simply on the earth, but so that we can attend to the divine conversation. Simplicity becomes not a chore, but a joy.

As we attend to the divine conversation, we are able to put more and more of our lives under the direct guidance of the Holy Spirit. The more we open ourselves to receiving and following this guidance, the more there is. It turns out that God is interested in every aspect of our lives, and is constantly equipping and guiding us to live very well—to live in harmony with the Creator and the creation.

My favorite example of this comes from a gathering of ministers in Ohio that I attended about a decade ago. In the course of the various discussions, some farmers in the group began to describe their practice of settling into the silence each morning, to be guided about what they should do and where they should go that day. Sometimes they felt no more than an affirmation of the tasks human reason would have recommended, but sometimes they received unexpected direction. One spoke of being directed away from a planned trip to town to buy feed and other supplies, and being sent instead to a distant pasture. When he got there, he discovered a very sick cow. His prompt arrival undoubtedly saved the animal's life. Ordinarily he might have gone a couple of days before going to that particular pasture.

Even those of us who work in offices have a remarkable amount of discretion in our lives, both at work and at home. Making space for this sort of continuing guidance will produce a remarkable simplicity in one's life. Simplicity of this sort is more than a plainness of garb or a frugality in spending or consuming. It entails a re-ordering of life's activities so that they require less of our attention, thereby freeing up more of our attention to give to the divine conversation. This is, as the Gospel of John reminds us, so that we might produce better fruit, not more fruit.

Our faith community plays an integral part in this simplifying, subtracting process. Beyond the wonderful experience of corporate worship, we model the path for one another and share the struggles as well as the joys along the way. It is as the writer of Ecclesiastes said,

> Two are better than one, because they have a good reward for their toil. For if they fall, one will lift up the other; but woe to one who is alone and falls and does not have another to help. Again, if two lie together, they keep warm; but how can one keep warm alone? And though one might prevail against another, two will withstand one. A threefold cord is not quickly broken.[31]

Because the community is so important in this tradition, the work necessary to build and sustain community has a very high priority. I am talking about comm—unity: unity with the Holy Spirit of God, not just the fellowship of like-minded folks. As individuals and as a group, we need to devote time and energy continually to those practices that enable us "to keep the unity of the Spirit in the bond of Peace."[32] This is hard work, and frankly many folks put more effort into sustaining community in their workplace or neighborhood than in their faith community.

Among the community building and sustaining processes that seem to me to be of highest importance are the queries and advices. The spirituality of subtraction and the reality of immediate divine guidance have posed difficult challenges for spiritual formation among Friends. How could Friends direct one another's attention to what is spiritually important, and how could we pass on what we have learned to newcomers to the tradition? The answer discovered was unique and *apropos* to Friends: they developed an interrogatory theology, called queries and their answers. There are queries for individuals in my yearly meeting, and queries for the meeting of ministry and oversight; but the queries that seem most important to me are the queries for monthly meetings. The corporate queries are designed to direct one's attention—more accurately, the meeting community's attention—to the most important aspects

31 Ecclesiastes 4:9–12, NRSV.
32 *Discipline*, North Carolina Yearly Meeting (Conservative), 1983 revision, p. 3.

of Quaker spirituality. Rather than making a declaration of the truth, these questions are designed to engage Friends with important issues in such a way that the truth becomes clear.

By truth I mean truth with a capital "T," as it often appears in early Quaker writings. To paraphrase Douglas Adams, capital "T" truth means God, the universe, and everything—including how it all fits together and how each part relates to every other part—especially how God relates to thee and me. Friends have consistently held two things to be true about capital "T" truth that seem to be contradictory and certainly are in tension with one another. The first belief is that the truth is both complete in itself and unchanging over eternity—Christ the Son of God. The second belief is that truth is at the same time incomplete and constantly unfolding. The Divine is all and everything and always, but our understanding, our comprehension of the Divine is necessarily limited by our circumstances and spiritual maturity. This fits quite well with our *apophatic* understanding: the truth is complete and perfect, but nothing we can think or say about it quite captures its fullness. "That's not it."

The genius of the queries is that they will engage us wherever we are, spiritually and physically. When properly engaged, the queries will reveal that aspect of the total truth that is appropriate to our condition. Of necessity queries are stuck in the moment in time at which they were written down, and sometimes their wording seems archaic or the issues they address are not phrased as we would phrase them today. I would suggest that this is not a shortcoming, and that our efforts to wrap our understanding around the queries and make them real to us in this moment and place are part of the process of revelation.

Our discipline and our practice assume that the corporate queries will be answered by the meeting community in a single voice,33 and this is an important function of the query process. As the meeting for business builds a response to any query, many Friends may offer insight or observation. The community's answer, however, is not a listing of these insights and observations, but a refining and development of these individual responses into a

33 Ched Myers, *Who Will Roll Away the Stone*, Orbis Books, 1995, pp. 37–38.

single community answer. This means often that deep worship is necessary to integrate disparate, or even conflicting individual statements into a transcendent response with which all may find unity. In that worship I may come to see a situation in a whole new light because the query discussion opens new perspectives to my understanding; others may reorganize priorities as the whole community comes to a single answer.

As the queries act to elicit a single voice from the community in response, the tradition speaks to us in a single voice through the advices, "to challenge and inspire Friends in their personal and social lives."[34] The advices are indeed declarative statements of advice, rather than questions, and they are advice rather than doctrine, although most of the important doctrines of the faith are embedded there, explicitly or implicitly. The advices are the voice of earlier generations of my faith community, passing on their wisdom to those embracing the faith in the present day. They inspire me because I know in my heart the effort these Friends made to live up to them in their day; they challenge me because they are an unambiguous declaration that our inward spiritual condition will inevitably shape and direct our outward lives. If I cannot live in harmony with any part of the advices, I must undertake a serious self-examination to see whether I am straying from these underlying principles, or am lacking the courage to put my faith into action.

Of course, the advices themselves change over time, as we wrestle with them in faith. We live in a larger social context, and as that context changes over years and decades, the pressures it places on faithful Friends also changes. An advice on ownership of slaves, for example, would have been relevant in the early nineteenth century but not fifty years later. This is one way the faith tradition evolves as we wrestle with it as individuals and as a community.

While no formal, corporate response to the advices is expected, a continual engagement with them is an important part of "honestly examining [oneself] as to [one's] growth in grace."[35] Our discipline urges their "earnest and frequent consideration" by all members of the yearly meeting. Applying the advices to one's own

[34] *Discipline*, North Carolina Yearly Meeting (Conservative), 1983 revision, p. 1.
[35] *Ibid.*

life, and reflection on the places where the two do not seem to match very well does indeed challenge us to do better and inspire us to make that effort.

I have been spending some time recently with Robert Barclay, and in particular with his *Apology*. It is a remarkable document still, after several centuries. One of the strengths of Barclay's writing is his insistence that if experience contradicts theory, he must revise his theory—or his theology—to fit the facts. In the present day, we need to replace our theoretical insistence that everyone is identical with an acknowledgement that God loves diversity, and gifts each individual differently, in order to bring about the kingdom of God. Beyond our call to membership in the kingdom, there are those individuals among us who have heard and accepted a second calling, to re-order their entire lives around a particular service for God. When this happens, and in whatever form it takes, whether visiting those in prison or feeding the hungry or vocal ministry, the faith community needs to participate in recognizing and celebrating the work of God among us. Only as community can we provide the support and guidance these folks need in order to be faithful servants in these callings.

Recognizing God's gifts in various ministries and service does not create a Quaker hierarchy, or a "two-tiered system," as some have called it.[36] Neither does denying this diversity of gifts make them go away. Formal acknowledgement does enable the individual to make a fuller and proper use of the gift, as it involves the entire community in discernment of right action for the development and exercise of the gift. The community can discern and remove obstacles to use of the gift and encourage the individual to be faithful. If the individual seems to outrun her Guide, the community that has already formally recognized the gift has a ready channel to provide additional discernment and guidance.

God bestows on the faith community those spiritual gifts it needs to carry out its part in bringing the kingdom of God to fruition. Individuals become stewards of those gifts, but they are essentially the community's gifts. This mutual accountability of the individual and meeting for the proper development and use of spiritual gifts is a natural outgrowth of this reality.

[36] Chuck Fager, private communication, 2003.

Now some persons may and do bristle at the prospect of coming under the meeting's authority. Individual pride and a sense of "I know what is best for me" get in the way of a right relationship. If we are serious about spiritual growth, however, we will welcome the oversight and guidance of others. To the objection that "the meeting members don't know me well enough to know what is best," my response is that it is our responsibility as individual members to live transparent lives, so the rest of the meeting community can know us, and to make the effort to build and sustain community which is the means of knowing one another.

There is an even more fundamental truth here. One makes spiritual growth only in the context of a faith community and faith tradition, as I mentioned last night. It is only in the context of a community that we are equipped and enabled to dig our wells deep in one place, to find the Living Water. Community gives me location—gives me my bearings—so that I know where I am. Community interprets and provides context for understanding my spiritual experiences. I discover that other Friends, in my meeting or in earlier generations, have had similar experiences that had certain effects on their lives, and from that information I am enabled to understand my own experience more fully.

My faith community also holds my feet to the fire: it holds me accountable for doing the hard spiritual work of our tradition, not just the "fun stuff." Without this accountability any person, Friend or not, is susceptible to a sort of eclectic, "salad bar" spirituality that allows one to pick and choose among spiritual exercises, avoiding those things that are difficult or seem like less fun. Of course, it is those difficult things that more times than not are exactly what we need to be doing and experiencing.

OUTWARD WITNESS AND TESTIMONY

Walking this peculiar Quaker spiritual path brings one into increasing harmony: harmony with God, harmony with oneself, harmony with other human beings, and harmony with all the rest of creation. The fruits of this harmony are among the strongest and clearest witnesses which we Quakers have to make to the rest of the world. If we are clear about the source of these witnesses, I believe they will be more effective than heretofore in transforming the world.

Perhaps the clearest example of this involves an aspect of the larger testimony of harmony, called the peace testimony. When I was a young man, I had to write a couple of faith statements for conscientious objector applications—one to the air force, and then another to Selective Service. My argument was, I believe, typical for most liberal Quakers: there is that of God in everyone, so every human life is of infinite value, and attacking another human being is the same as attacking God. The air force and the Selective Service System found this to be a sound argument, at least for their purposes, and I was allowed to separate from the air force and avoid being drafted by Selective Service.

Having spent the following thirty years engaged in peace work in various ways, I have come to see two problems in my original position of basing a peace witness on that of God in everyone, or the inherent goodness of human beings. The first problem is related to the need for a religious witness to be persuasive to its audience—to those not yet in agreement. A witness based on that of God in every person is not persuasive because the untransformed person simply maintains that the argument doesn't apply. An important part of any war effort is to portray the "enemy" as evil. From this perspective, there is no visible "that of God" in this person or these people, so it is OK to make war on them—perhaps even a moral necessity. I say there is that of God in the stranger at the gates, they say there is not, and very little dialogue is possible, except to agree to disagree.

The second problem is that it does not address the roots of war in me: the reasons I am drawn to make war in the first place. An effective peace witness needs to do more than underscore the worth and dignity of each human being; it needs to address the things in me that lead me to contemplate making war on my fellow human beings. We may agree that human beings should not have war waged on them, because they have that of God in them or whatever, but that does not help much if I can't resist the urge to wage war.

A stronger witness, articulated by Fox and inherently wrapped up in the principles we have been discussing, is that I have been changed by my encounter with the Divine, and therefore it is neither necessary nor appropriate for me to wage war: "I told them I lived in the virtue of that life that took away the occasion of all war."[37] My current pacifist position does not depend on the good or evil in another person, or the presence of the Divine in them, but in my own condition. By the grace of God I have been freed from bondage to the lusts and desires which the Epistle of James says are at the heart of wars and conflicts.[38] By grace I have been enabled to abide by the precept and example of Christ, who did not fight when he would have been justified to do so, and who ordered the disciple to put up his sword.

I believe lives that embody this new life in the Holy Spirit are the strongest possible peace witness—a witness that cannot be undermined by the apparent evil in other persons or by its apparent "success" or "failure." George Fox's metaphor was that he had been brought through the flaming sword and returned to that state that Adam was in before the fall, and even beyond that to another more steadfast state in Christ Jesus.[39] The peace witness arising out of a transformed life will be persuasive because of the invitation it offers to others to be transformed themselves, not because it does or does not promise the defeat of apparent evil in other persons. I can urge the cause of peace as a realistic option for others because I know experientially that peace is possible in me.

Arguments such as Scott Simon's, that war is not moral but at times a necessity, because the other side is truly evil,[40] are pushed aside by this new reality. The other side may or not be evil—what is important is that I am not evil—I am God's new creation, no longer a slave to the forces that impel human beings to war. And I know from experience, as Friends have witnessed and testified for over three centuries, that God does not ever present us with circumstances in which we must choose between two evils. There is always a third way. There may be indeed a great cloud of darkness that seems at times to cover the earth—but I can testify that there

[37] George Fox, *Journal*, Nickalls edition, p. 65.
[38] James 4:1.
[39] George Fox, *Journal*, Nickalls edition, p. 27.
[40] Scott Simon, "A Response," *Friends Journal*, May 2003, pp. 18–21.

is a greater cloud of light, which will overcome the darkness as we are faithful to our Guide.

In the great silence we taste the gospel order of which George Fox spoke, the harmony that was in all creation before the fall from Eden. In that communion we learn how to live all of life more nearly in that gospel order. We can witness for peace among human beings not merely because it is rational, spares innocent lives, and makes better use of finances—although all those things are true. We can witness for peace because we know experientially that peace is God's will and peace is possible—for us, in the present day.

Based on our experience as a community of faith, Friends can testify that the kingdom of God is indeed both becoming in the present moment and not yet here in its fullness. In the words of the theme of New York Yearly Meeting a couple of decades ago, we are indeed "trapped between two worlds: one dying and one struggling to be born." What we can witness to the world is the extent to which it is possible to live in the kingdom in the present moment.

There is a risk in peacework, to which some Quakers from time to time fall prey, and that is to begin considering the peace witness anti-war work. When this happens our focus is on stopping the next weapons system, or preventing the outbreak of the next imminent conflict, or opposing the latest outrageous policy or plan from the pentagon. The risk is that one becomes what one fights against. Victory over war, or the makers of war, can never be our goal. Richard Rohr of the Center for Action and Contemplation in New Mexico has expressed this well: "You cannot build on death. You can only build on life. We must be sustained by a sense of what we are for and not just what we are against."

Our work can never be merely anti-war, or the replacement of one set of national leaders—in any nation—by another. Our goal, as seen by those who signed the declaration of 1660, must be the transformation of society, so that all governments are God's. This is not the work of a year or even a lifetime. We must be like those persons described by the writers of Hebrews, who acted in faith even though they were never to see the goal. We do not know the day nor the hour when the kingdom of God will arrive in its fullness, but we can be assured that our faithfulness speeds that day.

The emphasis on the local faith community as the focus of discernment and interpretation lends itself to a circle of action and reflection that, if followed faithfully, will continually reshape and hone the actions and witness of the community. Unfortunately, we do not spend as much time as would be helpful in reflecting on the fruits of recent actions. If we sent another letter last month to the President about this policy decision or that, what effect did it have? What can we learn from that? What should we do differently next time, or what else should we try?

Many Friends meetings do not adequately close the circle of action and reflection. I believe we do an adequate job of discernment before taking action, and work hard to implement that discernment faithfully. Where we fall short is in corporate reflection on the outcomes or consequences of our actions: an intentional corporate review of what happened, why, and what we should consider doing differently as a result. Friends have a bias toward precedent—we do what we did last time this situation presented itself. This is by and large a good thing, in my opinion. If we were to shift the focus slightly, from what we did last time in this situation to what happened as a result of what we did, it would be a better thing. Local meetings would soon discern more effective and appropriate actions to interpret and support our inward practice and outward testimonies.

We Friends can be comfortable with this local discernment and interpretation precisely because we believe, based on our experience, that there is indeed one truth which informs us all, and that as each community draws nearer to that truth it comes closer to every other community making that same spiritual effort. Our human faculties cannot express the wholeness of the truth in any word or action constrained by our limited vocabularies and our boundedness in space and time, but that does not mean truth—with a capital "T"—does not exist, or that we should not strive to understand it more completely.

In the same way, our experience in the great silence leads to an environmental witness that is beyond rational argument. Carl Magruder, among other Friends, argues that environmental concerns should be, and must be, the pre-eminent witness of Friends in this century. This may be so. I am not yet fully persuaded, but Carl and these other Friends are having their effect on me.

What I do know is that the harmony that builds in us as a result of our encounter in the great silence extends to nonhuman creation, also. Not only does it lead one away from the idea of having dominion over the earth toward being the steward or care-taker of the earth, but it leads us toward a style of stewardship, if you will: stewardship from within the existing harmony of creation. We can aspire to this relationship because we are enabled and equipped through our communion with the Creator: brought back into the gospel order that was and is the intended state of all creation.

We cannot live in peace with our fellow human beings and at the same time continue to wreak havoc on the environment. The same transforming experience with God that enables and equips us to be at peace with humans enables us to see that the same harmony with the rest of the creation is also God's will. If we are truly to be witnesses to the divine possibilities of peace, we must be searching out and implementing projects and policies that address our growing environmental problems with the same energy and intensity that we search out and implement projects that promote human peace. No Friendly activity should be undertaken without, at some level, a consideration of its impact on the divine creation. Our underlying assumption is that continued environmental degradation is not inevitable, that we are called not simply to lives of neutral impact on the environment, but to active restoration of what has been damaged. Our understanding is that "all God's crit-ters got a place in the choir" indeed. The assumption that human interests always outweigh those of the rest of creation must be abandoned.

This will take a great effort, expended over a very long period of time. The human impact on the planet is like a large ocean-going vessel: it has massive momentum, and can change its direction only a few degrees at a time. However, it can turn, and humans can change, to regain that harmony that was always the divine intention. Action will be required at every level: global, national, and local. It will be the local faith community—the monthly meeting—that is the primary locus for these efforts because it is the local community that can best discern what actions should be undertaken, and how to educate its own membership about relevant issues.

There is a potential for unified witness on a number of public issues that modern Friends have not begun to realize. We admire the Friends of Reading, who survived the arrest of all their adult males, the arrest of all adult females, and the burning of the meetinghouse—which left the children, who continued to meet in the ashes! What would be the effect if whole meetings began to adopt a particular witness in a similar fashion? Suppose a meeting community of say, 100 persons all stopped paying war taxes as part of a community-discerned peace witness? I think the effects would be profound.

Conclusion

I began last night by outlining some of the important issues facing people of faith in the present, post-modern world, and made the claim that classic Quakerism is well suited to address these issues. In a society where social norms and moral values that seem essential to a well-ordered life and even to physical survival are crumbling rapidly, Quakerism offers a way of life that promises wholeness and integrity, and also an accessible and acceptable basis for adopting that way of life and the associated norms and values. The local faith community can communicate and interpret right action and its application to specific local circumstances successfully when the methods of central authority, whether located in church organization or Holy Scripture, cannot. The gathered meeting can achieve insights that will remain forever out of reach to unaided human reason. In Quaker community, we can perceive and model a way of life that offers not only life and dignity to every human being, but works to restore the proper and divinely intended harmony between human beings and the rest of creation.

A final word of caution: there can be at times a sort of spiritual elitism that creeps into our thinking about reaching out to non-Quakers. Not everyone is amenable to this quietness, we say, and so we don't share our good news very widely or loudly. As a result, our meetings have a certain white-bread homogeneity that does not reflect either the kingdom or our cities and towns. In this age of ecumenism, not many Friends cling to the vision that the entire world will become Quaker. Nonetheless, every person is equipped and enabled to partake of the divine relationship that is at the heart of our faith, and every person is capable of beginning the path of spiritual subtraction. There is no reason why our meetings should not be much more broadly representative of their surrounding populations than they are now.

Friends, let us not be slow to give an account of the joy that we feel.[41] There is a world of difference between proselytizing and witnessing. While I share some of the reservations many folks have about proselytizing in an ecumenical world, it builds unnecessary barriers between us all if we fail to share what is moving and wonderful about our faith experience. I am convinced that if we are faithful in our witness, verbal and nonverbal, and faithful in our praxis, some will be moved to join us in our embrace of this peculiar faith tradition. Just as importantly, our faithful witness and praxis will challenge and inspire others who share the same taproot of faith to look inwardly to see what their own tradition has to say.

By grace we have stumbled onto this pearl of great price.[42] Let us indeed sell everything else and embrace the pearl wholeheartedly. Indeed, the stronger our embrace, the more nearly we are completely committed to preserving and sustaining and nurturing and keeping this faith tradition alive and growing, the better able it will be to guide and nurture us into becoming the persons who God has always intended us to become.

[41] I Peter 3:15.
[42] Matthew 13:45–46.

Encounter with the Taproot

This was a plenary address to the sessions of Lake Erie Yearly Meeting in 1997. I had begun thinking about the taproot imagery after attending a gathering in Ohio organized by Bill and Fran Taber called "Dialogue with the Taproot." One never knows whether one has communicated the message one has been given, but I was gratified when, near the end of yearly meeting sessions, the Young Friends report of what they thought was important about yearly meeting included a poster of a slow cow and a burning bush!

Last month, while I was preparing what I might say tonight, my mother called to let me know that the old home place had burned down: the farmhouse on the New River in the mountains of North Carolina which has been the focus of my experience of family roots and heritage. The farm itself has been in the family for over two hundred years. An even older farmhouse washed away in a flood some decades ago, and this newer house—"Uncle Will's place"—had become the center of life for the Bare family. Now not a wall stands. The only way to get to the main part of the farm, where the house stood, is to pole oneself across the New River in a flatbed boat—there are no roads on that side, and no bridges. So when lightning struck the house last month, the volunteers from the rural fire department had to park their pump truck on the other side of the river and wade across, dragging their hoses behind them through water up to their armpits. It was futile.

None of us will ever sit on that porch again, on the hillside overlooking the New River, rocking gently to the rhythms of the water, watching the chickens range along the riverbank and watching for signs of weather coming over the mountaintop on the other side. Gone, too, are generations of quilts that were stored in the attic. To appreciate this loss you must have some sense of the culture. Women in Ashe County were expected, well into living memory, to make a quilt for every year of their lives. When my grandmother died at 36 from complications of childbirth, her mother-in-law remarked that she had been somewhat of a slacker, having finished only 23 quilts in her 36 years. These quilts were in all the patterns and stitches one sees in museums today, and many others that I can describe only as "freehand:" the design of a quiltmaker with a vision. My mother describes her experience, as a little girl, of taking over 150 quilts out for spring cleaning, hanging them over clotheslines, fence rows, bushes, and whatever was available—even slow cows!—so they could be beaten clean of the winter's accumulated dust and must. All were made completely by hand—not only was there no sewing machine, there were no electric lights until my mother left the farm in the 1940s to find work and sent money home to have electricity run to the house so lights could be installed.

All this leaves me with a profound sense of loss. My family's story—my story—has been cut off, shortened, diminished. I could sit on that porch and feel my ancestors seep into my bones; I could snuggle under those quilts and feel the loving care of my foremothers who made them, and the presence of generations of Bares who had also slept under them. Now these physical symbols of who I am and what it means to be me are gone forever.

Each of us seeks for meaning in our life, either in our personal accomplishments and accumulations or in some outside cause, or group, or story. Being a member of the Bare family has been an important part of my understanding of the meaning of my life—to be part of the ongoing story of the Bares. This fire is a clear reminder that nothing lasts forever—everything in this world passes away, whether farmhouse or quilts or jobs or beauty, power or prestige. If my identity, the meaning of my life, is based on these physical talismans, my life has a very fleeting meaning, indeed— because I will die and everything I have touched will eventually pass away, whether done in by moth or rust or flood or stroke of lightning. The Bare family story is larger than my individual story, but it is still not large enough to last more than a few hundred years. Our national story is larger, and will survive any number of floods and fires and tornadoes, but history warns us it, too, will eventually come to an end.

You and I are part of a still larger and longer story—we have an identity and our lives have a meaning far beyond our family history or national heritage. We are inseparably caught up in the grandest story of all: the cosmic story of the eternally developing relationship between the Creator and creation. All the other stories of which we may be a part—as individuals, as members of a family or citizens of a nation, as residents of a region or members of a religious community—take their meaning from the part they play in this cosmic story. I am here tonight to talk about the cosmic story—the big story—with a fresh awareness that no smaller story will ultimately be enough or can give our lives the meaning we want and need so much.

The theme of these yearly meeting sessions speaks of "Sampling the Powerful Roots of Quakerism." My personal experience is that there is a single root of our faith and life as a religious society—a taproot that is much older and runs much deeper than Quakerism. The taproot is that large, central root for a tree that runs straight down from the trunk into the deepest soil, anchoring the tree against the storms of life and providing nurture from the very deepest of sources. There may be hundreds of secondary roots, but only the taproot is necessary for the tree to survive and thrive. The taproot of our faith is so vast, so powerful, so profoundly "other" that we cannot truly say that we can sample it, because one can sample only what one controls. It seems closer to the truth to say that we encounter the taproot. The big story—the cosmic story—is the story of creation's eternally repeated encounters with its taproot.

We understand God, and we understand the life that God yearns for us to live, primarily through these encounters. It is a blessing to each of us that we have, in the form of the Bible, a record of over 3,000 years of these encounters, accumulated and passed down from generation to generation to guide us in our understandings and warn us away from mistakes others have made before us. When we study this anthology, one truth that stands clear is that God is unchanging from age to age—but our understanding of God waxes and wanes, as we discover and forget basic truths over and over again. Some important truths we have yet to understand fully, or to accept and act upon consistently.

Bible study reminds us that our story, yours and mine, did not begin with our birth and will not end with our death. Our story did not begin with George Fox's birth; it did not begin with Jesus Christ's birth. Our story begins with God. Just as there is one God, eternal and unchanging, there is one story about the relationship between God and God's creation: the big story, of which Moses and George Fox and you and I are little sub-stories. For those with eyes to see and ears to hear, each of these sub-stories proclaims the truth of the big story of creation's repeated encounters with its taproot.

Let us go back now over three thousand years, to the oldest story in the Bible. Let me tell you a taproot story: the story of the encounter that Moses had with the burning bush on Mount Horeb, the mountain of God. This oldest of Bible stories illustrates some truths about God and the way God operates that had to be rediscovered by George Fox and the other early Publishers of Truth some 3,000 years later. It also makes some clear statements about our right relationship to God and to each other that Christians on the whole have still not grasped, whether Quaker or not.

A long, long time ago, in a place very far away from Ohio, the children of Abraham, Isaac, and Jacob fled to Egypt as refugees from a devastating drought and the resulting famine. They were well received there, and protected from starvation. The drought eventually ended, but the Israelites stayed on in Egypt. Gradually, however, their life there worsened, until they became virtual slaves in the land, forced to the harshest labor and the worst living conditions, so that the Egyptians could live lives of relative ease. This went on for a long time, and there seemed no hope for the Israelites.

From the Book of Exodus, chapter 2:

> During this long period the king of Egypt died. The Israelites, groaning in their slavery, cried out for help and from the depths of their slavery their cry came up to God. God heard their groaning; God remembered his covenant with Abraham, Isaac and Jacob. God saw the Israelites and took note. . . .

> Moses was looking after the flock of his father-in-law Jethro, the priest of Midian; he led it to the far side of the desert and came to Horeb, the mountain of God. The angel of Yahweh appeared

to him in a flame blazing from the middle of a bush. Moses looked; there was the bush blazing, but the bush was not being burnt up. Moses said, "I must go across and see this strange sight, and why the bush is not being burnt up." When Yahweh saw him going across to look, God called to him from the middle of the bush. "Moses, Moses!" he said. "Here I am," he answered. "Come no nearer," he said. "Take off your sandals, for the place where you are standing is holy ground. I am the God of your ancestors," he said, "the God of Abraham, the God of Isaac and the God of Jacob." At this Moses covered his face, for he was afraid to look at God.

Yahweh then said, "I have indeed seen the misery of my people in Egypt. I have heard them crying for help on account of their taskmasters. Yes, I am well aware of their sufferings. And I have come down to rescue them from the clutches of the Egyptians and bring them up out of that country, to a country rich and broad, to a country flowing with milk and honey, to the home of the Canaanites, the Hittites, the Amorites, the Perizzites, the Hivites and the Jebusites. Yes, indeed, the Israelites' call for help has reached me, and I have also seen the cruel way in which the Egyptians are oppressing them. So now I am sending you to pharaoh, for you to bring my people the Israelites out of Egypt."

Moses said to God, "Who am I to go to pharaoh and bring the Israelites out of Egypt?" "I shall be with you," God said, "and this is the sign by which you will know that I was the one who sent you. After you have led the people out of Egypt, you will worship God on this mountain."

Moses then said to God, "Look, if I go to the Israelites and say to them, 'The God of your ancestors has sent me to you,' and they say to me, 'What is his name?' what am I to tell them?" God said to Moses, "I am he who is." And he said, "This is what you are to say to the Israelites, 'I AM has sent me to you.'" God further said to Moses, "You are to tell the Israelites, 'Yahweh, the God of your ancestors, the God of Abraham, the God of Isaac and the God of Jacob, has sent me to you.' This is my name for all time, and thus I am to be invoked for all generations to come."[43]

43 Exodus 2:23–3:15, New Jerusalem Bible.

That's not the end of the story, but let's stop there and look with fresh eyes at this encounter between a shepherd and God in a burning bush. This story holds truths about holy ground, how God chooses to communicate with each of us directly, and the qualifications of God's ministers, which were hidden in plain sight, in the Bible of all places, for dozens of centuries until rediscovered by George Fox and the Valiant Sixty. It is surprising to realize that these supposed Quaker innovations can be found here in the very oldest part of the Bible. It is perhaps more surprising to realize that they were here in plain sight and not seen for so many centuries!

Before we become too content with our Quaker twenty-twenty spiritual insight, let me say that Moses and the burning bush contains other truth, about the nature of our relationship to God and each other, that Christendom has still not understood or taken to heart—and Christendom includes most Quakers. First, however, let us look at these three Quaker innovations to be found in this Old Testament story.

In contrast to most other Christians, Quakers hold that no outward act can sanctify or bless or make holy a specific part of the physical world, and certainly that no separated group of individuals have been given a special ability to do this. There is no Quaker "Blessing of the Boats" at the local marina, no sprinkling of holy water to bless the faithful, no holy ritual to dedicate and sanctify the meetinghouse. Friends do not take off their hats when entering the meeting room in deference to the holiness of the place. In this we are distinctive from the great mass of Christian practice over the past two centuries. Yahweh tells Moses to take off his sandals, because he is standing on holy ground. It is the presence of Yahweh that sanctifies the place, not the rituals or sacrifices of human beings that makes it holy. George Fox would have been quite comfortable taking his own shoes off here, as Yahweh directed.

One of my favorite Methodists shows up for meeting every so often, even though he pastors a Methodist church in a neighboring city. When he arrived at the beginning of meeting for business one First Day morning, a Friend suggested that he had made a mistake, and really wanted to come back in two hours for meeting for worship. "Oh, no," he replied, "I want to be here for business meeting. I always like to see how you Quakers deal with an uncontrollable God." Much of our concern with holiness and righteousness seems to be to be fundamentally a concern with controlling an uncontrollable God. By setting aside certain space as holy, by means of human action, we try to control what sort of encounters we can have with God in other spaces. The burning bush reminds us that God chooses when and where we will have a divine encounter, and that the Divine Presence makes that spot and time holy, not anything we do or say.

The second Quaker insight that turns out to be old news is that our line of communication with God is—in airline terminology—direct and nonstop. God communicates with Moses directly, without intermediary. George Fox's profound insights— "There is one, even Christ Jesus, who can speak to thy condition." and "Christ has come to teach his people himself"—are not brand new to the story, but rediscoveries of the earlier relationship between God and human beings. There is no priesthood to mediate between God and the Israelites at this point in history, and Moses is outside that community anyway. Nor does God choose to communicate through Moses' father-in-law Jethro, the Midianite priest. Yahweh goes directly to Moses, to whom he wants to communicate.

Up until this point in the story, God has always spoken directly with our ancestors. Angels have been as much the manifestation of God as God's messenger, and no priests or theologians have been required to interpret or communicate God's message to the rest of us. God calls Moses directly, and engages Moses in the dialogue that will send him to Egypt. From his first words, Yahweh emphasizes the personal and direct nature of the conversation. "Moses, Moses," calls Yahweh. In Semitic culture, this doubling of the first name is a sign of affection, of deep personal relationship.

Right here, at the point of an encounter that manifests this direct communication between God and the individual, human beings are going to begin the project of forgetting about it. A personal and direct link between God and common people is always uncomfortable and even threatening to those at the top of the social pyramid, and we see in this story, just beyond the point where we stopped reading, the priesthood inserting itself into the flow of events and asserting its importance. The priestly faction tells the story of Moses' call with a slightly different twist, emphasizing Aaron's importance as an intermediary, hearing the Word of God from Moses and interpreting it for pharaoh and the Israelites. They even go so far as to make clear that Aaron is the older brother—an important fact in Semitic culture.

The institutional church is always inserting itself in between the individual and God, claiming its role as necessary intermediary and interpreter of the Word. This is certainly to some extent the result of desire on the part of some individuals for power and prestige—and sometimes for possessions, as it can be lucrative to be a priest. However, we must confess that it is also to some extent the result of our own desire for orderliness and predictability—to control an uncontrollable God. There is some part of us that is comforted by tradition, by ritual, by knowing in advance that God (or at least, the church) expects us to do this and this, and not to do that or that other thing.

The difficulty is keeping the line of direct communication with God open, without filters, while also gaining the benefit of the wisdom and experience of our brothers and sisters in Christ who can help us understand the context and implications of what God has to say to us directly. We are rightly suspicious of anyone who tells us, "God gave me this message for you." On the other hand, all my communication with God takes place in the context of the big story. If I shut myself off completely from the insights and perspectives of others in the story, I lose the context of the big story itself and the place of my personal encounter with God in that story. We need the institutional church; we need the orderliness it brings and the many ways it preserves our story and reminds us of the context of our lives. At the same time, we must never forget that Yahweh is constantly calling, "Moses, Moses"—with deep personal affection.

A third supposedly Quaker insight that is manifest in this Old Testament story concerns the qualifications of God's ministers. One of the remarkable aspects of the early Quaker movement that swept across England and beyond was the ordinariness of the people who were called to be ministers of the gospel. To express it a little differently, some pretty unlikely people were called to the ministry. To the surprise and discomfort of many, George Fox pronounced that it is not Cambridge or Oxford that makes a minister, but the call of God. Anyone familiar with Moses and the burning bush should not have been surprised. To whom does God communicate God's concern for the suffering Israelites? Whom does God choose to carry out this great ministry, to set the foundation stone of God's relationship with human beings? A fugitive from justice, wanted for murder, who has deserted his people to live in the wilderness and has "gone native" to the extent of marrying the daughter of a pagan priest—Friends, Moses married out of meeting! Moses is not disowned by Yahweh, or called to repentance, or sentenced to penance. Yahweh calls Moses to ministry!

Here is a clear example of Friends understanding that it is the call of God, the divine leading, that authenticates and validates the ministry, not the academic or political or cultural or religious credentials of the minister. Moses' story of going out to pasture his father-in-law's sheep one morning and being sent on a "mission from God" by nightfall reminds one of James Nayler's experience of setting out from home one morning and being called of God to travel in the ministry, setting off without saying good-bye to wife and family. Neither Moses nor Nayler had the academic credentials that even in Quaker circles are sometimes seen as necessary, and perhaps even sufficient, to make a minister of God. What they did share was an unqualified acceptance of and commitment to God's call. In each case the rest of their life was devoted to carrying out God's call to minister to God's people.

Moses' dedication did not change the fact that he was a fallible human being; one of those failings kept him out of the promised land. Nayler also fell prey to his own humanity. Ministers aren't perfect; they are called and committed.

Holy ground, direct communion with God, and God's call the primary qualification for the ministry—these Quaker distinctives are clearly laid out in the Exodus story, many centuries before there were Quakers. This reminds us of God's unchanging nature, and the way that human understanding of God waxes and wanes over time. We can discover nothing about God that has not been true for millions of years—only our understanding is different. We grow from "simple mind" into a more complex and sophisticated understanding of these Scripture stories as our own experience and intellect develop. Then, if we pursue truth with integrity, we discover that complex and sophisticated understanding are not the end point of our journey, and we begin to pass beyond intellect to what some have called enlightenment, as we ponder the profound truths enveloped in these simple stories. The stories are the same, the truth unchanging—but we are different, engaging not with our mind or spirit only, but with our gut and soul as well. The truth is unchanged, but our comprehension of its meaning and implications for our own actions is profoundly changed.

I said this is a taproot story. These Quaker distinctives—however important to our identity as the Religious Society of Friends—are not the taproot of our faith. They are no more than sidebars to the real story in this tale of the burning bush: the encounter with Yahweh, and the nature of our relationship with Yahweh as revealed in this encounter.

To read again from Exodus, chapter two:

> The Israelites, groaning in their slavery, cried out for help and from the depths of their slavery their cry came up to God. God heard their groaning; God remembered his covenant with Abraham, Isaac and Joseph. God saw the Israelites and took note.[44]

> Yahweh then said, "I have indeed seen the misery of my people in Egypt. I have heard them crying for help on account of their taskmasters. Yes, I am well aware of their sufferings. And I have come down to rescue them from the clutches of the Egyptians and bring them up out of that country, to a country rich and broad, to a country flowing with milk and honey.[45]

This is the taproot, the solid foundation of our faith, that the God of all creation has chosen to love us and care about our circumstances and to intervene in ways that liberate us from our suffering. The Israelites were not crying to Yahweh for help—the writers of Exodus are careful to make that clear in their narrative.

---

[44] Exodus 2:23–24, New Jerusalem Bible.
[45] Exodus 3:7–8, New Jerusalem Bible.

Yahweh heard them anyway, and chose to care that they were suffering, and chose to take up their cause, to intervene in history to end their suffering, to bring them to a land flowing with milk and honey. Yahweh did that for the Israelites because Yahweh chose to be in this special, covenant relationship with them.

We know now, as Christ has revealed to us, that God has chosen to be in this same relationship with every human being who is on earth—or who has been, or who will be. We all share in God's love and protection, not because of anything we have done or said, or our genetic makeup, or geography of birth, but because God has chosen to love and care for all of us. Every human being is equal in the sight of God, because God loves and cares for us all equally—and that love and care set the standard for our relationships with God and one another.

Friends have been proud of their testimony of equality. We are all equal, Friends often say, because we each have a bit of God within us. We speak reverently and thankfully of our experience of the Inner Light, the Inner Christ, which guides us and heals us in daily life. I wrote in my conscientious objector application during the Vietnam War that if there is God within each one of us, as I believe, then an attack on another human being is an attack on God—blasphemy and sacrilege! Each human being should be treated with the respect and dignity appropriate to the temple of God. Here in Exodus we find a different twist on the basis for our equality. We are equal because God cares for each of us equally. To jump forward about fourteen centuries, we are equal because Christ died as much for you as for me, and as much for Adolph Hitler and Timothy McVeigh as for either one of us.

It is not wrong to say that we are equal because there is that of God within each of us, but it is dangerous. It is spiritually dangerous because we live in such an individualistic culture. We talk about the "me generation" but the phenomenon is much larger than any one generation. In all of North American culture—religious, political, economic, and social—the individual is supreme. The focus is on whether I will get into heaven, whether my rights have been recognized or violated, whether I am financially secure into my retirement, and whether I am fulfilled as an individual.

These concerns are not wrong in themselves, but they tempt us to substitute the good for the gospel—the most dangerous of substitutions. All of these cultural forces encourage us to put ourselves at the center of our story rather than God. When we add to that an emphasis on the God within, we must struggle fiercely against the temptation to become little gods in our own little universes, where the meaning of anything is decided by how it affects my own welfare and happiness. We have no responsibility for anyone or anything else because we did not create them and do not sustain them from moment to moment—forgetting that God created and sustains us always. At the center of our little story, the only meaning is "more for me," which ultimately is meaningless since ultimately "me" dies.

Yahweh revealed in the burning bush is not God within Moses, or God within the Israelites, but God the profoundly "Other"— the mighty Creator and Sustainer of all creation. I cannot be at the center of any story that includes Yahweh as revealed in Exodus— only God can be at the center of that story. Paradoxically, it is only when I am no longer at the center of my story, and Yahweh is, that my life assumes its deepest, truest, and eternal meaning.

Please don't misunderstand me. God is both immanent and transcendent—within and without—and has been since the beginning of creation. George Fox's realization of and emphasis on the direct communion with Christ, and the expression of that realization by Friends as God within, were an important manifestation of truth. In a time and culture that debated whether women had souls, that countenanced slavery and economic oppression, that denied the value of the individual human being in so many ways, early Friends emphasis on the immanent nature of God was a blessing and sweet savor to many souls. God has not changed; the God within is still there, as much as ever.

Time and culture do change. In the present day and in the North American culture, we do not need to emphasize the worth or rights of the individual—the secular culture is doing that to excess, and much of the so-called religious culture is also. Our challenge is to re-attach the individual to the source of meaning beyond the personal pronoun, beyond "I" and "me" and "mine."

Our call is to tell the old, old story in new and fresh ways, to re-acquaint souls with the Author and Perfecter of their very being—to help them hear the story with new ears and to see the world and their place in it with new eyes. Those who do will realize that the only story that is ultimately satisfying has God at the center—not them.

Every time we do this—every time we tell the big story from the heart—the one person we know will be changed is ourselves. As we say at Norfolk Quaker House, our work is to be spiritual midwives in a process of spiritual conversion in our clients—and the one person we know will be converted is the counselor. Considering the Exodus story, hearing and telling of this first encounter between Moses and Yahweh, I am transported by the transcendent God—Creator and Sustainer of the universe, profoundly Other—not human at all—yet filled with such love and care for suffering human beings. I am inseparably caught up in the cosmic story, with God at the center. The meaning of my life is expressed in God's infinite love for me: God created me, and God sustains me from moment to moment by continuing to will my existence; and the same is true for you and for all of creation. I have meaning because God's love affirms that I am indeed, for all my warts and flaws, very good.

That is the beginning of a new understanding of how you and I are called to be in the world. When I understand the transcendent God to be at the center of the cosmic story, then God's affirming and sustaining love for me calls me to act on behalf of my fellow human beings with new strength and courage and commitment. God's love and care for those who suffer calls each of us and all of us to care equally deeply—and like God, to take up the cause of the suffering and oppressed and to intervene on their behalf.

God cares about the Israelites because they are God's chosen people and they are suffering. Whether they have an Inner Light is never mentioned; whether or not they are living righteous, holy lives is not discussed; there is no intrinsic quality in the Israelites that makes them worthy or deserving of God's care and interven-tion. God cares about the Israelites because God chooses to care, God chooses to love. God loves without regard to the worthiness of the individual, and intervenes to end their suffering and oppression because of God's love. So should we.

God's love and care for those who suffer makes clear why I should care about my neighbor's plight: I should care because God cares. Realizing that God is the true center of my story and every story, and experiencing God's infinite and unmerited love for all of creation, will result in a change of the central faith question for most North Americans. The central faith question for Christians in North American is usually some variation of "How can I be saved" or "How can I be righteous enough to earn God's favor?"

That question comes from a number of sources, including our individualism, the richness of our society which gives us what the rest of the world would experience as limitless options to do or not do works of faith and religious discipline, and the desire of individuals at the center of their own story to control an uncontrollable God. "How do I get into Heaven?" is the question most of us are asking, and it also translates into "What is the minimum necessary for me to do that will force God to accept me?"

When God is at the center of the story, when my relationship to God is bound up in God's love and concern for me and my plight, and I experience that God loves and cares for every person and all of creation with the same intensity, then the central faith question is no longer "Am I saved?" or "How can I get saved?" I am justified not by my works, and not by my faith, but by God's unmerited grace. I am already saved, by God's initiative. I have only to respond to God's invitation. The central faith question then becomes "Why is the world this way, and what can I do about it?" Surely it is not God's will that there be so much suffering and oppression and grinding poverty in the world that God created and sustains from moment to moment and loves so much. What causes the suffering? Not generic suffering, but the suffering of this individual person, and that individual person: why do they suffer?

And what can I do about it? God's example in Exodus is clear—God not only hears the groans of the Israelites, God cares, God takes sides, and God intervenes in history on behalf of the poor, the oppressed, and the powerless. We are called to do the same in the present day.

In the Gospel of Matthew Jesus makes the one unequivocal promise of when we will meet him in our daily life: when we give food and drink to the hungry, hospitality to the homeless, clothing to the naked, when we visit the sick and the prisoner.[46] When we do this to the least of persons, we do it to Christ. The concern of the church—particularly the church in North America—has been for the nonbeliever: who has been saved so far and how do we reach the rest? From Moses to Jesus to John Woolman to Dom Helder Camara, God has been telling us that the more important concern is for the nonperson—those whom we discount and treat as being of no value in our society.

My wife Susan and I help out on the breakfast line with the Norfolk Catholic Worker folks one morning each week, on a side street not too far from the center of downtown. Salter Street runs between a parking lot and a cemetery. After forcing the breakfast line to move from several other locations more convenient to the people we serve, city officials have tolerated our presence on Salter Street—after all, as our homeless friends observe, "No one lives there to complain!" Working from three coffee tables in good weather or out of the back and side of a van when it rains, we give grits, coffee and a sandwich to as many as 125 homeless men, women and children. I realize that I can be present in that activity in many different ways that really center on me, not them: out of a sense of guilt and obligation, or a desire to record another good work on my spiritual ledger, or to enhance my reputation in the religious community, or other reasons you can name. And the hungry will get fed, and the institutions of power, prestige and possessions will applaud the work—see, we care about the poor— they get their meals at that breakfast line.

However, when I am feeding the hungry out of participation in God's love for them, when God is at the center of the activity, then simply feeding them soon becomes insufficient. If God loves these homeless people so much, then it cannot be God's will that they experience such poverty and pain. One has to ask the questions, "Why is the world this way? Why do these people suffer?"

46 Matthew 25:34–40.

Asking that question "problematizes" the situation, and brings the wrath of the same institutions of power, prestige and possessions that applauded the simple act of feeding the poor. If God does not will that some people be homeless, have no job or access to health care, who does? If we agree not to blame the victim, then why is the world this way? Who put the structures together so that these people suffer? Who benefits from their being kept where they are, where they suffer so much? These are not questions that those at the top of society like to hear. As Dom Helder Camara, former Archbishop of Recife, observed, "When I give food to the poor they call me a saint. When I ask why the poor have no food, they call me a communist."

Susan tells a story of discovering a baby in the midst of a river, about to drown. Naturally, you jump in and save the baby. Before too long, you see another baby, and jump in and save that one, too. Before too long, you have organized a rescue squad to watch the river and pull the babies out, built an orphanage to take care of them once they are safe and a school for the older children who have been at the orphanage for a number of years. You develop a network of supporters whose donations help finance better rescue equipment, buy food and clothing for the babies, and so on. You've gotten really good at pulling babies out of the river. When are you going to send someone upstream to find out how and why the babies are getting into the river to begin with?

Yahweh is not content to start a soup kitchen for hungry Israelites, or to arrange for better medical care, or supply better tools to ease their workload. Yahweh goes upstream, to change the structure of Egyptian society to liberate the Israelites from their oppression. Yahweh's word to pharaoh is not "Pay my people better" or "Overtime for more than forty hours per week" or "Free straw for brick-makers;" Yahweh's word is "Let my people GO!"

If we really experience the direct communion with God proclaimed by George Fox and multitudes of other Friends for 350 years, then we can't help but share God's concern for the poor and oppressed, God's preferred location among them, and God's commitment to intervention in human history on their behalf. We're going to have to live in solidarity with the poor—not just throw money over the wall at them—and work to establish an entirely new great economy that reflects God's values and God's love for all people and all of creation. We're going to have to build an economy of grace to replace the economy of debt that encircles and enslaves us all.

The story of the burning bush calls us to live in community, tells us who is in that community, and shows how it is to be done. Our basis for being able to be in community with one another is our covenant relationship with God. In the Exodus story God demonstrates the nature of that covenant: God initiates, and we respond. God heard the groans of the Israelites, even though they were not calling to Yahweh; God cared about their plight, and intervened radically on their behalf. We are called to emulate that relationship with one another by hearing and caring and taking radical action.

We can be in community with God only when our community includes those people for whom God has shown a loving preference: the poor, the powerless, the oppressed people who are at the periphery of society, at the bottom of the pyramid of power, wealth, and prestige. They are not the only members of God's community, but if they are not fully part of it, God is not fully present.

To include these folks in our community forces us to step outside the social, political, religious, and economic structures that serve you and me so well. We will have to see these institutions from the perspective of the bottom, of the margins, and understand their flaws as well as their strengths. And because these structures in fact do not work for all the members of our community, we will have to restructure ourselves in ways that more truly reflect the value God places on each human life.

I do not mean that we should dedicate our lives to opposing the structures and institutions of social and economic injustice, or political oppression. To quote Richard Rohr, the Franciscan monk:

> You cannot build on death. You can only build on life. We must be sustained by a sense of what we are for and not just what we are against.

Our struggle is not against the oppressors, or the powerful, or the rich, or the institutions that serve their purposes. That struggle is just another form of domination, and our victory would only perpetuate the old injustices, with different actors in the various roles. You become what you fight against, and if we fight against the structures of oppression hard enough we will succeed in placing ourselves at the top of the pyramid instead of who is there now—another failure. Our struggle is for the oppressed, for the suffering, for the poor and powerless, to relieve their pain and create a world free of all forms of domination.

To do this we must learn to create new social and economic relationships, new circles of community that embody God's great economy, God's divine plan for all of creation. It will not be easy, and those who benefit from the present system will not come flocking to join us. The parable of Luke chapter 19 warns us, as it warned the disciples, just how hard and painful this effort will be. It also will not be quick. Jesus said that if we exorcise one demon, seven more will come to confront us. If we exorcise those, forty nine more will come, and so on—you do the math. It will be the work of a lifetime just to start the journey toward the great economy.

This is, however, the work to which we are called, the commission arising from our encounter with the taproot of all creation. This is the point of the cosmic story, foreshadowed in the garden of Eden and modeled among the creatures on the ark in the midst of the flood. This is the promised land of the Exodus story, and this is the holy city foreseen in the revelation of Jesus Christ to John:

> Then I saw a new heaven and a new earth; the first heaven and the first earth had disappeared now, and there was no longer any sea. I saw the holy city, the New Jerusalem, coming down out of heaven from God, prepared as a bride dressed for her husband. Then I heard a loud voice call from the throne, "Look, here God lives among human beings. He will make his home among them, they will be his people, and he will be their God, God-with-them. He will wipe away all tears from their eyes; there will be no more death, and no more mourning or sadness or pain. The world of the past has gone."[47]

[47] Revelation 21:1–4, New Jerusalem Bible.

Biblical Basis for Quaker Peacemaking

This was a presentation to a regional gathering of peace-makers in early 2004, including both programmed and unprogrammed Friends in the Knoxville, Tennessee area. What will always be most memorable for me about this trip is that after the presentation on Seventh Day, upon returning to our hosts' home for the night, both Mike Arnold and I felt a deep spiritual unease. After an extended period of solid consideration, we felt that we were supposed to drive back to Mike's home in Snow Camp, North Carolina, and attend meeting for worship there with West Grove Friends rather than staying to worship with Friends in Knoxville as we had planned. We set out after dark to drive across the mountains in a substantial snowfall, unable to explain our actions to our hosts or to ourselves except to say that it felt like the right thing to do. I still have no explanation except that it seemed like the right thing to do, and Mike and I both felt a great peace when we gave up to the leading and set out into the night.

To inquire into the Biblical basis for Quaker peacemaking requires that one first come to an understanding of the role of the Bible in determining the ethics of the Religious Society of Friends. So our question is how does the Bible guide and inform our actions in general, and in particular in the ethical area we call the peace testimony.

The prior assumption here is that the Bible carries some important moral authority, or at least moral influence, on this and other ethical questions. Early Friends were at pains to demonstrate that this was so, although their conclusions about the nature and direction of that authority and influence were often at odds with those of their Christian fellows.

Mention the Bible to a modern liberal Friend and she will immediately reply with "continuing revelation." That's an important Quaker principle for understanding the Bible. Friends must remember, however, that genuine *continuing* revelation means that there has been genuine *previous* revelation in years past. Friends have always embraced the authenticity and reality of this previous revelation. As Barclay says in the third proposition of his *Apology for the True Christian Divinity*:

> From these revelations of the Spirit of God to the saints have proceeded the Scriptures of truth, which contain,
>
> I.   A faithful historical account of the actings of God's people in divers ages; with many singular and remarkable providences attending them.
> II. A prophetical account of several things, whereof some are already past, and some yet to come.
> III. A full and ample account of all the chief principles of the doctrine of Christ, held forth in divers precious declarations, exhortations and sentences, which, by the moving of God's Spirit, were at several times, and upon sundry occasions, spoken and written unto some churches and their pastors.
>
> Nevertheless, because they are only a declaration of the fountain, and not the fountain itself, therefore they are not to be esteemed the principal ground of all truth and knowledge, nor yet the adequate primary rule of faith and manners. Yet because they give a true and faithful testimony of the first foundation, they are and may be esteemed a secondary rule, subordinate to the Spirit, from which they have all their excellency and certainty: for as by the inward testimony of the Spirit we do alone truly know them, so they testify, that the Spirit is that Guide by which the saints are led into all truth; therefore, according to the Scriptures, the Spirit is the first and principal leader. Seeing then that we do therefore receive and believe the Scriptures because they proceeded from the Spirit, for the very same reason is the Spirit more originally and principally the rule.[48]

---

[48] Robert Barclay, *Apology for the True Christian Divinity*, Friends Book-Store, Philadelphia, PA, no date, pp. 72–73.

Setting aside the statement about prophetic accounts for the moment, Barclay makes two other strong assertions about Scripture: that it contains a faithful account of the actions of God's people at various times; and that it contains a full and ample account of the chief principles of the doctrine of Christ. To restate these affirmations in reverse order, Barclay is saying that Scripture contains all the chief rules for living a Christian life, as well as the story of God's people as they sometimes abided by these rules and sometimes did not. To use their own terminology, Friends found both *precept* and *example* in Scripture to guide them in discerning right action in their own lives.

So the Bible is a collection of stories, letters, and other writings that hold some authoritative revelation from God of precepts about how to live, and some examples of human beings who tried to understand and follow that revelation. Some biblical characters were more successful than others. By trying to understand this body of previous revelation the believing community comes to understand the parameters or boundary conditions of right behavior. Our first test for ethical decisions is therefore whether or not our leading falls inside or outside these biblical boundary conditions. That is not sufficient, for as Scripture itself tells us, not all things that are lawful are helpful.[49] So we must seek additional discernment, in concert with our faith community, to see whether the leading or behavior in question builds up or tears down our relationship with God and God's creation, including the community of faith and the community of all human beings. What is God calling us to do in the present moment, and how can we be obedient to that call?

In approaching the Bible for specific guidance about peacemaking, Friends are looking for principles that seem to express God's will about war and peace, and for stories—Barclay's "historical accounts"—of how human beings acted as they tried to live by those principles. We are not searching for proof texts that will provide an up or down ruling, but for themes and stories that illustrate and illuminate our own discernment and decisionmaking.

The first thing one notices in such a search is that the Bible contains many texts about war, both pro and con. Some of the most prominent of these are:

49 1 Corinthians 6:12.

Biblical Texts for War

God dislikes war, but people just can't get along: Campaign of the Four Great Kings and Abram's revenge,[50] Tower of Babel,[51] Abel & Cain.[52] In Matthew, Jesus says that we will hear of wars and rumors of wars, because they must happen.[53]

God approves of war: God commands the Israelites to invade and conquer all the time. God is characterized as a warrior in Exodus for defeating pharaoh's army,[54] and many of the Psalms invoke God's help in violent suppression of the Psalmist's enemies, with the assumption that God will accept and cooperate with such a petition. In some cases, God seems to command that whole peoples be destroyed. Moses believed God had declared war against the Amalekites "generation after generation."[55] The Book of Hebrews praises warriors who had been "brave in war and driven back foreign invaders" as persons of great faith.[56] And the Book of Revelation is full of warlike imagery, including the scene where war breaks out in heaven as Michael and his angels attack the dragon.[57]

Isaiah records that "There is no peace, says my God, for the wicked."[58]

Over the years, several active-duty military personnel I've conversed with have cited the New Testament incident where Jesus praises the centurion who has faith that Jesus has authority to heal his servant[59] as proof that God approves of war and warriors.

God is on our side in war: Sometimes it seems that God not only approves of war, but also is on our side in war. This includes events such as the Exodus battle against pharaoh.[60] Paul uses military

50 Genesis 14:1–16.
51 *Ibid.,* 11:1–9.
52 *Ibid.,* 4:1–16.
53 Matthew 26:6.
54 Exodus 15:3.
55 *Ibid.,* 17:16.
56 Hebrews 11:34.
57 Revelation 12:7.
58 Isaiah 57:21.
59 Matthew 8:1–10.
60 Exodus 15.

imagery in his Epistle to the Ephesians to describe a spiritual warrior.[61]

Jesus himself was violent when the occasion called for it: In the description of Jesus "cleansing" the Temple in the Gospel of John,[62] Jesus used a "whip" of cords. Here again, I have had more than one discussion with military personnel, especially military recruiters, who cited this passage as proof that Jesus approved of military action.

Biblical Texts Against War

War is idolatry: Putting our faith in military force for our protection is worshipping weaponry rather than God. " I am the Lord thy God, which brought thee out of Egypt, out of the house of bondage. Thou shalt have no other gods before me."[63] Nuclear weapons in particular are idols that we put in place of God, depending on them and worshipping them with our time and money.

Peace is the divine wish and intent: Thou shalt not kill.[64] Now in fairness I need to say it is probably a mis-use of this verse to make it anti-war, but certainly it has been and is used in this way, by modern Friends as well as others.

You shall not take vengeance or bear a grudge against any of your people, but you shall love your neighbor as yourself: I am the **Lord**.[65]

His authority shall grow continually, and there shall be endless peace for the throne of David and his kingdom. He will establish and uphold it with justice and with righteousness from this time onward and forevermore. The zeal of the **Lord** of hosts will do this.[66]

The wolf shall live with the lamb, the leopard shall lie down with the kid, the calf and the lion and the fatling together, and a

61 Ephesians 6:9.
62 John 2:13–16.
63 Exodus 20:2–3.
64 *Ibid.*, 20:13.
65 Leviticus 19:18.
66 Isaiah 9:7.

little child shall lead them. And the cow and the bear shall feed; their young ones shall lie down together: and the lion shall eat straw like the ox. And the sucking child shall play on the hole of the asp, and the weaned child shall put his hand on the cockatrice' den. They will not hurt or destroy on all my holy mountain; for the earth will be full of the knowledge of the Lord as the waters cover the sea.[67]

Jesus' teaching: Christ has set us a new precept and new example. Jesus said, "My kingdom is not from this world. If my kingdom were from this world, my followers would be fighting to keep me from being handed over to the Jews. But as it is, my kingdom is not from here."[68]

Well—if all these Bible passages make up a single, coherent revelation, its meaning is less than intuitively clear to the casual observer! In fact, the Bible appears to be very self-contradictory. No wonder that over the ages, Christians have understood Biblical teachings about war and participation in war in widely divergent ways. In recent centuries, however, the great majority of Christians have understood the Bible to endorse participation in a "just war,"[69] however that might be understood or defined.[70] Those few sects who have disagreed—mostly Mennonites, Brethren, and Quakers—have earned themselves the collective name of peace churches.[71]

Friends are in this small group because we have corporately and consistently, from very early on in the life of the Society, interpreted this variegated Biblical message in a way to conclude that Christians should not participate in armed conflict. Early Friends were able to do this by making a series of assertions about the Bible

[67] Isaiah 11: 6–9.

[68] John 18:36.

[69] For an example of just war theory, see:
http://www.mtholyoke.edu/acad/intrel/pol116/justwar.htm.

[70] Opinion polls reported in the *New York Times*, January 24, 2004, "A Tougher War for the U.S. is One of Legitimacy," indicate over 80 percent of Americans believe a war may achieve justice; less than half of Europeans believe a war—any war—can be just.

[71] This phrase invariably invokes for me the memory of Colin Bell, former American Friends Service Committee executive secretary, who would in ecumenical events reproach those who used the term: "Because if we're called peace churches, then what does that make you?"

and the interpretations of Scripture that had come to predominate among Christians in the sixteen hundred plus years since the time of Christ.

- The Church had been largely apostate "since the apostles' days,"[72–73] so that true Christians need not be bound by the dominant institutional church's understanding of Scripture.
- Christ brought a new understanding of previous Scripture,[74] and a new fulfillment to all Scripture, so that many aspects of the "old dispensation" were fallen away, no longer binding or even appropriate for Christians. A common Quaker reading of Scripture, whether applied to water baptism or war, was that if B happened after A in biblical chronology, B must be the current teaching for the church, and not A.[75]
- The individual, in a living relationship with the risen Christ and with the believing community, could partake of the Spirit that gave forth the Scriptures, and thereby come to a new and entirely holy understanding of the meaning behind the words.[76]
- The risen Christ has returned and dwells among us, with the power to enable believers to follow and incarnate God's will.[77] Christ makes no command of His followers that He does not at the same time empower us to follow faithfully; no expectation that we cannot meet with divine assistance.

This is the context in which Robert Barclay could advance his proposition about the Scriptures, which is quoted above.

[72] George Fox, "Christ the Substance," in *Early Prophetic Openings of George Fox*, Tract Association of Friends, Philadelphia, 1962, p. 46.

[73] George Keith, *Immediate Revelation*, 1675, p. 196, in Digital Quaker Collection, ESR.

[74] George Fox, "The Lord Would Teach His People Himself," in *Early Prophetic Openings of George Fox*, Tract Association of Friends, Philadelphia, 1962, pp. 8–9.

[75] Thomas Story, in *The Life of Thomas Story*, Friends Library Vol. 10, edited by William Evans and Thomas Evans, Philadelphia 1846, reports using this line of reasoning many times when arguing over the issue of water baptism.

[76] George Fox, "Reading Scriptures Aright," in *Early Prophetic Openings of George Fox*, Tract Association of Friends, Philadelphia, 1962, pp. 28–30.

[77] William Penn, "Primitive Christianity Revived," in *Twenty-First Century Penn*, edited by Paul Buckley, ESR, Richmond, Indiana, 2003, p. 275.

Declaration of 1660

In that context, then, let us examine the most famous of the various declarations of the Quaker peace testimony: the so-called Declaration of 1660. Some short quotation from this statement is often included in yearly meeting books of discipline or faith and practice, but the full text is based on a series of biblical arguments and is full of other biblical references and allusions. I have annotated the fullest text I can find of the Declaration with a representative sampling of the various Scripture quotations and allusions that it contains—there should be copies of that annotated text to pass around this morning. The full text is also available online.[78]

The Declaration of 1660 is actually a declaration of twelve individual Friends—the institution of the Religious Society of Friends was not well organized at the time. It was written to exculpate Friends from suspicion of involvement in any treasonous plots against the king of England, such as those of the religious extremists known as the Fifth Monarchy men.[79] The Quaker declaration was distributed just a few weeks after Venner's Rising,[80] a Fifth Monarchist attempt to overthrow the new Restoration government before it could get well established. About 100 Fifth Monarchists and 4,000 Quakers were imprisoned in the aftermath of that revolt, and Friends were concerned to clear Friends collective name and free their brothers and sisters in the faith. Their intent was not to produce an abstract statement of ideals or principles, but to demonstrate concretely that Friends could never be involved in an armed uprising like that led by Thomas Venner earlier that same month. Their case is clearly applicable to personal participation in all armed conflict, of whatever description.

THE ARGUMENTS AGAINST WAR

The Declaration makes four principle arguments against fighting outward wars:

[78] See http://www.qhpress.org/quakerpages/qwhp/dec1660.htm.

[79] Named after the vision of God's kingdom in Daniel 2:44, the Fifth Monarchists were a part religious group, part political party.
See http://www.exlibris.org/nonconform/engdis/fifthmonarchists.html.

[80] Steve Angell, ESR faculty, personal communication, January 23, 2004.

- Christ has freed us from the motivation or compulsion that causes humans to fight;
- Christ has given us command and example not to fight;
- Our goal, the kingdom of God, cannot be brought about by outward fighting; and
- We can't be involved in the conflicts between worldly kingdoms because they are all going to be replaced by the kingdom(s) of God.

Christians have no reason to fight wars: Wars are fought for a reason, and in Scripture Friends found both an explanation of the fundamental compulsion for all wars and freedom from that compulsion.

War comes from lust and covetousness (James 4:1–3), and the Lord has redeemed us out of lust and covetousness, and therefore out of the occasion for war. As Fox said about a decade earlier, when offered a military commission as a means of getting released from jail:

> I told them I lived in the virtue of that life and power that took away the occasion of all wars, and I knew from whence all wars did rise, from the lust, according to James' doctrine. . . . I told them I was come into the covenant of peace which was before wars and strifes were.[81]

Some thirty years later, in his preface to the first edition of George Fox's *Journal*, William Penn cites this same Scripture passage as the keystone in the Friends peace testimony:

> All wars and fightings arise in human covetousness, according to the apostle James, not from the meek spirit of Christ Jesus. Christ is the captain of a different warfare, carried out with different weapons. Just as swearing gave way to speaking truth, fighting yielded to faith and truth in their doctrines and practices.[82]

This seemingly minor passage from a short epistle near the end of the New Testament resonated deeply with Friends because it matched with a key experience in their spiritual lives: the power of

---

81 George Fox, *Journal*, Nickalls edition, p. 65.

82 William Penn, "A Brief Account of the Rise and Progress of the People Called Quakers," in *Twenty-First Century Penn*, edited by Paul Buckley, ESR, Richmond, Indiana, 2003, p. 365.

Christ to change their lives, to regenerate them as new beings freed from their previous bondage to sinful ways of life. James said wars come from a certain kind of imperfection; Friends experienced a personal rebirth that freed them from that (and all) imperfection.

Friends called this new state perfection,[83] and considered it crucial to their spiritual lives. Penn, in the same preface to Fox's *Journal*, calls it one of the three general doctrines of the faith:

> A general doctrine that they were led to declare as the prize that all Christians are called to [is] perfection from sin. The Scriptures of truth testify that this is the purpose of Christ's coming and the nature of his kingdom. His Spirit was and is given to us so that we might be perfect and holy because God is holy. . . . They called this a redeemed state, regeneration, or the new birth and they taught it everywhere. This was the foundation—without it, no one could inherit the kingdom.[84]

Christ in the office of redeemer saves us from the power of sin (i.e., lust), which we could never accomplish on our own.[85] Once we have been freed in this way, there is no reason, or occasion, to fight any outward war—there is no longer a motive for the crime, to use modern terminology. For a professed Christian to fight is to confess by outward testimony that she has not yet experienced this rebirth and liberation from the bonds of sin.

The doctrine of perfection had two roots: first, it reflected the personal experience of Friends that they were indeed reborn and freed from many things that formerly oppressed them. Secondly, it was unthinkable to this devout people that God would command them to do or be what God did not at the same time empower them to do and become. They knew by experience and preached to the world that Christ gives us power to do those things He commands of us.[86]

83 George Fox, "Possibility of Perfection," in *Early Prophetic Openings of George Fox*, Tract Association of Friends, 1962, p. 30.

84 Penn, "A Brief Account of the Rise and Progress of the People Called Quakers," in *Twenty-First Century Penn*, edited by Paul Buckley, ESR, Richmond, Indiana, 2003, p. 362.

85 John 1:12–13, "Power to Become Children of God." But to all who received him, who believed in his name, he gave power to become children of God, who were born, not of blood or of the will of the flesh or of the will of man, but of God.

86 "Be ye therefore perfect, even as your Father which is in heaven is perfect" (Matthew 5:48); "But Jesus . . . said unto them, with men this is impossible, but with God all things are possible." (Matthew 19:26)

Those who say that sin (including war and other things) are inevitable from our human nature, and there were as many in the seventeenth century as in the twenty-first, are in the terminology of early Friends "preaching up sin." The Quaker understanding has always been that Christ has empowered Christians to obey this (and all) command(s) and follow His precepts.

Christ's specific precept and example: When Friends found Jesus both stating a precept on a matter, and also giving a personal example, they were confident that they had discovered a principle which should be followed. In the scene of Christ's arrest before he was crucified they found both.

In considering the *precept*, Friends demonstrated an important principle of Quaker exegesis: later pronouncements or examples illuminate or even overturn earlier ones. In this case, Christ certainly said that he without a sword might buy one[87] to fulfill the law and Scripture,[88] as pro-war proponents pointed out then and now; but Friends noted that *after that was accomplished*, he told Peter to put away his sword, saying he that taketh the sword shall perish with the sword.[89] So the first saying was to fulfill Scripture, and the latter was the one binding on Christians.

The Declaration of 1660 then links Christ's statement in that moment with the parallel statement in the Revelation of John:

> He that kills with the sword must be killed with the sword. Here is the patience and faith of the saints.[90]

The implication here is that the sword is false protection—an act of idolatry. The faith and patience of the saints is to endure outward persecution without attempting defense with outward weapons—to rely on God alone.[91]

---

[87] Luke 22:36.

[88] Isaiah 53:12.

[89] Matthew 26:52.

[90] Revelation 13:10.

[91] *The Interpreter's Bible* sees this passage as a warning that if they are destined for captivity, this will be their fate (i.e., persecution and martyrdom); but those who persecute them are also destined for death; Christians should therefore demonstrate those characteristics which lead to martyrdom: faith and patience.

Fox cites this passage elsewhere, also. In "The Quaker's just Allegiance is to hurt none of God's Creatures upon the Earth, and their Supremacy is the Power of God," which appears in *Truth's Triumph in the Eternal Power, Over the Dark Inventions of Fallen Man*,[92] Fox writes:

> But here was the faith and *patience of the saints*, he that led captive, should go into captivity, and that he that killed with the sword, should perish by the sword, shewing the saints' patience and faith was it by which they overcame, which were the true worshippers of God, and not ravening, nor fighting with outward carnal weapons for their religion, for the apostle saith, "it is not only given you to believe, but also to suffer persecution."

It is only human nature to ask "why?" In this case, why would Christ give such a command (that believers in Him should not fight)? The Declaration gives a clear answer to that unspoken question:

> Christ's kingdom is not of this world, therefore his servants do not fight, as he told Pilate (John 18:36): Jesus answered, "My kingdom is not from this world. If my kingdom were from this world, my followers would be fighting to keep me from being handed over to the Jews. But as it is, my kingdom is not from here."

The writers of the Declaration then go on to identify themselves with Christ, in that they are being looked upon as seditious and as fighters (revolutionaries), just as Christ was.

Christ's own example at the time of his arrest supported Friends understanding of the scriptural precept. Christ had legions of angels at his disposal to prevent his own arrest and execution, the greatest sin of all, yet did not call on them.[93] If ever there was a "just war" this was it. The King (Christ) is present to give the legitimate order to wage war, no innocents would suffer, all other means of reconciliation were futile, a perfectly just cause in the protection of God's perfectly innocent Son, and—we trust—an actual use of force proportionate to the need. Nevertheless, Christ says no; he will not call on these angelic defenses.

[92] George Fox, *Works*, 1831, Vol. 4, p. 276.
[93] Matthew 26:53.

The Spirit of Christ is not changeable: Before and after this argument about precept and example the Declaration slips in almost unnoticed an argument about the consistency and dependability of the leadings of the Holy Spirit of Christ. Before the argument, they state the objection of outsiders:

> But although you now say, that you cannot fight or take up arms at all; yet if the spirit move you, then you will change your principle, you will sell your coat and buy a sword, and fight for the kingdom of Christ.

And immediately afterward, they give their response:

> That the spirit of Christ, by which we are guided, is not changeable, so as once to command us from a thing as evil and again to move unto it. We do certainly know, and so testify to the world, that the spirit of Christ, which leads us into all truth, will never move us to fight and war against any man with outward weapons, neither for the kingdom of Christ nor for the kingdoms of this world.

These Friends were invoking the words of the writer of Hebrews, who in describing God's promise to Abraham, wrote:

> Thus God, determining to show more abundantly to the heirs of promise the immutability of His counsel, confirmed it by an oath, that by two immutable things, in which it is impossible for God to lie, we might have strong consolation, who have fled for refuge to lay hold of the hope set before us.[94]

They were also referencing the passage in John's Gospel in which Jesus says the Spirit that is to come will lead his followers into all truth,[95] as well as Paul's second Epistle to the Corinthians:

> For though we walk in the flesh, we do not war after the flesh: (for the weapons of our warfare are not carnal, but mighty through God to the pulling down of strongholds).[96]

Skeptics, not understanding Quaker discernment, were concerned that the Friends were actually just as capable of believing next week that God led them to fight as they were today of believing the opposite. Couldn't they change their minds about fighting as easily

[94] Hebrews 6:17–18.
[95] John 16:13.
[96] 2 Corinthians 10:3–4.

and often as Roger Clemens and Michael Jordan change their minds about retiring? No, the Friends responded, God is not like that.

As you and I reflect on this argument, the earlier comments about the authority of Scripture are relevant. Early Friends were quite capable of saying at the same time that Scripture was authoritative, as they did here, and that revelation continued. Scripture is setting the outer bounds of Christian ethical behaviour, as I said earlier. War is clearly out-of-bounds. What is in-bounds is not all expedient or helpful,[97] and we need the immediate guidance of the Holy Spirit to discern that.

Means inconsistent with the end: The next argument the authors of the Declaration make is that the means of outward war are inconsistent with the end they desire, which is the kingdom of God. Their Scripture basis is the fifth vision of Zechariah, understood to be a vision of the kingdom of God, with God watchful over all the creation and with Zerubbabel and Joshua, the spiritual and secular leaders of the community, implementing the will of God.

How does this kingdom come about? "Not by might, not by power, but by my Spirit,"[98] says God. Though the opponents may be great mountains, they will become a plain before the coming kingdom. So if you really want the kingdom of God to come about, say these Quakers, war is not the way. You really can't fight for peace; you can't wage outward war for the kingdom. God says that's not how the kingdom is going to come.

Remember always that this Declaration was written for a purpose, to allay fears that Quakers were political extremists like those who had recently revolted against the government. So they add here an explicit denial of any association or approval of any persons who might use any outward weapon to fight for the kingdom of God—an explicit reference to the Fifth Monarchy men, who were fighting to establish the Fifth Monarchy implied in the Book of Daniel: Friends deny the spirit, principle, and practice of any such persons.

[97] 1 Corinthians 6:12.
[98] Zechariah 4:1–14.

The kingdoms of this world are become the kingdoms of our Lord, and of his Christ; and He shall reign for ever and ever: The authors of the Declaration are saying here that they cannot prefer one worldly kingdom over another, either to covet some other kingdom (or its wealth) or to fight for the one where they live, because all the kingdoms are destined to end, and to become God's kingdoms. Their basis for this claim is Revelation 11:15, about which the Interpreter's Bible says, "Here, in a brief liturgical sentence, is the main outline of Revelation."[99]

> There were great voices in heaven, saying, the kingdoms of this world are become the kingdoms of our Lord, and of his Christ; and he shall reign for ever and ever.

There is a greater story at work in the world than the story of human kingdoms and governments: the cosmic story of creator and creation. What happens between kingdoms, however important to their rulers, is only a subtext of the greater story of which Scripture tells us: the story of God becoming once again reconciled to creation; the restoration of the gospel order in which creation came to be. The eye of the Quakers is on this greater story, and the transformation it promises. When this transformation comes to pass, then the prophecies of Isaiah and Micah quoted here will also come to pass, that nation shall not lift up sword against nation, neither shall they wage war against one another.[100]

Peace comes not by the Pax Romana or Pax Britannica, or even by the Pax Americana, but by the rule of Christ in human hearts. Our best defense, on every level, is evangelization: promoting the true knowledge of Christ in every heart. That will protect us (and everyone) from the mugger as well as the invader.

Summary

Here then, is the biblical basis for the peace testimony as expressed by the first generation of Friends. Note carefully that the peace testimony is a result, not a cause. Many modern Friends have

[99] *The Interpreter's Bible*, Vol. 12, p. 450.
[100] Isaiah 2:4, Micah 4:3.

come to Quakerism because of the peace testimony; early Friends
came to the peace testimony because of their experience of the spiritual truths of Quakerism. Fox did not set out to beat his sword
into a ploughshare, and early Friends did not set out to establish a
peace testimony. The peace testimony is the inevitable consequence
of the fundamental doctrines of Quakerism.

Two principles that flow all through our study of the Biblical
basis of the peace testimony are that it is a consequence of changes
Christ has made in our inward natures, not on some assumed goodness in other human beings, and that it is based on faithfulness, not
success. To express this in personal terms, I am peaceable because of
changes the risen Christ has made in my deepest being, and I live
out this new reality in order to be more like Christ, not in order to
be successful. Because they understood all who had not undergone
this rebirth in Christ to be still under the sway of lusts and other
sins, early Friends more or less expected to suffer for their beliefs—
Penn even headed his section on the peace testimony "Not fighting,
but suffering."[101] At the same time, they expected that the witness
of their words and their suffering for truth would have its effect:
Penn wrote, "We hope in our lifetimes to achieve real change in the
world."[102] The desire and ability to live peacefully with one's neighbors comes from the work of regeneration accomplished by Christ
in the heart of the believer. It is the Christian's condition after
entering into the new covenant, giving allegiance to Christ above
all and receiving Christ's redemption. Once that has happened,
says Fox, we cannot (literally are unable to) learn war or fight with
outward weapons, because we are changed beings. We are new
persons in Christ, as Paul says in his Epistle to the Corinthians.[103]

Fox's contemporaries considered him a transgressor and a
promoter of sedition, even as Christ was. Our response is the
same—not to seek justice or good reputations for ourselves, but to
rely on God's justice on judgment day. The Lord will plead our
cause with all people on earth at the day of their judgment.[104]

101 Penn, *op. cit.*, p. 364.
102 Penn, *op. cit.*, p. 341.
103 2 Corinthians 5:17.
104 Psalm 43:1.

It is of interest to note that war tax resistance, which many Friends consider the "cutting edge" of the peace testimony in the present day, received almost no attention during the first century of Quaker history.[105] George Fox seems to have paid taxes that were identifiably for the promotion of war, and wrote an epistle[106] endorsing such practice.[107] William Penn, who personally accepted the position of captain-general of the armed forces of Pennsylvania when the colony's charter was granted, also expressed approval of payment of these taxes, Philadelphia Yearly Meeting's 1970 minute notwithstanding.[108]

MOVING FROM PEACE TESTIMONY TO PEACEMAKING

This Quaker peace testimony is strong stuff, as far as it goes; but I share the assessment of Ron Mock and others that a peace testimony is not sufficient for Christians today.[109] We cannot be content with a testimony that is merely negative, against our own participation in wars and preparations for war. Our call goes far beyond this, to a positive testimony of how the kingdom can be firmly established in the visible world. Remember Barclay's assertion about the Bible as prophecy: "A prophetical account of several things, whereof some are already past, and some yet to come." One of the strongest prophetic themes in Scripture is the coming of the kingdom of God in all its fullness. Quakers today must be concerned to address all the systemic evil that prevents the inbreaking of the kingdom of God in the present day, and that evil includes a great deal of nonviolent oppression.[110] A peacemaking

105 Edwin Bronner, *A Quaker History*, Friends Committee on War Tax Concerns, Washington, DC, 1986, p.23.

106 Epistle #177, 1659, in *The Power of the Lord Is Over All*, edited by T. Canby Jones, Friends United Press, Richmond, IN, 1989, p. 136.

107 Edwin Bronner, *A Quaker History*, Friends Committee on War Tax Concerns, Washington, DC, 1986, p.6.

108 Edwin Bronner, A Quaker History, Friends Committee on War Tax Concerns, Washington, DC, 1986, pp. 6–7.

109 Ron Mock, *What Can the Bible Teach Us about Peacemaking?*, 2001 Quaker Peace Roundtable, http://quaker.org/qpr/ronmock-2.htm.

110 The tendency among some contemporary Friends to extend the definition of violence to include all injustice seems to me unpersuasive, as it results in a discussion of what is violent, rather than what is just. We need to reclaim use of vocabulary such as "evil," and "sin," which places the devil's advocate in a much more difficult position: arguing whether the activity being considered is moral or just, rather than whether it is violent.

testimony for Friends for the present day must include direct action to address all the ways oppression is at work in the world, all the ways our collective lust prevents shalom, all the ways our idolatry prevents the Spirit of the Lord from completing its work in the creation.

Opposition to systemic evil: We have today a much greater sensitivity to, and understanding of, systemic evil than I see evidenced among the first generation of Friends. Walter Wink has done much to help us see how Paul understood this phenomenon,[111] but this understanding seems to have been lacking among the early Friends. We must avoid what Richard Rohr[112] calls the "Protestant fallacy" that the world will be won over by winning each soul one by one.[113] Our efforts must be directed to relieve the systemic oppression that afflicts so many of the humans of the world, especially around the margins of our North American society.

Jubilee: One enduring image that should pattern Friends work in this area is the biblical vision of jubilee: when everyone has enough, and no one has too much; when debts are forgiven and ancestral lands are restored.[114] Now it is very true that the Israelites themselves apparently did not practice jubilee in any systematic way, but our understanding of Scripture is that it is a mixture of God's precepts and the story of imperfect attempts by imperfect humans to understand and follow them. So we should not be overly discouraged by the Israelites' failure here. The jubilee image is still a strong one—I would say a compelling one—and we should explore ways that we can corporately move closer to it. For those who would like to explore jubilee economics more deeply, I strongly recommend becoming familiar with the work of Bartimaeus Cooperative Ministries,[115] and especially Ched Myers.

---

[111] Walter Wink, *The Powers that Be: Theology for a New Millennium*, Galilee Doubleday, New York, 1998. Also the "Powers" trilogy: *Naming, Unmasking, Engaging*.

[112] Richard Rohr, OFM, is founder of the Center for Action and Contemplation, a school for prophets in Albuquerque, NM, www.cacradicalgrace.org

[113] Richard Rohr, personal communication, c. 2001.

[114] Leviticus 25.

[115] http://www.bcm-net.org/.

Harmony with the environment (gospel order): Fox's under-standing was that he had come into a new relationship with God, identical to the one Adam was in before he fell. This experience was available to all who opened themselves to the work of Christ within. Well, one of the characteristics of Adam's life and Eve's life before they fell out with God, while they were still in the Garden of Eden, was that they were in perfect harmony with the rest of creation. This is part of the restored gospel order of which early Friends and more modern ones, including myself, have written and spoken. God who has the power to regenerate our inmost being so as to live in harmony with our fellow human beings also has the power to restore our ability to live in harmony with the environ-ment, to use the modern phrase. One of the most powerful Quaker prophets in this area is a young man named Carl Magruder[116] from Pacific Yearly Meeting and Friends Community on Unity with Nature.

Friends are doing these things already, one might say. To some extent this is true, but our collective efforts fall short of our spiri-tual inheritance. To move effectively in these areas, Friends will have to regain a much stronger commitment to and practice of close community than is seen almost anywhere in our North American yearly meetings. We must incarnate the kingdom of God here on earth, demonstrating by our lives together that we have experienced the regeneration that we read about in Fox and other early Friends, and offer that same experience to our neighbors. Only corporately can we effectively address the challenges of systemic evil in our society, or build the practice of a jubilee society, or find and practice ways to live fully in harmony with the rest of creation. As we learn these things, we will be developing a testimony of peacemaking to extend and bring to completion the peace testimony Friends have declared since 1660.

[116] camagruder@earthlink.net

The Declaration of 1660

A declaration from the harmless and innocent people of God, called Quakers, against
all sedition, plotters and fighters in the world,
for removing the ground of jealousy and
suspicion from both magistrates and people in
the kingdom concerning wars and fightings.
[And also something in answer to that clause
of the king's late Proclamation which
mentions the Quakers, to clear them from the
plot and fighting which therein is mentioned,
and for the clearing their innocency.]

Presented to the king the 21st day of the
Eleventh month 1660.

Our principle is, and our practices have
always been, **to seek peace and ensue it**;* to
follow after righteousness and the knowledge
of God; seeking the good and welfare, and
doing that which tends to the peace of all.
We know **that wars and fightings proceed
from the lusts of men** (as James 4:1–3), out
of which lusts the Lord hath redeemed us,
and so out of the occasion of war. The occasion of war, and war itself (wherein envious
men, who are lovers of themselves more than
lovers of God, lust, kill, and desire to have
men's lives or estates) ariseth from the lust.
All bloody principles and practices we, as to
our own particulars, do utterly deny, with all
outward wars, strife, and fighting with
outward weapons for any end, or under any
pretence whatsoever: this is our testimony to
the whole world.
And whereas it is objected:
'But although you now say, that you
cannot fight or take up arms at all; yet if the

Psalm 34:14

First Argument
James 4:1–3

---

* Throughout this section bold type has been added to
assist the reader.

spirit move you, then you will change your principle, you will sell your coat and buy a sword, and fight for the kingdom of Christ.'

To this we answer, **Christ said to Peter, 'Put up thy sword in his place';** though he had said before, **he that had no sword might sell his coat and buy one** (to the fulfilling of the law and Scripture), yet after, when he had bid him put it up, he said, **'He that taketh the sword shall perish with the sword.'** And further, Christ said to Peter, **'Thinkest thou, that I cannot now pray to my Father, and he shall presently give me more than twelve legions of angels?'** And this might satisfy Peter, after he had put up his sword, when he said to him **he that took it, should perish by it,** which satisfies us. (Luke 22:36; Matthew 26:51-53). And in the Revelation, it's said, **'He that kills with the sword shall perish with the sword; and here is the faith and the patience of the saints.'** (Revelation 13:10.) So **Christ's kingdom is not of this world, therefore do not his servants fight, as he told Pilate, the magistrate who crucified him.** And **did they not look upon Christ as a raiser of sedition?** And did not he say, **'Forgive them?'** But thus it is **that we are numbered amongst transgressors and amongst fighters, that the scriptures might be fulfilled.**

That **the spirit of Christ, by which we are guided, is not changeable,** so as once to command us from a thing as evil and again to move unto it. We do certainly know, and so testify to the world, that **the spirit of Christ, which leads us into all truth, will never move us to fight and war against any man with outward weapons,** neither for the kingdom of Christ nor for the kingdoms of this world.

Second Argument
Matthew 26:52
Luke 22:36

Matthew 26:52

Matthew 26:53

Luke 22:36
Matthew 26:51-53

Revelation 13:10

John 18:36

Luke 23:2

Luke 23:34
Mark 15:28

Hebrews 6:17

John 16:13

2 Corinthians 10:4

First, because **the kingdom of Christ, God will exalt, according to his promise, and cause it to grow and flourish in righteousness, 'Not by might, nor by power [of outward sword], but by my spirit, saith the Lord.'** (Zechariah 4:6.) So those that use any weapon to fight for Christ, or for the establishing of his kingdom or government, their spirit, principle, and practice in that we deny.

Third Argument
Zechariah 4:6

Secondly, as for the kingdoms of this world, we cannot covet them, much less can we fight for them, but we do earnestly desire and wait, that (by the word of God's power and its effectual operation in the hearts of men) **the kingdoms of this world may become the kingdoms of the Lord, and of his Christ**; and that he may rule and reign in men by his spirit and truth; that thereby all people, out of all different judgments and professions, may be brought into love and unity with God, and one with another; and that **all may come to witness the prophet's words who said, 'Nation shall not lift up sword against nation, neither shall they learn war any more.'** (Isaiah 2:4; Micah 4:3.)

Fourth Argument
Revelation 11:15

Isaiah 2:4, Micah 4:3

So, we whom the Lord hath called into the obedience of his truth, have denied wars and fightings, and cannot again any more learn them. This is a certain testimony unto all the world of the truth of our hearts in this particular, that as God persuadeth every man's heart to believe, so they may receive it. For we have not, as some others, gone about cunningly with devised fables, nor have we ever denied in practice what we have professed in principle; but in sincerity and truth, and by the word of God have we **laboured to be made manifest unto all men**, that both we and our ways might be witnessed in the hearts of all.

2 Corinthians 5:11

And **whereas all manner of evil hath been falsely spoken of us**, we hereby speak the plain truth of our hearts, to take away the occasion of that offense, that so we being innocent may not suffer for other men's offenses, nor be made a prey of by the wills of men for that of which we were never guilty; but in the uprightness of our hearts we may, under the power ordained by God **for the punishment of evil-doers, and for the praise of them that do well**, live a peaceable and godly life in all godliness and honesty. For although we have always suffered, and do now more abundantly suffer, yet we know that it is for righteousness' sake; **'for all our rejoicing is this, the testimony of our consciences, that in simplicity and godly sincerity, not with fleshly wisdom but by the grace of God, we have had our conversation in the world'** (2 Corinthians 1:12), which for us is a witness for the convincing of our enemies. For this we can say to all the world, we have wronged no man's person or possessions, we have used no force nor violence against any man, we have been found in no plots, nor guilty of sedition. When we have been wronged, we have not sought to revenge ourselves; we have not made resistance against authority, but wherein we could not obey for conscience' sake, we have suffered the most of any people in the nation. We have **been accounted as sheep for the slaughter**, persecuted and despised, **beaten**, stoned, wounded, stocked, whipped, imprisoned, haled out of the synagogues, **cast into dungeons** and noisome vaults where many have died in bonds, shut up from our friends, denied needful sustenance for many days together, with other the like cruelties.

Matthew 5:11

1 Peter 2:14

2 Corinthians 1:12

Acts 8:32

Acts 16:37

2 Corinthians 11:25

And the cause of all these our sufferings is not for any evil, but for things relating to the worship of our God and in obedience to his requirings of us. For which **cause we shall freely give up our bodies a sacrifice**, rather than disobey the Lord. For we know, as the Lord hath kept us innocent, so **he will plead our cause**, when there is none in the earth to plead it. So we, in obedience unto his Truth, do not love our lives unto death, that we may do his will, and wrong no man in our generation, but seek the good and peace of all men. He who hath **commanded us that we shall not swear at all** (Matthew 5:34), hath also **commanded us that we shall not kill** (Matthew 5:21), so that we can neither kill men, nor swear for nor against them. And this is both our principle and practice, and hath been from the beginning, so that if we suffer, as suspected to take up arms or make war against any, it is without any ground from us; for it neither is, nor ever was in our hearts, since we owned the truth of God; neither shall we ever do it, because it is contrary to the spirit of Christ, his doctrine, and the practice of his apostles, even contrary to him for whom we **suffer all things**, and **endure all things**.

And whereas men come against us with clubs, staves, drawn swords, pistols cocked, and do beat, cut, and abuse us, yet **we never resisted them, but to them our hair, backs, and cheeks have been ready.** It is not an honour to manhood nor to nobility to run upon harmless people who lift not up a hand against them, with arms and weapons.

Therefore consider these things, ye men of understanding; for plotters, raisers of insurrections, tumultuous ones, and fighters, running with swords, clubs, staves, and pistols,

Romans 12:1

Job 16:19, 1 John 2:1

Matthew 5:34

Matthew 5:21

1 Corinthians 9:12
2 Timothy 2:10

Matthew 5:39
Luke 6:29

one against another, we say these are of the
world and have their foundation from **this
unrighteous world, from the foundation
of which the lamb hath been slain**; which
**lamb hath redeemed us from this
unrighteous world; we are not of it, but
are heirs of a world of which there is no
end and of a kingdom where no corrupt-
ible thing enters.** Our weapons are spiritual
and not carnal, **yet mighty through God to
the plucking down of the strongholds of
sin and Satan**, who is the author of wars,
fighting, murder, and plots. And **our swords
are broken into ploughshares and spears
into pruning-hooks, as prophesied of in
Micah 4**. Therefore **we cannot learn war
any more**, neither rise up against nation or
kingdom with outward weapons, though you
have numbered us among the transgressors
and plotters. The Lord knows our innocency
herein, and will plead our cause with all
people upon earth **at the day of their judgment, when all men shall have a reward
according to their works.**

Therefore in love we warn you for your
souls' good, not to wrong the innocent, nor
the babes of Christ, which he hath in his
hand, and tenders **as the apple of his eye**;
neither seek to destroy the heritage of God,
nor turn your swords backward upon **such
as the law was not made for, i.e., the righteous; but for the sinners and transgressors**,
to keep them down. For those are not peace-
makers nor lovers of enemies, neither can
they **overcome evil with good**, who wrong
them that are friends to you and all men,
and wish your good and the good of all
people on earth. If you oppress us as they did
the **children of Israel in Egypt**, if you
oppress us **as they did when Christ was**

Revelation 13:18

John 1:29
James 2:5
1 Timothy 1:17, Titus
3:7, Isaiah 9:7

Luke 1:52

Micah 4:3

Isaiah 2:4

Matthew 16:27

Matthew 11:25
Deuteronomy 32:10

Romans 12:21

Exodus
Matthew 2:16

Acts 4:4ff
Acts 4:17

born, and as they did the Christians in the primitive times, we can say, "The Lord forgive you;" leave the Lord to deal with you, and not revenge ourselves. If you say as **the council said to Peter and John, "You must speak no more in that name,"** and if you serve us as they **served the three children spoken of in Daniel**, God is the same as he ever was, that lives for ever and ever, who hath the innocent in his arms.

Daniel 3:6ff

O friends! Offend not the Lord and his little ones, neither afflict his people; but consider and be moderate. Run not hastily into things, **but mind and consider mercy, justice, and judgment**; that is the way for you to prosper and get the favour of the Lord. Our meetings were stopped and broken up in the days of Oliver, under pretence of plotting against him; in the days of the Committee of Safety we were looked upon as plotters to bring in King Charles; and now our peaceable meetings are termed seditious. Oh! That men should lose their reason, and go contrary to their own consciences; knowing that we have suffered all things, and have been accounted plotters all along, though we have always declared against them both by word of mouth and printing, and are clear from any such thing! Though we have suffered all along, because we would not take up carnal weapons to fight against any, and are thus made a prey upon because we are the **innocent lambs of Christ, and cannot avenge ourselves!** These things are left upon your hearts to consider; for we are out of all those things in **the patience of the saints**, and we know as Christ said, **"He that takes the sword shall perish with the sword."** Matthew 26:52. Revelations 13:10.

Matthew 23:23

1 Peter 1:19
Leviticus 19:18

Revelations 14:12

Matthew 26:52
Revelations 13:10

This is given forth from the people called Quakers, to satisfy the king and his council, and all that have any jealousy concerning us, that all occasion of suspicion may be taken away, and our innocency cleared.

Given forth under our names, and in behalf of the whole body of the Elect People of God who are called Quakers.

George Fox	Gerrard Roberts
Henry Fell	Richard Hubberthorn
John Bolton	John Hinde
John Stubbs	Leonard Fell
John Furley Jr.	Francis Howgill
Samuel Fisher	Thomas Moore

Postscript—Though we **are numbered amongst transgressors**, and have been given up to rude, merciless men, by whom our meetings are broken up, in which we edified one another in our holy faith, and prayed together to the Lord that lives for ever, yet he is our pleader in this day. The Lord saith, **"They that feared his name spoke often together," as in Malachi**; which were as his jewels. For this cause, and no evil doing, are we cast into holes, dungeons, houses of correction, prisons, (sparing neither old nor young, men nor women) and made a prey of in the sight of all nations, under pretence of being seditious, etc. so that all rude people run upon us to take possession; for which we say, **the Lord forgive them** that has thus done to us; who doth and will enable us to suffer; and never shall we lift up hand against any man that doth thus use us; but that the Lord may have mercy upon them, that they may consider what they have done. For how is it possible for them to requite us for the wrong they have done to us? Who to all nations have sounded us abroad as seditious

Mark 15:28

Malachi 3:16

Luke 23:34

or plotters, who were never plotters against any
power or man upon the earth, since we knew
the life and power of Jesus Christ manifested
in us, who hath redeemed us from the world
and all works of darkness, and plotters
therein, by which we know the election
before the world began. So we say, the Lord
have mercy upon our enemies, and forgive
them for what they have done unto us.

Oh! **Do as ye would be done by; do
unto all men as you would have them do
unto you; for this is but the law and the
prophets.**

                                        Matthew 7:12

All plots, insurrections, and riotous
meetings, we deny, knowing them to be of
the devil, the murderer; which we in Christ,
who was before they were, triumph over.
And all wars and fightings with carnal
weapons we deny, who have the sword of the
spirit; and all that wrong us, we leave to the
Lord. This is to clear our innocency from
that aspersion cast upon us, "that we are
seditious or plotters."

Added in the reprinting: Courteous reader,
this was our testimony above twenty years
ago, and since then we have not been found
acting contrary to it, nor ever shall; for the
truth that is our guide is unchangeable. This
is now reprinted to the men of this age,
many of whom were then children, and doth
stand as our certain testimony against all
plotting, and fighting with carnal weapons.
And if any, by departing from the truth,
should do so, this is our testimony in the
truth against them, and will stand over them,
and the truth will be clear of them.

The Argument

We have no reason to fight wars.

- War comes from lust (James 4:1–3)—an intense, overmastering desire to possess or enjoy. One may lust for power, fame, wealth, et cetera.
- The Lord has redeemed us out of lust, and therefore out of the occasion for war. Our relationship with Christ reorients us away from the world which contained the objects of our lust and toward God. This shift is so dramatic that James says love for the world is enmity toward God.
- Christ in the office of redeemer saves us from the power of sin (i.e., lust), which we could never accomplish on our own.

Christ commanded us not to fight—Christ as king: a simple direct command.

- Christ said that he without a sword might buy one (Luke 22:36) to fulfill the law and Scripture (Isaiah 53:12); but after that was accomplished, he told Peter to put away his sword, saying he that taketh the sword shall perish with the sword (Matthew 26:52). Christ in the office of king orders us not to fight.
- He that kills with the sword must be killed with the sword. Here is the patience and faith of the saints (Revelation 13:10). The sword is false protection—an idolatry. The faith and patience of the saints is to endure outward persecution without attempting defense with outward weapons—to rely on God alone.
- Christ had legions of angels at his disposal to prevent his own arrest and execution, the greatest sin of all, yet did not call on them (Matthew 26:53). If ever there was a "just war" this was it. The king (Christ) is there to order it, no innocent suffering, all other means of reconciliation futile, force proportionate to the need, and a just cause (one side all right, one all wrong): and Christ says no.
- Christ's kingdom is not of this world, therefore his servants do not fight, as he told Pilate (John 18:36). Christ as king:

our allegiance is to Christ, not our worldly government; Christ's servants do not fight.

- God who commanded us not to swear at all (Matthew 5:34) also commanded us that we shall not kill (Matthew 5:21).

Christ's kingdom flourishes by peaceful, not warlike means.

- Christ will never move us to fight with outward weapons because the kingdom of Christ will grow and flourish "Not by might, nor by power [of outward sword], but by my spirit, saith the Lord" (Zechariah 4:6). An unusual reference! Zechariah is speaking of the (hoped-for) reign of Zerubbabel, a messianic kingship characterized by the rebuilding of the Temple—the kingdom of God.
- Our weapons are spiritual and not carnal . . . And our swords are broken into ploughshares and spears into pruning-hooks, as prophesied in Micah (Chapter. 4). This is not the first step—Fox did not set out to break his sword into a ploughshare. This is a description of the Christian's condition after entering into the new covenant, giving allegiance to Christ above all and receiving Christ's redemption. Once that has happened, says Fox, we cannot (literally are unable to) learn war or fight with outward weapons.
- The Lord will plead our cause with all men and all people on earth at the day of their judgment (Psalms 35:1, 43:1). Fox's contemporaries considered him a transgressor and a promoter of sedition, even as Christ was considered the same. Our response is the same—not to seek justice or good reputations for ourselves, but to rely on God's justice on judgment day.

Our desire is that the kingdoms of this world become the king-doms of Christ.

- Christ will never move us to fight with outward weapons because we (Friends) cannot covet the kingdoms of this world (James again) much less fight for them (Revelations?), but wait and pray that Christ may rule in [all] men by his spirit and truth, and the prophecies will come to pass that nations shall not lift up sword against nation, neither shall they learn war any more (Isaiah 2:4, Micah 4:3).

- Peace comes not by the Pax Romana or Pax Britannica, but by the rule of Christ in human hearts. Our best defense, on every level, is evangelization: promoting the true knowledge of Christ in every heart. That will protect us (and everyone) from the mugger as well as the invader.

"Why Do You Still Read that Old Thing?"

This was given as part of the Pendle Hill Monday Night Lecture Series in the spring of 1996. My intent was to give a personal account of the importance of the Bible in my life, rather than an intellectual report of what role the Bible should play in the life of a good Christian.

Introduction

Visiting Canadian Yearly Meeting in 1982 was a wonderfully eye-opening experience for me. Among other things, I was fascinated by their schedule—they are still the only yearly meeting of which I am aware that schedules general interest events to begin at midnight! These Friends had traveled as much as three thousand miles to be together, and they were not about to waste a minute; they could sleep next week!

I was taking a short walk one afternoon during a break in the formal sessions, my Bible under my arm as usual, when a twenty-something Canadian Friend approached me and struck up a conversation. After some preliminary greetings she got to the point. Pointing to my Bible, she asked, "Why do you still read that old thing when there is so much more modern material available?"

I was caught short by the question, and constructed an incomplete answer on the spot. I've been answering that same question, in many forms, for the fourteen years or so since that day. Tonight I can give you a progress report.

Asking this Canadian Friend's question, as so many other Friends do, in one form or another, implies that the questioner has made some assumptions about the Bible and those who read it: the Bible is old and therefore out of date, not historically accurate, full of violence, oppresses women, contradicts itself, etcetera, etcetera; and those who read the Bible believe it is literally, historically and factually true in every detail. Like many of our assumptions about people and things we don't know well, these are only half true at most.

What does seem to me to be completely true is that a Christian life and the Bible go hand in hand. Ignoring the Bible is like trying to go through life unable to remember anything that happened before today. The Bible is not documentary history, as contemporary Western-educated people understand history. It is larger than mere history, because it connects us with the big story—God's cosmic story that incorporates all of creation and that gives our individual lives and personal stories true meaning.

Yes, the Bible is old. The Bible stories have been sifted through many centuries and many different cultures. Only those stories that have been consistently helpful in these very different times and settings have been remembered and passed down to the next generation. The age of the Bible is not a detriment, but a clue as to the real value of its contents.

As for violence, the Bible is about as violent as the front page of my daily newspaper. The world is violent. The Bible is about living in the world. Unlike the newspaper, television, or movies, the Bible is not interested in violence for its own sake, to boost readership or win viewers away from the competition. The Bible is interested in violence only as part of the context in which the big story unfolds.

Likewise, the Bible stories are set in the context of a society that did not recognize many groups as equals, including women. That is not an endorsement of that society or its practices, but the context of a story. Much of the meaning of that story is that God hears, cares, takes sides, and intervenes in imperfect human societies, working through flawed people on behalf of broken people. It is precisely because Bible societies are inequitable in ways we can now see so easily—the mote in our brother's eye—that God's actions have such symbolic importance for us today. If God cared and helped then, God will care and help now.

There are many ways for Christians to relate to the Bible, including fundamentalism. Quakers are not fundamentalists—but we started with such a close relationship to Scripture that it was said that if all the printed Bibles should disappear, the Scriptures could be reconstructed from the mouth of George Fox. Esther Murer has documented thousands of Scripture references in the writings of Fox, Penn, Penington, and other early Friends. Why, one might ask, was such a flawed document so important to our spiritual forebears? What should be the role of the Bible in our faith community's spiritual life in the present day?

Rather than address these issues *a priori* from first principles and conclude whether or not the Bible should be important to Friends, I want to proceed *a postiori*—from my experience with the Bible—and let you conclude whether or not there is something there that could enrich your life.

The Bible in My Personal Spiritual Life

I have three kinds of personal, daily experience with the Bible: daily devotions, directed Bible study, and Bible reading.

Daily devotions: Our family has daily devotions, after breakfast and before the children leave for school and adults for work. We read a passage from the daily lectionary, often from another devotional book as well, and have some silent worship and/or vocal prayer. Susan or I may preface the Scripture reading with a brief explanation of the context of the passage for the benefit of our children, or make some comment after the reading about what is important in the passage for us, or how the passage affects our daily life.

These devotions accomplish several purposes. I began reading the lectionary passages several years ago, in order to be connected with Christians outside the Religious Society of Friends. Following the lectionary means reading the same Scripture passages as Christians all over the world. I feel this connection most strongly when we worship with other Christians and have been reading their liturgical Scripture all week, but the connection is there all the time. God's interest in human beings didn't begin with George Fox and is not limited to the Religious Society of Friends. Staying connected with other Christians both reminds us of the big(ger) story and keeps us in touch with other ways in which God is in relationship with human beings, outside Quakerdom.

A second effect of our daily lectionary reading is a more complete connection to the many ways we can encounter and experience God, through the seasons of the liturgical year. The structure of the liturgical year embodied in the lectionary keeps me balanced in my devotions—I can't spend all my time in Easter and ignore the Christmas story. We have to engage the big story in all its fullness, and the lectionary helps us do this.

The third effect of our daily devotional Bible readings is that it helps teach our children the big story. The most important inheritance we can give our children is not a trust fund, and it is not a good education or a trade. The most important inheritance we can give our children is an understanding of the big story of God's involvement with creation through the ages and how that involvement extends directly to them right here and right now. We attempt to do this by all our words and deeds 24 hours a day. The importance of daily devotions, with this structured reading of the Scriptures, is that it gives them a resource to which they can turn when Susan and I are no longer around. We are seeding the ground for a harvest we will never see in its fullness, but I believe that a familiarity with the Bible stories will help my children in their life choices over and over again. What does Noah's story say about the Endangered Species Act? What does the parable in Luke 19 say about how it is going to feel to try to live a kingdom life in this world? I couldn't put the answers to these questions in their minds, even if I thought that would be right or helpful—but through these daily Bible readings Susan and I can give them grist for the mill—the resources to help them find their own answers.

By encountering the range of the Bible story through the lectionary readings, our children learn that the Bible is a collection of different books on different topics, each useful in a range of varied situations. They know the Bible is not simply about an old man in the sky telling the Israelites to kill everyone else, because they have sampled bits and pieces of the big story throughout the Bible. When life crises come to them, and they inevitably will, they will have another resource they know can help—the Bible.

The importance of familiarity with the Bible as a resource when other resources may not be available is shown in the experience of one of our Norfolk Quaker House clients, currently serving on a carrier off the coast of Bosnia. When he began to have the first twinges of conscience about his military service, there were no pacifists or sympathetic counselors on board ship. He did have his Bible, though, and remembered passages that were relevant to issues of war and peace. He went back to Scripture, studying in private, and became a conscientious objector.

Directed Bible Study: The second type of regular Bible experience I have is directed Bible study: a process of "cleaning the lens" so I can see the big story more clearly. Bible study helps me break through what one of our Norfolk Quaker House clients calls the cultural sugar coating over the Scriptures, and get to the real meaning of the Bible stories. I am able to do this with the help of people who have put their own insights and understandings into a Bible study or commentary that I can then engage in depth. Ched Myers has helped me and many people like me see the gospel from a new perspective through his book *Binding the Strong Man—A Political Reading of Mark's Story of Jesus.* For well over a year I have been studying the Gospel of Mark with the help of this book, discovering meanings in the symbolic actions of Jesus that had previously been invisible to me. What I'm learning, over and over again, is that Jesus was so radical and so revolutionary that the dominant culture of every generation has to sugarcoat his message to make it less threatening to the institutions of power and wealth. I say learning over and over again because I am part of the dominant culture, and the gospel afflicts me as much as it comforts me. Directed study like this helps me understand Jesus' real import in a new way, and enables me to be more faithful in my own actions.

The gospel calls us to a new life so different from our old life in every way that it is like being born again. That is uncomfortable living. We Christians and the world both work to smooth over those differences so we can be more comfortable. Directed Bible study takes the smooth patina off old familiar stories and restores their sharp edges, so we can see them more nearly as those who witnessed them at first hand.

Another author who has been helpful to me and to others is Robert McAfee Brown. His small book, *Unexpected News—*

Reading the Bible with Third World Eyes, showed me the real power in the new Scripture exegesis being produced by the base communities of Latin America. Brown's translation of their experience into words I could understand helped me find a new perspective on Scripture and the big story and see truth that had previously been hidden from me.

One needs the help of other people to understand the Bible because what we are able to see in the Bible depends greatly on what we bring to the Bible: our own questions, our own life experiences, and our own predispositions. The Bible was written by and for the underclass of the world, but it has been interpreted in Western society by the overclass. We twentieth-century North Americans are in the difficult position of trying to understand a book written in a different historical era for a different social class of people—understandably, some nuance has been lost. Those who bring different questions and life experiences to study of the Bible can illustrate the Scripture for us in new and revealing ways. For example, the underlying question for us in North America has long been "Do you believe?" In the third world, it is "Does God care?" This different question leads one to very different understandings about the meaning of Scripture stories.

These have not been for me purely intellectual exercises. Clearly the Holy Spirit has been active in me, opening my eyes and ears to the hidden Scripture message; as Quakers know, it takes personal inspiration to understand the inspired Scriptures. Without God's breath in our souls, the Bible remains mostly a closed book. However, if we want to go where God's wind would carry us, we had best raise the sail and grasp the rudder—that's the Scripture.

Bible reading: My third type of Bible experience is what Conservative Friends call "Bible reading"—soaking up the Scriptures. We don't always know what we need to study. Simply soaking up the Scripture gives God grist for our mill, and a context in which Bible study and devotional reading can be richer experiences. When we bump up against an experience in real life, the storehouse of Scripture stories we have soaked up can help us understand what is happening to us right now. Our leadings, understandings, and admonishments from God are enriched by the Scripture that has become part of us. You don't have to have a "good reason" to read any particular part of Scripture in this way. I've been reading Ezekiel for several months, since I purchased a used Blazer to drive, because the Blazer brought to mind the "wheels of fire" passage from Ezekiel. I wasn't expecting Ezekiel's theological message that God's forgiveness comes to us before we repent of our sins, but there it is.

Every so often I get the urge to listen to Scripture as I'm driving around. I keep the New Testament on tape in the center console of my Blazer, and just pop a cassette into the tape deck. This is strictly "Bible reading:" No commentary, no exegesis or exposition, just the words of the Bible in great chunks—10-15 minutes or more of uninterrupted Scripture. It doesn't have to "do" anything for me immediately (though it often does); it takes its place in my mind, ready for use when the time comes.

One hears passages unexpectedly this way, before one can set up defenses against their message. I have filters that tell me what a particular passage means; when listening to the Bible in this way, a parable or incident can get to me before I filter out other possible meanings, and I learn something new! The context of when and where Jesus told a parable, or when the gospel writer placed it in his narrative of Jesus' life and ministry, is often a clue to its meaning and significance. When we read selected passages we are often reading "out of context;" hearing long passages read to me reminds me of these contexts. Finally, hearing the Bible in large chunks sows the ground of one's mind with Scripture stories and parables that will bear fruit in their own season. I hear passages that I would not otherwise have picked out to read, and they have their effect on me, consciously or unconsciously.

The Bible in the Work of Norfolk Quaker House

Norfolk Quaker House is a Christian peace witness in Hampton Roads, Virginia—the most heavily militarized region in the world. Now in its second year, Norfolk Quaker House does military coun-seling, counter-recruitment, peace training, and evangelical work in our faith communities. My wife Susan is the founder and clerk of the board of directors; I am the part-time staff person. The Bible has several functions or roles in the work of Norfolk Quaker House: it builds up the faith of those we counsel and helps them articulate their beliefs; it helps the board and staff build up our own faith and faithfulness; it helps us communicate and connect with other people of the Book, especially Christians; and it helps us understand our work in the context of the big story, which both guides us and protects us against burnout.

Articulating and building up the faith of those we counsel: A common story among our clients is that a shocking experience early in their military life led them back to the Bible, which they had read as a child but neglected in recent years. In the Bible they found old familiar stories that now had new, different meanings and specific applicability to their circumstances. They now saw that Jesus taught that we should not wage war on one another. This scriptural affirmation of their inner convictions is a source of tremendous inner strength to them, as well as a continual goad to change their life.

Each of our conscientious objector applicants entered the service with an understanding of the Bible that supported or at least was neutral toward military service. When they began to question their continued military enlistment and the Bible's support of it, they had to wrestle with authority figures who quoted the Bible against them. Family members and personal pastors have often bought into the "cultural Christianity" understanding that being a good Christian and being a patriotic American go hand in hand. I myself grew up with this notion that male churchgoers should all serve their country in the military. Military members whom the conscientious objector approaches for counsel and guidance may quote the Bible in defense of military service. One of our clients was told, in detail, that when Jesus blessed the centurion he blessed all soldiers and military service in general, thus justifying war.

To resolve these contradictions, these young people have to be able to claim the Bible for their own: to learn to come to their own understandings and be able to defend them. Given their heritage, it would be almost impossible for many of these young people to adopt and defend a position of conscience that was in fact contrary to the teaching of the Bible. If they can't be confident that Scripture supports their inner promptings of conscience, they won't pursue a conscientious objector discharge—to everyone's detriment including the branch of the military involved.

When they do understand personally that Jesus Christ of the Bible is calling them to be peacemakers, they have an inner strength that makes them more than equal to the task of extricating themselves from the war machinery.

Building up our own faith and faithfulness: Study of the biblical bases for the Quaker peace testimony helps build up our own faith and faithfulness. Bible study is a way of understanding how and why God wants Susan and me to be active in this particular peace witness in this specific way, and increasing our ability to be faithful in this way. It is important to us because we know experientially that activism without deep roots will quickly burnout—no results, and no nurture. We also know that misplaced activism wastes time and energy without accomplishing the divine will. Our goal is not to accomplish great things, but to fulfill God's divine intent for each of us and for the world. What happens outwardly as an apparent result of our faithfulness is in God's hands.

A key piece of directed Bible study for us has been a study of the Declaration of 1660 (see p. 92). In the course of this study we have found our own inner leadings confirmed by the witness of the early Friends who wrote this document, and all of this solidly based on Scripture. Susan and I have gathered the fullest text of this document we can reconstruct, and searched out the many, many Scripture references embedded there. This effort has both confirmed and given words to the inner promptings of the Holy Spirit. We have been confirmed that our leadings are those of the early Friends, in that we understand as they did that we are called to be peacemakers because we have been converted/born again in the Holy Spirit, and redeemed from the lusts that are the occasion of war—no longer ruled by the greed, lust for power and fear that push men and women to war against one another. (James 4:1–3).

We understand as they did Christ's command not to fight in wars from whose power we have been redeemed (Matthew 26:52).

We understand as they did God's kingdom is not and cannot be brought forth by fighting, but only by God's own spirit (Zechariah 4:6).

We pray, as they did, not that the kingdoms of this world be conquered for Christ, but that they be converted and become the kingdoms of the Lord (Revelation 11:15).

Through this and other bible studies, with Quakers and non-Quakers, we have come to understand that our work is not about fighting the navy in Hampton Roads, not about opposing the military ideology that permeates everything about the community in which we live, and not about extracting as many people as possible from military service. Our work is being spiritual midwives to a conversion experience in those we serve, helping them be birthed into a new world that, in the words of George Fox, "gives forth a new smell."

Helping us stand in the river of both Quakerism and Christianity, soaking up the nurture that comes from being an integral part of both those traditions: Being a Quaker, which has historically meant being a "primitive Christian," means being a prophetic witness to the coming kingdom of Christ. You have to be standing in the river to be a prophet. If not, you won't be heard and you won't be strong enough to persevere. The river of Quakerism in which we stand, a small part of the larger river of Christianity, is filled with the witnesses of those who have gone before us, whose understanding and faithfulness have been shaped and strengthened by their own rootedness in Scripture.

In Virginia, the witness of Quakers for peace includes George Wilson—a soldier turned Friend—who died in Jamestown jail for the crime of being a Quaker, and Henry Vaux—the first Virginian to be convinced into Quakerism—who died shortly after being released from prison. Vaux' crime was giving shelter to William Robinson, late of the *Woodhouse* and soon to be hanged on Boston Common.

In Virginia, where we live and minister, the struggle for state recognition of the rights of conscience regarding military service dates to 1692. Our work at Norfolk Quaker House has deep roots. Like those Friends who carried the first petition to the colonial House of Burgesses, we are nurtured by the witness of those who have gone before and particularly by the Scripture record, which tells us both what to expect and how to deal with it.

Communicating and connecting with other people of the Book, especially Christians: There are many biblical paths to nonviolence; the Bible is not monolithic or monotonal. For example, Catholic writings on pacifism voice a particular concern with the idolatry of depending on nuclear weapons rather than God. The mainline Protestant emphasis seems to be on obedience: to Jesus' commandments to love rather than to kill. The Brethren in Christ church cites Jonah as a warning story about the evil of nationalism and idolatry of the state. The Quaker emphasis, in contrast, is on the redeeming power of Christ, and the conversion experience that frees us from the bonds of lust that are the cause of war. Knowing and understanding how people of different denominations have come to their understanding of Christian pacifism helps us explain ourselves in understandable ways, and to respect that others may support our work for reasons different than our own, but that are still authentic and valid.

Understanding our work and ministry in the context of the big story: The Bible helps us keep this ministry in gospel order and keep us from burning out in frustration. This ministry is about faithfulness and conversion, not production or success.

Scripture teaches that all persons have the potential for conversion no matter what their station or circumstances—Jesus' centurion and tax collectors, Peter's jailer, et al. Conversion leads to healing—is a healing. All healing is spiritual and incarnational. The Bible teaches that the incarnation is very good! Anyone may be converted as an outcome of our work—sailors, commanding officers, navy chaplains, spouses. Everyone with whom we deal is seen as a person in whom God is at work toward conversion. The person in this whole group we know will be converted is the Norfolk Quaker House counselor, because we know we are in a process of continual conversion ourselves.

Because we undertake this work as helping individuals through a conversion process rather than as a war of ideologies versus the military industrial complex, we have been able to form collaborative relationships with military and civilian personnel to assist those we serve. Because we understand the work to be the Lord's, not our own, we do not insist that the people we help use our vocabulary or even that they have discharge from the navy as their goal. We are a Christian peace witness that counsels Christians who feel they may be conscientious objectors. We also counsel non-Christians, theists, and wiccans who feel they may be conscientious objectors. We also help folks who know they don't fit in the military but who don't object to participation in war per se, and folks who simply need someone outside the service to hear their story and lend a compassionate hand.

We are protected from burnout in this work because we have been released from the need for results. Like Peter on his way to the temple, our shadow also falls behind us, where we cannot see, and bears fruit we know nothing about. Our need is only to be faithful, not to see great changes in the visible world.

My Vision for the Role of the Bible in the Religious Society of Friends

My vision of the role of the Bible in the Religious Society of Friends involves our past, present and future. The role of the Bible in our past is to help us remember and understand our own history—George Fox, Robert Barclay, Henry Cadbury and all the others who have written our story as a people of faith with their testimonies and witness. Proverbs says, "Without vision, the people die." I submit that without a past, the people can have no vision of who they are—and so they will die out. We cannot truly know and understand our own past as Quakers without knowing and understanding the Bible and its role in our story as a faith community.

When he gave the keynote address at North Carolina Yearly Meeting (Conservative) sessions some years ago, Wilmer Cooper was asked by an attender why Quakers spend so much time talking about ourselves. Wil's response was that we have to tell our story to remember who we are. We are a faith people deeply rooted in the Scriptures, whose understanding of the meaning and usefulness of the Bible has enriched most of Christendom. We isolate ourselves from our own history, unable to understand our own forebears, if we cut ourselves off from a deep understanding of and familiarity with the Bible. A close engagement with the Scriptures shaped the leadings of the Friends whose witness built the Religious Society of Friends, and shaped their lives and testimonies that inspire us today. We can understand the meaning they gave to much of their actions only if we understand Scripture as thoroughly as they did.

In the present, the Bible helps us remember that our story as Quakers is part of the big story. We lose much of the meaning of who we are today as a faith people if we do not value and nurture our connectedness with the big story—not the story of the Quakers over the past 350 years, but the story of God's covenant relationship with all of creation since the beginning of time. We find that story expressed most fully and meaningfully in Scripture

Because we are an individualist faith tradition in an individualist age, it is easy to forget that our personal story and the Quaker story in general are only part of the big story of God's covenant relationship with creation. The Bible reminds us of these true relationships, which is both humbling and reassuring. The dominant culture works on the premise that I am at the center of my story: my rights, my pleasures, my pains, my gains and losses. The Bible reminds us that God is at the center of the big story, and my story is only a small part of that. If I am at the center, the meaning of life is "more for me"—which is ultimately nothing, since ultimately we each die. If God is at the center, then the meaning of life is that God created and sustains me moment by moment, saying of me as of the rest of creation, "This is very good." God has a great love and a divine plan for all of creation, and I am a very good part and very loved part of that plan.

As we live into the future the Bible confirms for us—as it did for George Fox and other Friends throughout our history—the promptings and leadings of the Holy Spirit, giving us the confidence and understanding to act clearly and faithfully.

The Bible confirms the leadings of our conscientious objector clients toward pacifism. My yearning for the Religious Society of Friends is that it would rediscover what these young people are discovering for themselves: the Bible is a living document of a living God—not the God of the dead, but of the living—and it teaches us in the present moment how to live into the promise of the coming kingdom of God.

The Bible confirms our leadings to begin Norfolk Quaker House and continue this work, and guides us to a fuller understanding of how we are to go about this work in gospel order. The dominant order is constantly at work on us, pushing and pulling us back toward its assumptions, understandings, and values. The Bible is an instrument of our continual conversion, over and over again drawing us into new understandings of the big story and how it is unfolding in *kairos,* and how we should understand and interpret current events. Friends have long cherished this sense of being a separated people, "in the world but not of it." I yearn that Friends would rediscover the Bible as a resource in the struggle against assimilation into the dominant culture.

The Bible can have these roles of affirmation and discernment only if we give it the authority to withhold affirmation—if we believe, as did early Friends, that the Holy Spirit is not changeable, so as to lead us toward a thing as right at one time (in Scripture) and later to lead us from it as wrong (in the present). Our experience, as Friends, is that spiritual authority is acknowledged by the affirmation in one's own heart of the truth of what is being said, and is borne out by the fruits of following what is said. I bear witness that the Bible has that authority, and that acknowledging it bears good fruit.

How to make the vision come true: The Bible can help us in these ways only if we learn, individually, how to strip away all the personal, cultural, and historical veils that hang between us and God's truth in Scripture, preventing us from seeing and understanding the word God has for us. By personal veils between us and God's truth in Scripture I mean the barriers and biases that you and I as individuals place between us and understanding the Bible story, including the very human desire to see our own circumstances approved by Scripture, or at least not condemned. We expect to read something in the Bible, and sure enough there it is! By cultural veils I mean the ways that the dominant culture has softened or blunted the Scripture's warnings about the dangers of power, prestige, and possessions. By historical veils I mean the changes in culture and historical context that make the original symbolism and meaning of events or stories obscure to us. Learning and teaching one another the cultural context of both Old and New Testaments so we understand the symbolism of the story and not get stuck in the apparent literal meaning takes real work.

A passage where all three veils have been at work is Matthew 5:39–41: turning the other cheek, walking the extra mile, and giving the shirt as well as the cloak. Historically, we no longer understand the context of these admonitions. Culturally, they have been re-interpreted to encourage submissiveness and passive acceptance of authority by the great majority of the population at the bottom of the pyramid. Personally, the re-interpreted passages ring so false that many persons turn away from such a crazy book. I am grateful to Walter Wink for opening my eyes to these passages during a Bible study in Greensboro, North Carolina.

If someone slaps you on the right cheek, turn and offer him your left. Remember those period movies where a backhanded slap was a challenge to a duel? Since biblical times, the backhanded blow has been a sign that the person being struck had inferior social status compared to the one doing the striking. The forehand blow, or punch, was delivered between social equals. That is the first point of context one must remember to understand this statement of Jesus. The second point of context is that in Semitic societies from Biblical times to the present day, the left hand is and has been unclean. To do anything with the left hand, other than certain toilet functions, makes one unclean and requires purification.

Now think about this statement once again. It will help if you can act it out with another person, or visualize it carefully. Because my attacker can use only his right hand, a blow on my right cheek is a backhand blow: a declaration of his dominance and my inferiority.

To turn and offer my left cheek is to turn the tables on my attacker completely. By standing my ground I deny the power of the blow itself to defeat me. By simply turning my head, I have changed the circumstances so that my attacker can no longer reach my right cheek with his right hand. He now has the choice of striking my left cheek a backhand blow with his left hand, making himself unclean in the process, or striking my left cheek a forehand blow with his right hand, admitting that I am his social equal!

Jesus is not encouraging us to become victims here. He is telling us to look for nonviolent ways to recast the structures of domination that oppress us, to "bind the strong man" (to use Jesus' phrase from Mark) and proclaim our true dignity and worth. Jesus' next two statements confirm and extend this theme.

If a man wants to sue you for your shirt, let him have your coat as well. Jesus' audience was primarily the lower half of the economic pyramid of his day. Rich and powerful followers were so unusual that their appearance merited special mention in the gospels. This statement is directed at the poor, who had no funds to pursue a court suit, but did find themselves the object of a court case from time to time—even though they had little that could be taken from them other than the clothes on their back.

The cultural context to remember here has two relevant facets. The first is that men of that time and social class wore only two garments, an inner coat and outer cloak—and to paraphrase Michael Jordan, they were *not* "briefed." Undergarments as we think of them were unknown in Biblical times and culture. The second fact to remember is that in Biblical times and culture, viewing a naked man made the men who saw him unclean. This is crucial: it is not unclean to be naked, but it is unclean to look upon a naked man. A man who does so must undergo a purification.

Jesus is making another statement about the use of the judicial system to enforce unfair economic practices on the poor, and his advice is to find a way, by obeying the court's instructions literally, to recast the situation so that the truth comes out. Imagine the courtroom as our poor defendant takes the shirt off his back to pay the rich man who has sued him—and then continues by removing his coat as well, insisting that the plaintiff receive it, while everyone present tries to avoid looking at him. The defendant has made a symbolic statement about the court itself while obeying its commands literally: a system that takes the clothes off a man's back is indeed unclean and needs purification.

If a man in authority makes you go one mile, go with him two. The once-proud kingdom of David and Solomon was, in Jesus' lifetime, the Roman province of Judea—an occupied nation. Roman rule and Roman law were enforced by Roman troops stationed throughout the country. The "man in authority" who could make you go one mile was the Roman soldier, who had the legal right and authority at any time to conscript any civilian and make him carry the soldier's pack and gear for a mile. You could be plowing your field, on your way to synagogue, or rushing to see your dying father before he passed away—when the Roman soldier picked you, everything else had to wait while you carried his pack for a mile and then walked back to where you started.

This practice eased the load on the Roman soldiers, making their life easier and enabling them to travel farther in a day and arrive less fatigued. It also emphasized to the general population that the Romans were in charge, and that even the least Roman soldier had more power than the most prominent Jew. To prevent abuse of the population, no soldier was allowed to conscript a single individual for more than a mile. The person who was responsible for seeing that this regulation, and all army regulations, were carried out properly was the centurion, who had the power of life and death over the troops in his command.

Imagine now the Roman soldier who conscripts a farmer trying to do his spring planting. After the obligatory mile, the soldier tells the farmer he is free to go home, but the farmer refuses to go! "This is such an honor, I'll go an extra mile, sir! Your pack is really quite light!" The centurion is certain to notice that a civilian has been with the troops longer than usual, and will make an inquiry. The soldier will be hard-pressed to explain why he has apparently broken regulations by keeping a civilian in service for more than a mile. "Well, sir, this civilian insists on continuing to carry my pack—says it is an honor." Honor or not, regulations are regulations and the army must see to it that all are obeyed. Our Roman soldier has broken a regulation and will be punished. If this happened often enough, soldiers might well decide to carry their own packs.

Jesus is again pointing out a way to turn a common, oppressive situation around so that truth and real justice are revealed. The historical and cultural veils between us and the political, cultural, and social realities of Jesus' time make it difficult for us to understand what he is really saying. The dominant system in our own time draws its own veil, teaching us that Jesus wants us to be wimps—willing victims in our own oppression. We draw our own veils over such an outrageous assertion, refusing to engage the Scripture that makes such unreasonable demands. Only when we learn to strip away these veils can we learn what Scripture is really teaching—and we will be surprised and deeply thankful to find such a treasure.

My Vision for the Role of the Religious Society of Friends in the Contemporary Use and Understanding of the Bible

Just as the Bible has a role for us, we have a role in the church universal regarding the Bible. Part of this role has been our task for over three centuries: to remind Christians of the proper place of the Bible in Christian life—a secondary authority. We can't give effective testimony about the over-importance given to the Bible in some quarters unless we are willing to give it the importance it deserves, as a unique guide and resource second only to the direct inspiration of Jesus Christ, which is available to all.

A second aspect of our role in the wider arena is to remind Christians of what the Scripture really says. The cultural veils to understanding Scripture affect all Christians; those in strong institutional churches have institutional veils as well. Because Friends are relatively free of institutional momentum and somewhat separated from popular culture, we can provide a bridge back to a clearer understanding of the Scripture message in every generation. If you think Friends can't contribute importantly or be taken seriously by

Bible scholars and theologians of other faith groups, first refresh your memory of the contribution of Henry Cadbury to *The Interpreter's Bible*, then consider the contribution of Latin American peasants to the understanding of Christians everywhere in the world of the story in Luke 19.

Conclusion—Encounter with the Bible

Rabinadrath Tagore said, " A tree does not become independent by cutting itself off from its roots." The Bible is an important part of our spiritual root system as Christians and more broadly as people of the Book. We cut ourselves off from a richer spiritual life and from real help and sustenance in our life in the physical world when we allow our connection to the Bible to languish or die. Our lives draw their meaning from their connection to the big story—God's cosmic plan for all creation. The Bible is an account of the big story to date; without it, we tend to lose sight of the big story and try to give meaning to our "little stories"—nations, ethnic groups, or even individuals. We take the little truth of these stories and call it the truth—take what is really death and call it life.

Why do I still read that old thing?

- It helps me stay rooted in the big story when so much of daily life is trying to uproot me;
- It turns my face toward God when so much of our world is calling me to look elsewhere;
- It guides and nurtures me when I would otherwise wander like a lost sheep in the desert.

Could I be a good Christian without the Bible? Of course— but it would be a little like descending a ski slope in galoshes instead of skis. It could be done, but why?

Part Two

Practice

Gathered with One Accord

The meetinghouse in McNabb, Illinois was the setting for this plenary address, delivered to Illinois Yearly Meeting during its annual sessions in Seventh Month, 2001. Later in the week, I was active in the vocal ministry during meeting for worship. Afterward, a young Friend approached me to ask whether it might be possible that I had been brought to Illinois to deliver that ministry, not this planned message. I told her that the last words Susan had for me as I was leaving home were, "Remember, thee doesn't know why thee is going to Illinois—the lecture is only the excuse!" I have tried to keep this attitude in my heart throughout my travels in the ministry.

"I've been thinking." Rufus Jones began a piece of vocal ministry with this statement one First Day morning many years ago. At the rise of meeting, one of the elders of meeting approached him as they made their way out of the meetinghouse. Looking him in the eye, she said, "Rufus, thee shouldn't think!"[117]

The Conservative Quaker tradition in which I have put down my roots shares this skepticism about too much thinking. Nevertheless, I must admit to doing a good bit of it over the past several months. I've been thinking about the nature of the Christian life—what does it mean for me to be Christ's man in pharaoh's world. We who have had the experience of the Living Christ are a small minority in a much larger world and a much more powerful culture. How do we survive, and thrive, and even carry out some of the tasks that God may be giving us? Somewhere in the midst of all this thinking came your invitation to speak, which seemed to be an opportunity to share some of the fruits of this inner work. If at the conclusion you say to me "Lloyd Lee, thee shouldn't think," at least I'll know I'm in good company.

117 Recounted in Cadbury, Henry J., "With All Thy Mind," *Friends Journal*, Vol. 10, No. 1, Philadelphia, January 1, 1964, p. 4.

We are called to grow in our faith, and also called to transform the world. The hard truth is that we are caught up in a powerful culture that is as intent on transforming Christians as we are intent on transforming it. One way of looking at this struggle is to say that our calling as Christians is to put God at the center of our story. The dominant culture wants to put me there. Put you there. Put the individual person at the center of that person's story.

The pervasiveness of that effort is reflected even in our religious thought. Let me give you four examples of the way the dominant culture's individualism has gotten a foothold amongst us.

- "The great Christian question is, 'How can I be saved?'" In fact, the Christian life isn't really about personal righteousness. It is certainly not about getting into heaven. Our vocation as Christians is to heal the world, not to get saved.
- "The path to holiness is to separate myself from the world." In fact, the Bodhisattva principle is true: you can't be holy until the entire world is transformed anyway. You can't get away from it. So even if personal righteousness is your thing, the path to righteousness is to heal the world.
- "One person standing alone can change the world." In fact, the faith community, not the individual, is the means by which the world is to be transformed. No single individual is strong enough to overcome the powers that be,[118] and the changes that are needed are systemic and institutional, not just individual.
- "I grow in grace most by personal spiritual disciplines and practices." In fact, individual growth in grace comes from life in community, which is the mechanism for that growth. We receive what we most need when we focus our attention outside ourselves and our needs, immersing ourselves in our chosen community.

So the kingdom is not about personal righteousness or piety. We won't bring about the kingdom of God by living a lot of disconnected holy lives, but by helping one another become whole people,

---

[118] Walter Wink, *The Powers that Be: Theology for a New Millenium*, New York, Doubleday, 1999.

in holy community. My own personality makes me wish the path favored becoming recluses, hermit scholars with relatively little contact with other people; but it doesn't. The gospel of the kingdom is about a way of life in relationship; a life of loving servanthood to all of creation. Not only servanthood, but suffering servanthood. Only in servant relationship to others (and to all of creation) can we fulfill our role as a people "in the world but loyalists of Christ."

How do we do this community thing? I can't say. I can't say for several reasons. First, community is messy and unpredictable. It is a living thing, not a crystalline structure like a gemstone that is beautiful only when it is "right" in components and crystal bonds. Community is not the same from place to place, or even from time to time in the same place.

Second, describing community in advance is the law all over again—do this and this, but not that, and everything will be all right. Life isn't like that—and the life of the Spirit is certainly not like that. Community can't be described or regulated *a priori* because it doesn't exist *a priori*—only after the fact can we identify that yes, that was community that happened then.

We don't have a set of *a priori* rules to determine how we should behave in order to nurture and sustain community, or what the community should do in order to be faithful. We do have another way to direct our actions. Community comes out of our common *praxis*—our practice. Community is nurtured when we try something together, and reflect together on what happened and why, and then try again—but this time something a little different, based on the fruits of our common reflection.

As a beginning point for our *praxis*, we do have the example of those first Christians of two thousand years ago, as recorded by Luke in the book of Acts. This description is especially valuable because this community was so close chronologically to Jesus' life and teachings that we can assume with some confidence that they had an accurate understanding of what that life and those teachings meant. These folks were even weaker than we are, and the surrounding culture was more overtly hostile, so we may be able to learn some valuable lessons from them.

Let's take some time to examine the example of the early church in Acts 2:41–47.

41. Those who believed were baptized, and about three thousand were added to their number that day.
42. They devoted themselves to the apostles' teaching and to the fellowship, to the breaking of bread and to prayer.
43. Everyone was filled with awe, and many wonders and miraculous signs were done by the apostles.
44. All the believers were together and had everything in common.
45. Selling their possessions and goods, they gave to anyone as he had need.
46. Every day they continued to meet together in the temple courts. They broke bread in their homes and ate together with glad and sincere hearts,
47. praising God and enjoying the goodwill of all the people. And the Lord added to their number daily those who were being saved. (Paraphrase of New International Version)

- they believed
- they devoted themselves to the apostles' teaching and fellowship
- they devoted themselves to the breaking of bread
- they devoted themselves to prayer
- they all believed
- they spent time together
- they treated their belongings as held in common
- they shared their material wealth according to need
- they spent much time together in daily worship
- they broke bread together daily
- they ate with glad and generous hearts
- they praised God
- they had the goodwill of all the people
- the Lord added to their number

This is a wonderful description of community—I want to sign up now! How did this come about, and how can we have that same experience? The first couple of verses of this chapter give us two important principles:

Verse 2: Community is a gift.

"Suddenly there came a sound from heaven as of a rushing mighty wind." (King James Version)

The Holy Ghost came upon them as an unexpected gift. After we've done everything right, after we've dotted every i and crossed every t, community is a gift. We are not in charge—we can't build community or achieve community on our own; community is a gift. Hard to learn, in this culture, but once we're in community we're glad we're not in charge!

Verse 1: You have to prepare to receive the gift!

"They were all with one accord in one place."(King James Version)

The dominant culture works to persuade us not to believe in community. To the extent that we are persuaded, we act in ways that make community more difficult, if not impossible. Individualism is king in the dominant culture—look out for number one! Our western paradigm of dualism—either this or that—has convinced us that we are each independent entities, working out the progress of our lives in isolation.

Individualism is a myth. It doesn't work, and the more effort we put into it the more absurd it becomes. Think of the millions of dollars spent in advertising to convince thousands of people that if they just buy this particular mass-produced car they will be more unique than if they buy that other car mass-produced by another corporation.

Community is a gift—a miracle. So we have to prepare to receive the gift. Expect a miracle! Order your life to make room for the gift. "They were all with one accord gathered in one place."

How do we prepare? The body of the passage I read earlier lays out the principles early Christians found to be central to their life. I believe that a large part of our preparation lies in orienting our lives to be in harmony with these principles.

Verse 41: They believed.

Those that gladly received Peter's message were added to the community.

This was a covenant community. The basis on which they were drawn together was not compatibility, or special interests, or similar backgrounds—they were together because they had received the gospel message of Jesus Christ, and accepted it gladly. Another way of putting it is that this was a "Believers' Church."[119] The new Christians were not forming a national church in political or geographic terms, nor one based on a creed or liturgy. The new community consisted of those who voluntarily confessed their belief in Jesus Christ as Lord.

Conflicts and differences of opinion abounded (e.g., the controversy about circumcision in chapter 15), but they shared a single orientation, like sunflowers. They were all oriented toward Jesus.

What you don't read in Scripture is sometimes as important as what you do. This passage says next to nothing about an expected belief "system." This is a confessional community, not a creedal one. They shared an experience of the power of the risen Jesus, but Luke is much more concerned with describing their right practice—*orthopraxy*—than right belief—*orthodoxy*. They had not accepted any specific creed, dogma, or vocabulary. They had accepted Jesus Christ into their lives. To use my wife's expression, they were all looking in the same direction: toward God as revealed by Christ. God was now at the center of their story.

Verse 42: They devoted themselves to the apostles' teaching and fellowship.

These were not folks intent on changing the group to meet their own predispositions. They were eager to learn more about Jesus and about the gospel, and were ready to hear more from those who knew more. In traditional Friends terminology, they were humble learners in the school of Christ. They valued what these more seasoned Christians could tell them about Jesus' life and message.

On the other hand, the apostles' teaching at this time would have been almost entirely stories and reminiscences about Jesus' teaching. What we share with one another should be mostly what our experience with Jesus has been, not our intellectual ideas about what God must be like.

---

[119] Donald F. Durnbaugh, *The Believers Church*, Macmillan Company, New York, 1968, p. 32.

These folks had been through a transforming experience, and now they wanted to put down new roots, to dig down into this newly discovered truth. In modern times we often act as if the way to honor other religions is to take an eclectic approach to them all, taking a little from this one and a little from that one to suit ourselves. This is like trying to find deep water by digging dozens of shallow wells all over the landscape. When drought brings tough times, the shallow wells will go dry. The same effort spent digging one deep well will bring us to the aquifer, to the living water that will never go dry. When we've done that, we'll realize that the same living water feeds all the great religions.

The newly convinced Christians devoted themselves to digging deeper wells. To do that, they listened to the stories of those who were more experienced. They undoubtedly also asked some hard questions, and talked long into the night about what had happened to them and was still happening to them.

Verse 42: They devoted themselves to the breaking of bread.

It is unlikely that this phrase refers to a practice of Eucharist as such, but rather to Jesus' practice of table fellowship. In both his gospel and in Acts, Luke reports on a great number of meals. Jewish identity was defined in large measure by the people with whom one ate. Dietary laws, cleanliness regulations and the like defined who was a real Jew. Remember how the Pharisees were constantly offended by the people with whom Jesus ate. Luke in particular tells us Jesus was constantly sharing table fellowship with folks who were excluded from Jewish society by purity and debt laws.

Now this community was devoted to the apostle's fellowship. What do you think the apostles told them about meals in the kingdom of heaven? Remember Luke's story of the messianic banquet and think whom this community must have been inviting to eat with them. Were these invitations themselves not gospel—good news—to those who received them? "Blessed is anyone who will share the meal in the kingdom of God!"

They were devoted to breaking bread together. If you eat with someone often enough, you get to know their likes and dislikes, their table manners, the pressures and commitments that sometimes make them late to dinner or call them away early. These folks were getting to know each other in a very intimate way. You can be on your best behavior for a while, but sooner or later at mealtime the real you comes out. Good for that!

The new community was inclusive, not exclusive. Everyone who believed the good news was welcome, whether they were "moral" people or not. We Quakers keep forgetting that we're all sinners, not one worthy of the table. Personal righteousness is not the issue—our love of God is all that matters. Love God, and love one another.

Verse 42: They devoted themselves to prayer.

What prayer had Jesus taught his disciples?

> Now once he was in a certain place praying, and when he had finished one of his disciples said, "Lord, teach us to pray, just as John taught his disciples." He said to them, "Say this when you pray:
> Father, may your name be held holy
> Your kingdom come.
> Give us this day our daily bread,
> And forgive us our sins,
> For we ourselves forgive each one who is in debt to us.
> And do not put us to the test."[120]

Now there are lots of commentaries about that prayer; I encourage you to spend some time with it, in study and/or contemplation. A couple of points are particularly relevant to our topic.

"Your kingdom come"—if we are praying for that occurrence, our behavior should be consonant with our prayer. Act boldly for the kingdom—lean on God! You have not yet suffered to the shedding of blood, as Paul reminds us. Don't pray for the kingdom and at the same time live a life that keeps that day distant from us.

"Give us this day our daily bread"—Money is one of the great destroyers of community. Dependence on God rather than our individual piles of money is important to all of gospel life, including community. Let us each consider the lilies of the field, and look at our own lives, and repent.

[120] Luke 11:1–4.

"And forgive us . . . for we ourselves forgive each one who is in debt to us."—It is well to be reminded of just how central the matter of forgiveness is to Jesus' message. This is not forgiveness in exchange for repentance or apology or sacrifice, but forgiveness as the first step. Two thirds of the gospels can be read as encouragement of the practice of forgiveness. Community is in large part the practice of forgiveness. God's love is not conditional, and our being righteous (or repentant) is not going to make God love us more. Our love for one another is also to be unconditional, and we are to forgive those we love. The prophet Ezekiel in the Hebrew Scriptures realizes that God forgives us in advance, and that our repentance comes as a reaction to the realization of God's forgiveness. Two millennia later, after all that Jesus has tried to tell us, we still get it wrong. We think that God doesn't love us until we repent, and we withhold our love from other humans until they repent to us. This moral one-upmanship is contrary to the gospel.

So these new Christians prayed. What do you think they prayed about? What did they ask for? Something like, "Gee, God, this is great! Keep it going and if possible make it better! Help me share this with Aunt Bessie back home and Joe and the gang at the office!"

Richard Rohr, the Franciscan monk I admire so greatly tells the story of an interview he had with his novice master. After the usual discussion, the novice master said to him, "Remember, you will get what you pray for." "Of course," Richard replied, and got up to leave.

"No," said the novice master, "You really will get what you pray for."

"Well, yes," said Richard, or words to that effect.

"I am absolutely serious," was the response. "You will get exactly what you pray for."

The lesson for me and thee in this story is to be careful what we pray for—because prayer works. Therefore, let us pray to be in harmony with the divine will.

Verse 44: They all believed.

Now this is a repetition of what has been said before, which is always important in Scripture. Remember, writing materials were expensive, and not to be wasted on unnecessary words. Acts is just about long enough to fill up one scroll completely. Luke used up all the available space, and had no room to repeat ideas that didn't merit repeating.

The basis of church community is belief. Not political stands or peace testimonies, but belief. And the belief on which community stands is not affirmation of a creed or assent to dogma—it is our "yes" to the experience of God's centrality in our lives. To believe is, among other things, to make ourselves vulnerable to that in which we believe: to take a risk. Using our intellect to keep a safe distance from the presence of God is not belief. Falling into the hands of the living God is belief. Until we can let go that much, our belief is incomplete.

Verse 44: They spent time together.

> One in heart, they all used to meet in the portico of Solomon. (see also 5:12)

How important this is to strong community. We want community, but we don't invest our time in being community. These folks wanted to be together, so they spent their days together. Fact—you can't be community with an investment of one hour per week. We create space for community to happen by spending time with people, and we naturally want to spend time with the people in our community.

It is surprising to me how many Friends want to have community, and how few show up to participate in meeting for business. There are a hundred reasons why meeting for business is frustrating, or irrelevant, or the stronghold of stick-in-the-muds: I know every reason, and have expressed most of them myself at one time or another. All that aside, nevertheless, meeting for business is when community is made manifest: when the body of Christ discerns how it is called to be kingdom in this world, and how to carry out that call. Think it is irrelevant? Come add thy relevancy to the mix. Is it held at an inconvenient time? Be sure and tell God when it is convenient for thee to receive leadings and carry them out. Does it seem fractious and argumentative? This is where community is forged—absent thyself at thy own risk. Does it not seem to do anything relevant or important? How can thee tell without being present to participate in the corporate discernment? Maybe thee would learn that some things are more relevant than they seem; maybe thee would learn more humility; maybe the corporate body would benefit from thy contributions to accurate discernment and end up acting differently.

Beyond formal activities, it is important to seek one another out in all our activities, in work and recreation. When I have belonged to a meeting that included a physician among its members, I have made that Friend my primary physician. When a fellow member was an architect and I was working in nonprofit housing, I enlisted that architect in every project I could. It seems to me that living in community involves helping one another out that way.

It also involves sharing meals together, and projects at one another's homes and in the community, and all the different ways we can spend time together. To some extent, we should spend time together to build community; to some extent, we want to spend time together to enjoy the community we share.

Verse 44: They treated their belongings as held in common.

(see also chapter 4:32–37)

The whole group of believers was united, heart and soul; no one claimed private ownership of any possessions, as everything they owned was held in common. The apostles continued to testify to the resurrection of the Lord Jesus with great power, and they were all accorded great respect. None of their members was ever in want, as all those who owned land or houses would sell them, and bring the money from the sale of them, to present it to the apostles; it was then distributed to any who might be in need. There was a Levite of Cypriot origin called Joseph whom the apostles surnamed Barnabas (which means "son of encouragement"). He owned a piece of land and he sold it and brought the money and presented it to the apostles.

The members of the community evidently still had personal possessions, but had given up their sense that they had a right to them—they treated their possessions as held in common. The verb is imperfect, i.e., "used to sell," meaning that they sold things from time to time, as there was need—not that there was one great yard sale.

The year 2000 was a jubilee year, and with great fanfare this country proposed to forgive a little international debt. This church in Acts is practicing jubilee with a vengeance. They are not just forgiving debt, they consider themselves stewards of all their material possessions, and are giving out of their own 401(k) plans to help other folks! Radical! This flies in the face of our dominant culture individualism.

Certainly the society that surrounds us today is quite different from that of first-century Palestine, and we can't blindly transfer financial practice from one era to another. But what remains constant is that how we use money illuminates our priorities in many areas. How do we use the material wealth that has been entrusted to us? Are we building up a stronghold to protect ourselves and our blood kin, or are we building up the community of faith, to ensure that everyone has enough and no one has too much?

About now some of you are getting a little uncomfortable, and a few are saying to yourselves that this made sense only because these Christians thought the world was going to end any day—who needed money? I suggest something quite different was operating here. People who thought the world would end in a few weeks or days would not have bothered to write a history of the beginnings of their earliest church—it would be a needless labor. Luke wrote this story, and others preserved it, precisely because they believed in an unfolding future that would need this story. And naturally, they put in it what they thought would be most important to remember. So far from discounting these early Christians' attitudes toward money and possessions, we must read their account in boldface, as something of utmost importance to us today.

Verse 45: They shared their material wealth according to need.

(see also chapter 4:34)

There was not a needy person among them! This is not simply charitable giving as we practice it today, not simply giving out of our excess and surplus, but giving out of the need of the other person—giving until their need is gone.

Note also that they shared their material goods according to need, not according to worthiness, either moral worthiness or standing in the community (seniority, positions filled, etc.). In fact, the people making the gifts aren't even the ones deciding who receives it—the apostles do that (4:35).

Jewish teaching ascribes different levels of blessing to different kinds of gifts. The least blessed is the gift where the giver knows the recipient and vice versa. It is more blessed to give so the recipient will not know the identity of the giver, and most blessed to give so that neither giver nor recipient knows the identity of the other. This flies in the face of our desire to limit giving to the identifiably "worthy poor," but the church in Acts was doing just this: the givers gave to the Apostles, who then distributed where there was need. Soon, of course, the Seven were appointed to take this task off the Apostle's hands.

When was the last time any of us gave until the need was gone, trusting that God will give to us until our need is gone, as well? These Christians set a hard example before us, but I think it is an important one. We aren't community, at least in this sense, while there is unmet need among us.

That there is "no unmet need" does not mean every person or every household has exactly the same resources, or the same amount of money per person. But the community knows—if it does not go into denial—true unmet need when it exists among its members. When the burden of that knowledge is placed on our hearts, our response is revealing.

Verse 46: They spent much time together in daily worship.

Think about our own faith tradition, with its relatively short history of less than four centuries. Friends used to attend two meetings for worship on First Day, each considerably longer than an hour, and gathered as well on Fifth Day mornings—closing down their businesses and unhitching their plows to do so. Beyond this, daily devotions including reading the Bible and waiting worship were the standard practice in every household.

The church in Acts is meeting in one another's homes on a regular basis. Are we ready to bring one another home for meeting for worship? Are we ready to bring meeting for worship into our home?

Worship is the foundational and formational act of our faith community. In meeting for worship our covenant with God is articulated, renewed, strengthened, extended. In meeting for worship we are knit together with each other by the presence of God. In worship we receive our "marching orders" as God's hands and feet and voice in this world. We, too, should spend much time together in daily worship.

Verse 46: They broke bread together daily.

The importance of this practice is underlined by its repetition here. This is not a monthly potluck, but a daily gathering for what we often call the Quaker communion—the common meal. You can't be on your best behavior every day at mealtime. Sooner or later the pressures of life are going to break through (Hallelujah!) and your fellows are going to know a little bit more about you. Wonderful! Slowly we learn that we are all broken, all less than perfect, and that God loves us, each one, wonderfully even so. Slowly we learn that the real love for one another we crave is not the ideal love of my personal façade for your façade, but the imperfect intent to love that my flawed self can offer to the real you.

Verse 46: They ate with glad and generous hearts.

Well, who do you want to hang out with—glad and generous people, or curmudgeons and Scrooges? The kingdom of God is a party—a wedding feast—a banquet—a celebration of finding what has been lost—the joy of a bountiful harvest beyond all expectations. Remember the parables of losing and finding in Luke 15, and the rejoicing at the end of each one. Think of Zacchaeus called out of the tree by Jesus, and the joyful way he greeted Jesus.

We Quakers often appear a dour, sober-faced people; it is no wonder that folks don't flock to our meetings for worship. Creation is good, God is in charge, and Christ has come to dwell among us. What's not to celebrate?

Verse 47: They praised God.

Let's remind ourselves again of just who is throwing this party, and who issued all the invitations, and why we're so fortunate as to be invited. God is at the center of the story, not any one of us or even all of us together.

These folks knew why their lives had been changed, and were unashamed to claim that—praise God, the author and perfecter of our faith!

Now Luke concludes his description with two statements about the fruit of community:

Verse 47: They had the goodwill of all the people.

Not the officials and power brokers, mind you, but the people: the ones at the margin.

And why not? The Christian life should be a mighty attractive one. Christian community is a testimony—a prophetic voice of God to those not yet included—see how those Christians love one another! It seems to me that one of the tests of a healthy community is whether it generates the good will of ordinary people, and especially of people at the margins of society.

Verse 47: The Lord added to their number.

Many Quakers today seem to think that there are only a few people in the world who have the special talents or inclination to be Friends. This is an elitism that has no analog in the experience of the early church. The church in Acts had the opinion that everyone was invited to participate in the life of Christ, and the Lord added to their number in very dramatic ways: from 120 persons (1:15) to 3,000 at Pentecost (2:41) and 5,000 more after the miracle at the Temple (4:4).

If there is fellowship every day, glad and generous hearts breaking bread together and sharing their blessings with those in need, don't you believe that would be an attractive life—that folks would want to join in! Proselytizing is almost a dirty word among liberal and conservative Friends. The matter here is not building up the church membership, but sharing the joy of the kingdom with other folks. If we've truly had the experience of the Holy Spirit, we will want to share that joy with other people—and they will want to be part of the experience.

Conclusion

Sometimes proudly, sometimes humbly, the Religious Society of Friends has always considered itself "primitive Christianity revived." This claim continues to be true only if we seek to understand and emulate these first, "primitive" Christians. It has merit only if early Christians continue to have something to teach us. I believe they do, and this description of their common life is one of the most important messages we have to receive from them, to understand, and to put into practice in our own lives.

The church in Acts was gathered on the basis of belief, not assent to a creed or catechism, not as a kinship group or political action organization. Each one knew that something very special had happened to them and their response was to believe that God was at work in and among them.

Rather than telling us of personal rules of piety and spiritual discipline adopted by individual Christians, Luke describes four principles of corporate praxis adopted by the community:

1. devotion to teaching and learning;
2. table fellowship and other time together;
3. prayer and worship and praise of God; and
4. sharing material wealth according to need.

Community is and has always been a blessed gift from God. Like all of God's gifts, we can place ourselves in position to receive this gift more readily, or we can make it harder. When we open our hearts to believe, and adopt these four corporate practices, we make ourselves ready to receive and nurture the divine gift of community. In so doing, we become, and act as, the body of Christ in this broken world.

Friends Testimonies in the Marketplace
On Living an Integrated Life

This was a Pendle Hill Monday Night Lecture in 1995 as was "Why Do You Still Read that Old Thing?" placed earlier in this book (but a year after in actual chronology). As I look back over these words from a distance of almost a decade, it is gratifying to see at least a consistency of intention in manner of living, if (as in all things) the actuality has at times fallen short of the intent.

The Quaker doctrine of integrity requires an integrated life. Our spiritual practice is not limited to holy ground, or to family observances, but includes—must include—our life in the marketplace, where we interact with the rest of the world. I have been asked to reflect on Friends testimonies in the marketplace considered narrowly—in the realm of business and commerce—but I will take the liberty of considering the marketplace in the broader sense, as the place, as all the places, where we encounter other people in daily life.

To speak about Friends testimonies one must start with the words testimony and witness themselves, to understand what they symbolize and why they are important. The terminology of "witness" and "testimony" comes from the courtroom, where one hears a witness to an event give testimony as to the truth about that event, to the best of the witness's knowledge and ability to communicate. Our testimonies as Quakers are in their essence an attempt to communicate by direct action what we have witnessed about the truth of God and God's creation. The jury is the world's people, who must judge the truth of the testimony presented to them. If we do not give our testimony, in clear and unequivocal terms, the jury is deprived of important information about the truth.

It is important to communicate what we have witnessed because we understand that we have been entrusted with a glimpse of absolute truth: of God's intent for creation, and of the grand divine plan of which we are only one part. There is a single divine order in and for the universe, a divine harmony among the various and diverse parts of creation, and between each of them and the godhead. That divine order is good news for all of creation—hence its name among Friends: the gospel order. Gospel order tells us that the universe is orderly; apparent disorder is simply our inability to perceive and understand the greater order that is God's plan for creation.

If this divine order were only applicable to Friends, there would be no cause for testimonies; but we understand the good news is for everyone, and it is therefore our joyful responsibility to share what we have seen and heard and tasted for ourselves of the gospel order. Hear me carefully. I am not saying that my perception of the truth, and that of others who share my perceptions, are the only way to perceive the truth, or that they incorporate all that is important about the truth of the divine order. What I am saying is that what God shows us, when we open ourselves to the Inner Teacher, is part of the great truth of God and God's divine order. I believe we have been given a prophetic witness for the nations, which we fail to proclaim in words and deeds to our own peril and the world's suffering.

So although I do not understand everything I see or hear, I have heard the gospel with great joy, and am convinced it is good news for everyone. I want to share my joy and its roots with others in the world, to bear witness to the truth as I have been able to perceive it. Following the example of my Teacher, I have used a number of symbolic acts to announce the good news and create the "teachable moment" in which truth can be communicated and perceived. These symbolic acts we Friends call testimonies.

The discipline of North Carolina Yearly Meeting (Conservative) calls simplicity and harmony the primary testimonies, and Wilmer Cooper makes a strong case for Integrity as the keystone testimony. I want to start by sharing share a little about my experiences with these historic Friends testimonies. As the outward world changes, old symbols lose their original meaning and new circumstances call for new perspectives and new testimonies. I want to share some changes we need to make in order to see this broken world more clearly, and suggest some new testimonies that will symbolize the truth about the ways we see and experience God breaking into history at this moment.

In sharing these reflections and experiences I am only a blind man reporting on his encounter with an elephant. What I have felt and heard are true, but they are not the whole truth and not the only truth. Other Friends will encounter the elephant in different places and different times, and their experience will undoubtedly be different from mine.

Simplicity

Perhaps the testimony one thinks of having the most striking effect in the marketplace is simplicity. It does play a visible role in one's daily walk in the marketplace, but not always in the ways one might think. Simplicity is a testimony of single-pointed awareness, not an economic doctrine. The point is not to make oneself as materially poor as possible (though there is nothing wrong with evangelical poverty, if undertaken in the right spirit), but to remove from one's life everything that distracts one's attention from God. Testimonies are directed at oneself as well as one's colleagues and counterparts; testimonies of simplicity are a great aid to me in my effort to stay focused on God throughout each day. Testimonies of simplicity help me return over and over again to contemplation of the reality of God in the midst of all the distractions of life.

Trying to make simplicity an economic doctrine can rebound to leave me worse off spiritually than before. When I was a newly convinced Friend, the executive secretary of Friends Meeting of Cambridge, Massachusetts, Elmer Brown, drove a large expensive-looking car—probably a Lincoln, though I don't remember for sure. What I remember is my disapproval that this weighty Friend should drive such an un-simple car! I was so upset that I finally cornered him in the parking lot and asked him how he could be so un-simple when our meeting looked to him to set an example for others. "Well," Elmer replied, "A Friend at the last meeting I served gave me this car so that I would have something to drive to carry out my responsibilities to the meeting. I didn't pay anything for it and it serves me well. That seems simple to me." Elmer was right and I was wrong: he was freed from a material worry to center his awareness on God, and I was distracted by the car away from attending to God.

The first and strongest testimony of simplicity that I make in the marketplace is that God is worthy of my primary loyalty and attention, and that my career is secondary to that loyalty. Hence the question for me is not how do I incorporate these peculiar practices into my career as a manager, but how do I be faithful to my God and God's plan for me while pursuing some competency which will supply my true material needs? Over and over again, I have tried to choose service to God in preference to conventional career, beginning with my decision in graduate school to leave the "fast track" of an MIT Ph.D. in favor of some more direct service to human beings. At present my wife and I run a small business providing management services to a number of nonprofit organizations in Hampton Roads. We are the only two employees, although we subcontract some work to other small businesses. This arrangement allows us to choose how much we will work and for what projects. Recently we decided to end a $20,000 per year consulting contract in order to have more time to devote to the work of Norfolk Quaker House, a Christian peace witness addressing the huge military establishment where we live. I believe these actions are a witness and testimony to those who observe them about what is really real and what is illusion.

Plain Dress

I have chosen to make a symbolic statement about simplicity in the way I dress, which in some ways evokes the "plain dress" that has almost completely passed from the Quaker scene. There is no integrity in dressing for a role. It is as counter to the gospel order to "dress for the part" of old-time Quaker as it is to "dress for the part" of prosperous banker. There is integrity, however, in choosing clothes that remind oneself and others of our historic testimonies and values, in the hope of influencing our current decisions and choices for the better. The point is not to make some protest against style, but to live outside the boundaries of style. The story goes that when John Woolman decided for the sake of simplicity to give up his dyed hat for an undyed version, he was somewhat distressed to discover that just then undyed hats were in fashion. After some hesitation, he decided to go ahead with the headgear he felt led to wear, in spite of its being fashionable. For some years I took my shirts to a tailor to have the collars removed, for the sake of simplicity—as a visible reminder of the need for single-pointed awareness centered on God. Recently my wife Susan and I were at first joyful to discover some collarless shirts in a mail order catalog. Soon we discovered them in another catalog, and then another, and another, until it became clear that they are now in style. Susan points out that if we are patient, the style will change again and I can have this testimony back.

In addition to removing my collars, I have over time given up wearing suits and ties, my favorite pocket watch and gold chain, and even my beloved "brass rat:" the MIT class ring which symbolized so much of my family's aspirations for my generation of children. In their place have come broad-brimmed hats and a desire to reduce my wardrobe to as few "looks" as possible: one for clean activities, one for dirty activities, and one (I do live at the beach) for sandy activities. Again, the point is to eliminate the need to devote time and energy to my clothing and the decision about what to wear, so that time and energy is available to attend to God.

I have been informed, by one who has seen the official list of seventeen "plain Friends" worldwide, that I am not plain. Among other things, my shirts have too many buttons down the front— some of them are even dyed in various colors and patterns! Nonetheless, I don't resemble any of the people with whom I do business; the difference is helpful to me and I believe an important reminder to others. I spend considerable amounts of time meeting with bankers, lawyers, and government officials in an attempt to create safe, decent, and affordable housing for low-income persons. Unlike many of my colleagues in the nonprofit world, I do not blend in. My odd clothing helps remind them, I hope, that the accumulation of material wealth symbolized by their own attire is not the highest value to which they should aspire. It certainly is a valuable reminder to me of the self-same fact.

Ironically, the one employer over the years that expressed some concern about my plain dress was Friends General Conference. At the end of my interview with the search committee, I was asked whether I had anything I felt I should share with them. Having noticed that all the other men were wearing sport jackets and ties, I said I had a testimony about plain dress and did not own any suits or ties. The committee immediately began discussing whether it would be possible to address Philadelphia Yearly Meeting sessions without wearing a suit and tie. For better or worse, they decided to hire me anyway.

Another aspect of plain dress, which is for me personally very important, is that my distinctive dress helps me behave properly when I might otherwise slip and slide. My clothing reminds me continually of the commitments I have made in life, and of my real priorities. It helps me remember, and helps me act in accordance with what I remember, to be dressed in a plain fashion.

PLAIN SPEECH

Which leads me to the matter of plain speech. Plain speech for me means choosing my words carefully, so that I say exactly what I mean, to the best of my ability, not speaking beyond my certain knowledge, not speaking ill of other persons, and speaking with economy. A rule of thumb among conservative Friends is "If thee can't add to the silence, keep quiet!" This can lead some to conclude that I am hoarding information, but not so. I was reassured of the value of careful speech as a testimony to others when a non-Friend who is the executive director of my largest business client volunteered recently that my economy of speech seemed to her to be part of my testimony of simplicity.

This understanding of plain speaking has also had impact on my correspondence. I have found it difficult to close business letters with a routine or perfunctory "Sincerely" or "Respectfully" since the first implies that sometimes I am not sincere and the second might be construed to imply a social distinction I do not feel. Most of my letters close with "In Peace," since until I do feel a sense of peace with the contents and intent of the letter I will not send it. I have been understood at times to be making a radical political statement, though none was intended. The significance of this closing is clearly as a reminder to me rather than a witness to other persons. Interestingly, I find the one time I do consistently use "Sincerely" to close a letter is when I am engaged in the unpleasant but necessary duty of reminding a tenant of their obligation to pay their rent. I tend to give tenants a much greater latitude than most landlords, but there comes a time when the tenant must either pay what they owe or leave—their failure to do so will put the other tenants the property at risk. My letters at these times lay out in plain English what the delinquent tenant must do in order to bring their accounts into order, and when it must be done, and what the consequences of failure to comply will be. These letters I do sign "Sincerely," because I most certainly am.

Plain speech means to me that I will keep my word. On the front end, I am inclined to say outwardly "I will try to do so" rather than promise, and to add, "if God is willing" to my intentions to attend a particular meeting or complete a particular task on schedule. On the back end, I try to do what I have said I will do, even (as the Psalmist says) to my own hurt. This honoring of one's own word is not generally understood in a business world of contracts, lawyers, and looking out for number one, but I am convinced it carries a witness into those hearts that have been prepared. Even if it did not, I would continue to strive to be true to my word because of what it says about and means to me before God.

Equality

As Friends we believe in the equality of all persons: that God's grace and mercy are distributed throughout all of creation, to every person without limitation or distinction or need for mediation or intercession. In the marketplace this principle is usually thought of as meaning that various current and potential employees, customers and suppliers should be treated equally, without respect to national origin, race, gender, sexual orientation, et cetera. In my own career a concern for equality has found expression from my very first real job after college, when I joined in the effort to provide a single standard of care for all ambulatory medical patients at Massachusetts General Hospital, regardless of economic or social class. Contrary to previous practice, we provided care to both private patients and "teaching clinic" patients in the same offices, with the same staff, at the same time. Along the way I managed to integrate the previously all-white, all female administrative staff of about twelve persons both racially and sexually. In my more recent jobs I have consistently worked to hire minority-owned subcontractors, to recruit women and minorities for jobs, and to ensure equal pay for equal work.

Harmony

Harmony is for me the over-arching testimony, upon which all the others rest. The concept of a gospel order implies a divine harmony among the parts of a cosmos created by a God of order and not of chaos. Our testimony of harmony is a witness to the reality of that gospel order among the parts of creation, and to the ability of human beings, with divine assistance, to live in harmony with all parts of creation.

Environmental Concerns

A testimony for "living lightly upon the earth" has been part of my life in business throughout my career, expressed most unequiv-ocally in my work in housing. The design of Friends Community in North Easton, Massachusetts, was shaped consciously to preserve existing wetland, minimize the use of cars, and use solar power to provide the bulk of space heating needs—before the wetlands preservation act was even proposed legislation. For a decade I helped run the largest weatherization program in the Commonwealth of Virginia—we had weatherized the homes of more than 5,000 low-income families by the time I left. I placed a high value on the reduction in heating and cooling costs we were making available to our poor clients, the benefits in improved levels of health, performance in school, and other facets of the quality of life. An aspect of our work that loomed almost as large for me as these personal benefits was the number of gallons of fuel oil and tons of coal that would not be used for space heating each year as a result of our work. In the same way, my work at JAUNT, Inc. in Charlottesville, Virginia had meaning to me both for the way it enabled the poor and handicapped persons we served to get to their destinations, and for the thousands of gallons of gasoline that we saved by substituting a small number of passenger vans for a multitude of cars and trucks. More recently my concerns have come to include water conservation—a real issue in Hampton Roads, where I live and work. Use of low-flow toilets and shower-heads has become a personal requirement in my housing rehabilitation work and property maintenance work. I'm happy to say that hundreds of toilets and showerheads have been replaced with more economical models, and hundreds of wasteful heating and air conditioning systems have been replaced with more energy-efficient systems in the course of my work.

PEACE

The peace witness is a special case of the testimony of harmony. Given my career choices, it has not been difficult to avoid working in the military-industrial complex, once I was convinced as a Friend and obtained my conscientious objector discharge from the air force. Also, being self-employed as I have been at several points in my career has made it relatively easy to practice war tax resistance of various sorts. There are two other incidents that stick out in my memory where the application of the peace testimony had particular impact on my work life. The first happened in 1979 at JAUNT, Inc., a rural transportation company that served low-income persons in the region surrounding Charlottesville, Virginia. JAUNT had a policy that gave employees time off for reserve duty in the summer in addition to their annual vacation. Feeling that this policy encouraged participation in war and the preparation for war by our employees, and was de facto participation by JAUNT as an organization, I advocated for and obtained a decision from the JAUNT board of directors revoking the policy. From that point on, employees who wanted to go on reserve duty in the summer had to do so on their own time.

The second incident happened more recently, as my former business partner and I were managing a 56-unit rental property in Newport News, Virginia that had a bad reputation for crime, including drugs. We hired a security service to patrol the property on Friday and Saturday nights, with the enthusiastic support of most of the tenants. However, we found that no one would work at this property without carrying a weapon. With difficulty, I came to agree with my partner that the residents deserved to receive the protection they wanted from on-site security, and that we should not deprive them of that protection by imposing our own value system on the situation. I was never completely comfortable with this outcome, and am glad not to be employing armed security personnel anymore.

Integrity

Wilmer Cooper has described integrity as the central Quaker testimony. Integrity is a synonym for such words as honesty, honor, virtue, morality, and principle. Thinking about the testimony of integrity as a testimony of honesty brings to mind a business meeting about ten years ago between Virginia Mountain Housing, for which I was then the director of field operations, and a potential client in Northern Virginia. The executive director of Virginia Mountain Housing and I were proposing to run a weatherization program for this local community action program, and this was the pivotal meeting. After a little more than an hour, one of the representatives of our potential client remarked, "You guys are perfectly honest—what a sly sales technique!" Obviously our integrity had been communicated to the other person—but he could understand it only as an instrument of dishonesty and deception. This illustrates both the power of our testimonies and the need to be faithful even in such mundane matters as being completely honest.

One of the principles guiding the behavior of much of the western world is that of the zero-sum game. If you and I are going to share a pie, and you get an extra piece, I must necessarily get one fewer piece. The sum of extra pie and pie lost is always zero. For every winner there is always an equal loser. Part of the fruit of a belief in the gospel order is a conviction that there is a solution to every problem or response to every circumstance that works out well for everyone: the world is not a set of zero-sum games, as the dominant culture believes, but a series of synergistic opportunities in which cooperation results in win-win relationships. Everyone can get more: we can make more pies, we can put ice cream or whipped cream on top, and we can make cake, or muffins, or brownies in addition to the pie. It has been my practice, throughout my career, to look for ways to structure win-win relationships in every business transaction. Since so much of my career has involved real estate transactions of one sort or another, I have often appeared naive to the people with whom I have been dealing. Other times I appear soft, because I'm "leaving money on the table." In the short run, I believe happy people give better service; in the long run, I discover people call me up asking for opportunities to do business with me again. They can feel the gospel order, even if they don't know what it is and can't name it.

Under the heading of integrity as a testimony of morality and principle I would put the social testimonies that have had the most impact on my business life: gambling and alcohol. Working with numerous nonprofit organizations has exposed me from time to time to the frequent desire of these groups to make some quick, easy money—for a good cause, of course—by operating some sort of gambling program. If their cause is really that important, I often ask, why not just ask for a direct donation? People's eyes glaze over and they seem to find something important about their shoes when I ask this question.

Our company's largest client is Samaritan House, a battered women's shelter in Hampton Roads with a budget of about $1.1 million per year. Last year, the Samaritan House board of directors decided to sign up for a monthly bingo night in a local bingo emporium, with the promise of making $1,000 or more each month for a few hours work. Staff members were to be "strongly encouraged" to help staff the operation, which involved spending an evening in a thick haze of tobacco smoke, selling game boards and concessions. Faced with the potential of handling a considerable amount of gambling proceeds, I went to the elders of my meeting and asked for their advice. Could I continue to work for this group if it were to participate in gambling in this way? It is all right to continue for now, they said, but keep us informed of how things develop.

At the next board meeting I shared my deep concern about gambling and the tobacco use in the bingo hall, and let the board know that I had asked the elders for guidance about whether I could continue to serve Samaritan House. Once I had "gone public," several staff members expressed their own hesitations about the gambling issue, and the board of directors decided that no staff would be expected to participate; they would staff the operation on their own. Well, the upshot was that after two months the bingo operation had actually lost money, not made $1,000 per night, and the shelter pulled out of the program.

Just three months ago the director of development for this same organization announced at a board meeting that this winter's big fundraising event would be a casino night, with gambling and drinks at a local establishment, with expected net revenue of about $10,000. Board members expressed pleasure at the news, but I was dismayed. Finally, near the end of the meeting, I spoke up about the discrepancy I perceived between the service the shelter provides and the means being proposed to raise money. Gambling and alcohol contribute to the domestic violence and homelessness which the organization seeks to prevent—how can they use gambling and alcohol to raise money to accomplish that goal? There was no immediate response to my comments, and there did not have to be; I was simply testifying about perception of truth. However, at last week's board meeting the same director of development announced that now this winter's big fundraising event would be a silent auction at a local restaurant, with the same expected net revenue as before.

Testimonies for Today and Tomorrow

I have been speaking so far about the conventional testimonies—the historic witnesses which connect us to all the generations of Quakers who preceded us, those glorious sons and daughters of the gospel morning which we read about in any number of books and journals. They are products of a particular historic moment, and center on individual righteousness: How can I be in right relationship with God? I want now to shift gears and talk about some symbolic actions which aren't testimonies yet but should be, and why.

I would suggest that Friends should be testifying about the universal nature of the gospel order: that it applies to all of creation and connects every part of creation to every other part. To a world chained by oppressive social structures and systems that reward only individual ambition and greed for power, prestige and possessions, God offers a path of integral liberation: the freedom of the gospel for all aspects of the creation achieved together. The hitch is that we cannot obtain this liberation for ourselves to the exclusion of the rest of creation—including all other people, all the living creatures who share this world with us, and the non-living physical environment. Friends should be offering a *testimony of integral liberation* as people who have witnessed the truth of both the world's brokenness and God's healing presence in new ways. This testimony of integral liberation expands the old testimony of simplicity—single-pointed awareness focused on God—to include the totality of God's creation and its present brokenness. Integral liberation extends our perception of harmony to include not only our individual actions in relation to the divine order, but the effects of the institutional and cultural structures of which we are a part. Integral liberation calls us to speak with integrity in word and deed—not only for ourselves, but to speak with integrity for all those who have no voice, no advocate among the powers and principalities of the world. From the Exodus story to the present day, God has continually demonstrated a consistent pattern of caring for those who suffer and of intervening on their behalf. I believe Friends are being called to symbolic actions that bear witness to God's concern and intervention and our common human need to repent of our unwillingness to love the world as God loves it: every human being, from womb to tomb, every plant and animal, every rock and stream.

This will require a break with the prevailing culture as profound as the break those first Publishers of Truth experienced in England over 300 years ago. I suggest that the symbolic actions that will bear our witness and testimony will call people away from our modern idols by a series of radical changes in the way we see and live in the world.

A Change in *Perspective*

As part of the dominant culture of the First World, North American Quakers share a view from the top of the pyramid: the power, prestige and possessions are up here with us; down below are all the other people who must suffer to hold us up. To bear witness to the seamless unity of all creation, we must act out a new perspective on the world: the view from the bottom. Over against the viewpoint of the dominant class we are called to symbolize God's "preferential option for the poor." Through our actions we should be testifying about God's preferential option throughout history, from Exodus onward: God as liberator—hearing, caring, choosing sides, and intervening in human history. The dominant culture interprets the Bible for its own purposes; we need to proclaim that Scripture was written by and for the underclass, and carries that same meaning and message today. We here tonight have benefited so much from the privileges of our position that most of us can never be truly poor, but we need to learn how to be with the poor as well as to be for the poor: simply to be with them, to begin to see the world from their perspective, and by our very location with the poor to call symbolically for a radical change in perspective from the dominant culture's point of view.

I bear witness to the view from the bottom as part of a "soup kitchen" breakfast program organized by the Norfolk Catholic Worker House to serve the homeless people of Norfolk, Virginia. Four mornings a week, rain or shine, hot or cold, the Catholic Worker van arrives at a deserted street in Norfolk and, with volunteers from several local churches, feeds breakfast on the sidewalk to 75–100 or more homeless folks—nearly all men. Grits are the mainstay of their meal, with lots of sugar and a little butter, washed down with hot coffee. Each one gets a sandwich as well, to take with him or her on the day's journey.

I have been amazed at the ways in which the dominant culture has attempted to disrupt this simple act of mercy. Jesus said we will encounter him when we feed the hungry—that he is the hungry one himself. The city of Norfolk was too uncomfortable when Jesus was being fed in front of the federal building downtown, so the Catholic Worker people were forced to move to Sacred Heart Church in the fashionable Ghent neighborhood. More complaints there moved the feeding program to a vacant lot and former dump site. The city built a parking lot on that site and then complained because people were walking on the landscaped grass on their way to the meals. Now breakfast is served next to a graveyard, "because nobody here can complain about us," as one homeless man observed. The city health department showed up one morning to take the temperature of the grits and sandwiches to make sure the grits were hot enough and the sandwiches cold enough to meet their standards, and that all the food had been prepared in a health department-approved kitchen. The city government, acting on behalf of people like you and me, is unwilling to feed these hungry people—but they will act to ensure that we feed them according to their standards.

Susan has participated in this breakfast program longer than I have; occasionally our ten-year-old daughter Morgan joins with us. I believe that our actions incarnate the Scripture, bringing the Gospel of Matthew to life once again; that we symbolize God's presence with and among and for the poor of the world, that God hears and cares and intervenes on behalf of those at the bottom of society. "These people," our actions say, "these people are the Christ."

A CHANGE IN *QUESTIONS*

As Dom Helder Camera, former archbishop of Recife, discovered, "When I fed the poor, they called me a saint. When I asked why there are poor, they called me a communist." The dominant religious culture is obsessed with questions of individual success: "How can I be righteous or holy?" "How do I succeed religiously?" and "How do I get to heaven?" Our testimony, in contrast, should be about the importance of questions like "Why is the world this way?" "How can I respond to these circumstances with God's love?" The profound importance of this change in questions is clearly recognized by the dominant culture, and as profoundly resisted. The public debate at the moment is the extent of the churches' responsibility to help the poor: "How much help do I have to give in order to get to heaven?" It is far different to ask, "How can I embody God's infinite love for this poor person? How have I contributed to her poverty?"

I mentioned my work with Samaritan House, the battered women's shelter, earlier. Their mission is to intervene on behalf of families in crisis and victims of domestic violence, and to work toward eliminating the root causes of homelessness and domestic violence. My heart can't help but break when I think about the joy of the gospel order as it exists in the mind of God and compare it with the broken world of pain and suffering that these women and children must live in, day after day after day. God's heart must break to see the ones God loves so deeply hurt so much. I keep the books, make sure the monthly reports to funding agencies are accurate and payroll goes out on time, unstop the toilets and fix the garbage disposals. What I do enables others to work directly with the women and children who are our clients, to begin the healing process, to prepare them for living independently, and to build the skills and insights that will keep them from entering into another similar relationship.

The question symbolized by our work is not "What spiritual path will get me to heaven?" but "Why is the world this way and what can I do about it, in faith?" As an example of the dominant culture's question, I offer you the magistrate who recently told a battered woman who had pressed charges against her spouse to kiss and make up, because marriage is a sacred commitment. We need as Friends to take up symbolic actions that point to the truth that it is more important to love my neighbor than for either of us to be religiously correct (righteous).

A Change in Goal

For too long devoted religious folk have labored to build up the institutional church: to strengthen the congregations and meetings of their faith, to enable the church to recruit more members so that more people can get to heaven. Our witness, in contrast, should be about beginning the reign of God irrespective of the condition of the institutional church. We should be de-emphasizing the institutional church as a way station to heaven. We Quakers are not some spiritual elite who have the special traits needed to be Friends, and are not any steps closer to God or heaven than other people who worship differently or not at all. We are nobody special, and our task is to build up the reign of God, not our meetinghouse or our meeting's treasury.

All that we value as Quakerly: our meetinghouses, our committees and meetings for business, our endowments and our membership lists, are not ends in themselves, but tools for beginning the reign of God on earth. Our task is not to put people into Quakerism, but to bring the reign of God to the people. When Dwight D. Eisenhower was president of Columbia University, the administration brought him the problem that they couldn't make the students walk on the sidewalks—they kept cutting across on the grass. How could they change the students? "Don't!" said Ike, "put sidewalks where the students walk!" By our actions we should be bringing God to people where they are, not bringing people to the institutional church.

A CHANGE IN *MEANS*

The dominant culture operates on what Paulo Freire calls the "banking theory" in many arenas, from education to welfare. Under this paradigm the people in control operate as a bank which contains the good to be distributed: education, or economic welfare, neighborhood development, or what have you. Development consists of opening an account in the name of the individual to be helped, and transferring some education, training, money, or what have you into the individual's account. There is no room in this model for the indwelling Christ that inhabits all beings, or for the poor and oppressed to assist in their own liberation. We must from the outset be suspicious of any mechanism by which the power structure purports to volunteer to assist those who suffer under the system. Our testimony should be about a change in the means by which we help one another: from the banking theory to what some are calling conscientization: from the institution "saving" the individual to self-liberation (by grace). I can't free anyone else from their oppression—only they can do that. But by trying to help them do it themselves I can be liberated myself.

In my own life, two current activities illustrate this change in means. In 1992 I left the large nonprofit organization with which I had worked off and on for a decade and formed New Dominion Housing, Inc., as a nonprofit Community-based Housing Development Organization, or CHDO. In contrast to the conventional model of nonprofits as organizations of those who have helping those who do not, a CHDO is formed expressly to give a voice and real power to those people who will benefit from the programs and activities of the organization. As a nonprofit organization formed to provide safe, decent, sanitary, and affordable housing to low income persons, New Dominion Housing was structured so that the poor people who are the intended beneficiaries of our actions have a voice—and real power—over how our programs are chosen, developed, and carried out. While the requirement is for one-third low-income membership on the board of directors, the New Dominion Board of Directors has for the most part been between one-half and two-thirds low-income persons, including all of the presidents of the board.

A second activity embodying this testimony is my work counseling military personnel as part of Norfolk Quaker House. Our understanding of what we are about is being present to assist with a spiritual conversion that the counselee is undergoing on his/her own. It is not our goal to dismantle the military, or even to get as many people as possible out of the service, or keep people from enlisting. Our goal is to assist with a process of conversion that is going on in the individual, and to stand in solidarity with that individual no matter how that conversion works itself out: visiting them in the brig, helping them prepare a conscientious objector application, helping them apply for a transfer to another duty station, or providing a safe place to come and talk while they continue to serve out their enlistment.

Both of these activities have humbled me and taught me a great deal. I ended up thanking our first set of naval prisoners for letting me visit them in the brig (a federal penitentiary), because I had learned so much from the experience.

A CHANGE IN *SIN*

Individual sin—our universal experience of missing the mark in our attempts to live rightly—is an important facet of the Christian life. I believe there is a moral ethic to which individual Christians are called; at least to which this individual Christian is called. However, the institutional church has collaborated in using an overemphasis on individual wrongdoing to mask a pervasive and equally important pattern of structural, corporate evil. We obsess on a small number of individual behaviors such as sexuality or tobacco so that we don't have to look at our complicity in much larger societal and cultural sins.

For example: South American religious leaders such as Dom Helder Camara point out the reality of a "spiral of violence" which illustrates this need for a change in how we understand and react to sin. In the spiral of violence incidents of crime and civil unrest, either individual or organized, which are one level of violence, are answered by government troops or heavily armed police, which are another level of violence. The use of force by the institutions of government is justified by the individual crimes that preceded it. What we ignore, Camara says, is the violence done to the poor and powerless by the institutions of society, which oppresses them and leaves them without options to meet their basic needs. That is the first stage in the spiral of violence, which those who are benefiting from the institutions of society never discuss.

The monthly meeting to which I belong is typical of many in its emphasis on certain individual sins to the exclusion of corporate, structural sin. Virginia Beach is part of Hampton Roads, the largest naval military installation in the world and one of the most heavily militarized regions on the face of the earth. This past year Friends in Virginia Beach Friends Meeting have spent many hours, in and out of meeting for business, trying to decide whether or not visitors to our meetinghouse/school campus should be allowed to smoke outdoors when school is not in session, and whether the teachers and staff should be allowed to smoke in one room of the school (smoking is banned indoors everywhere else all the time).

The deeper problem, as Dom Helder Camara points out, is that we obsess on these issues while ignoring the structural sin of militarism all around us. That sin is too hard to face; it involves the 30 percent of the population who are military personnel or civilian contract employees, and $7 billion per year pumped into the local economy. Our meeting is thunderously silent on the preparations for war that fly over our meetinghouse and sail past our beaches every day and night.

By labeling use of tobacco a sin, I can feel righteous about myself and not address these broader issues. Even if I smoke, I can look only at my smoking and ignore my position on top of the pyramid of power, prestige, and possessions. Let us refocus our under-standing of sin away from the idea that "I can be righteous if I do this thing, or don't do that thing," toward "Is it my goal in daily life to help bring about the reign of God?" Tobacco smoking may still be a sin after we've shifted focus this way, but it will take its rightful place in relation to the blight of our inner cities, the Persian Gulf War, military interventionism in general, and the blasphemy of building a nuclear warship and naming it *Corpus Christi*.

A Change from *Orthodoxy* to *Orthopraxy*

The dominant culture has emphasized *orthodoxy* over *ortho-praxy*—right belief over right action. This has two benefits for those in power. First, it tends to divide and weaken those who are being dominated, since their ability to cooperate with one another is debilitated by their arguments over doctrine. Secondly, no matter what doctrine is most widely believed, the emphasis on orthodoxy minimizes the need for individuals to act on their beliefs. This leads, in the extreme, to devout Christians being able to make the transi-tion from worship in their congregation to work in the nuclear weapons industry without a tremor. The Religious Society of Friends has bought into the dominant culture's position in this matter hook, line, and sinker. We argue and agonize and suffer over whether this Quaker or that Quaker is orthodox enough to be a member of the Religious Society of Friends, or does their personal belief traumatize me so much I can't continue to be a Friend myself? So much time and effort spent on trying to find or create doctrinal conformity, and so little left over to do God's work in the world.

What difference does it make if there is a wiccan somewhere who considers herself a member of the Religious Society of Friends? We don't believe an intermediary is necessary to connect us to God—do we believe another person can thwart God's will to be in relationship with us? The relevant question is not "Do you accept this specific belief structure?" but "Can you and will you share our practice and reflect on our common experience together?" Theology must become the second step, as a reflection on praxis in the light of faith—praxis comes first (a shift from *a priori* thinking). Through reflection on our common experiences—our praxis—we can and will come to a shared understanding of God's message to us and God's desire for our next praxis. Reading the account of the last judgment in Matthew 25 had no visible effect on my practice of prison visitation or feeding the homeless, but visiting our friends in the Navy brig and feeding our homeless friends by the graveyard has profoundly affected the way I understand Matthew 25.

If we are so different we can't share our practice, or if our understanding of what is going on is too radically different for common reflection to be meaningful, then we probably can't be in the same community. But until we've tried that, arguments over orthodoxy are the adversary's joy.

Clear testimonies about our understanding of the difference between the gospel order and the dominant culture's idolatry in these half-dozen areas are needed if we are to continue to be God's leaven in the world, and not become a mostly irrelevant remainder of what used to be an inspired people. May God grant us the vision and courage to see the really real and to be clear witnesses to the truth.

A Lively and
Harmonious Exercise

*This was delivered as the closing message at the 2004
sessions of North Carolina Yearly Meeting (FUM) at
Black Mountain, near Asheville, North Carolina. Earlier
in the week Tony Campolo, the well-known evangelical
Baptist, spoke twice to the gathered Friends. Tony is articulate, energetic, a powerful speaker, clean-shaven, and
mostly bald.*

I need to begin our time together this morning with a confession. I am not Tony Campolo. I am not anything like Tony
Campolo. I have more hair. But you knew that already—and that's
not the confession I have to make. My confession is that I love you
all. John Woolman wrote of love as the first motion;[121] I have
written myself of love for unknown Friends as the first step toward
traveling in the ministry. The invitation to speak to you all this
morning came several months ago; but I fell in love with you on
the evening of August 5, 2004, in the middle of an intensive course
at the Earlham School of Religion. Suddenly, as I composed myself
for sleep, I felt a deep affection for you as individuals and as a
community striving to be faithful to the God we both love. Then I
knew that all would be well today, and all would be well, and all
manner of things would be well.[122]

It is exciting for me, as a Conservative Friend, to be invited to
speak to your yearly meeting today. These are exciting times for
Conservative Friends in North Carolina—although I have to use
the word "exciting" carefully. A neighbor who was present with my
wife and me when we received some exceptionally good news asked
Susan, "Doesn't he ever get excited?" To which the reply, of course,
was, "Oh yes, look at him—this is as excited as he gets!"

---

[121] John Woolman, *Journal*, in *Works of John Woolman*, 1775, p. 150.
[122] Julian of Norwich, *Showings*, Paulist Press, 1978, p. 225.

Next month North Carolina Yearly Meeting Conservative will mark the 100th anniversary of its first separate yearly meeting sessions. Our representative body will meet at Cedar Grove Meetinghouse in Woodland on October 30, 2004, to commemorate the organizing sessions held there from October 28 to October 31 in 1904. I don't know exactly what form that commemoration will take, but I do invite any and all of you to join us. We would love to see you there!

One of the reasons this centennial is exciting for us is that we have been much more intentional about understanding and articulating our own history in the past few years. Friends in the conservative yearly meeting had not paid enough attention to educating ourselves in our own history, in the foundations of our small tributary of Quakerism. We weren't very good at telling our story, because in fact we didn't know it well enough ourselves.

The intervening years have been important ones for us, as we have made several efforts to understand our own history and to be able to articulate it to each other, to newcomers and attenders, and to interested persons at a distance who would like to know more about us. The publication of the *Journal* of North Carolina Yearly Meeting (Conservative), published sporadically on subjects such as vocal ministry, the queries, and the advices, is only one of many positive outgrowths from those joint yearly meeting sessions.

As I have contemplated this morning, my thoughts have been drawn to part of the Advices to Meetings of Ministers, Elders, and Overseers (nowadays also called the Meeting of Ministry and Oversight) in the Discipline of North Carolina Yearly Meeting (Conservative). The passage I have in mind reads like this:

> Be tender at all times of each other's reputation, and watchful lest you hurt each other's service as servants of the same Lord, with diversities of gifts, but the same spirit. Maintain a lively exercise harmoniously to labor for the spreading and advancement of the truth.[123]

The last part of this advice seems to me to be especially applicable to our two yearly meetings: we are indeed servants of the

---

123 *Book of Discipline*, North Carolina Yearly Meeting (Conservative), 1983, p. 36.

same Lord, with diversities of gifts, but the same spirit; and I believe we are called to maintain a lively exercise harmoniously to labor for the spreading and advancement of the truth. We have developed differently over the past century, but we share a common heritage that affects all we do. And we both live in the same suffering world, which is presenting us with a powerful set of challenges as well as a growing set of opportunities for Christian witness and Christian service.

The world is suffering. As individuals, we know more about the scope and degree of suffering across the world than any previous generation; and the scope and degree of that suffering at times seems about to overwhelm any of us. Who could imagine humankind's ability to be inhumanely cruel to other humans if we did not see the evidence all around us, and brought to us electronically every day. In the midst of this pain, another change is overtaking us all, especially in North America. The old structures of religion and government and civic relations seem to have lost their ability to convince a growing segment of the population that they offer any meaning at all. People are suspicious of hierarchy, suspicious of truth proclaimed from on high, suspicious of tradition and familiar teachings precisely because they are traditional and familiar.

How can we, as Quakers, be relevant to this suffering, postmodern world? Can we be relevant at all, or are we doomed to wither away, becoming more and more marginal as the world spins down to an uncertain end? I believe not only that we can be relevant, I believe that Quakers have a heritage and practice that is uniquely positioned among North American Christians to speak directly to the needs and questions of the generation around us.

Classic Quaker spirituality can and should survive in all the branches of contemporary Quakerism, it seems to me; and that classic spirituality speaks directly to the condition of the world around us. Let me share three pillars of classic Quaker spirituality—no, let us remember them together—and remind ourselves how important they can be in the times we live in.

The classic Quaker spirituality is not fully observable in any contemporary yearly meeting, but pieces of it are available and in use here and there across the country. It is not the spirituality of George Fox and Elizabeth Hooten, but it has roots in the gospel they preached 350 years ago. A faith tradition is a living thing; it grows and branches and changes over the years, drawing nurture from its roots and energy from the sun; we who commit ourselves to the tradition water it with our sweat and our tears, and we prune it with the witness of our lives. Classic Quaker spirituality is the living tradition that has honored its roots in seventeenth century England while opening itself to change through the struggle of those who have wrestled it with integrity, like Jacob and the angel.

The first pillar of classic Quaker spirituality is the spirituality of subtraction. This is a direct consequence of Fox's life-changing moment, when he heard one who said, "There is one, even Christ Jesus, who can speak to thy condition!"[124] If Christ can speak to my condition, then I better arrange my life to hear what Christ has to say! This is the basis for the *apophatic* spirituality that is characteristic of classic Quakerism—which I, along with others, call the spirituality of subtraction.

There are two great ways of knowing God. By far the most common path among Christians in the western world is known as *kataphatic* theology. This path can be described as knowing God through the set of all-true statements that can be made beginning with the words "God is ___." On this spiritual path, one seeks a deeper understanding of and relationship with God through positive images, symbols, and ideas. It is the most common form of spirituality throughout the Christian church (Roman, Orthodox, and Protestant). Younger people typically start with a *kataphatic* spirituality. It is easier to learn about what and who God is, how God acts in the world, etc., than to start out by trying to grasp God by considering what God is not. It is easier for their Sunday School teachers and First Day School teachers as well.

Classic Quaker spirituality, the heritage you and I share, is something quite different. Friends have followed an *apophatic* path. *Apophatic* theology can be described as knowing God through the set of all true statements that can be made beginning

124 George Fox, *Journal*, Nickalls edition, p. 11.

"God is not ___." This is also called the negative road, or the spirituality of subtraction. One approaches God by subtracting from one's consciousness, from one's entire life, everything that is not God. This may remind some folks of Sherlock Holmes' comments to Dr. Watson about detective work—after one subtracts everything that is not true about a case, whatever is left is the truth. Classic Quaker spirituality is heavily *apophatic*.

Kataphatic spirituality is a spirituality of immanence, of the Word made flesh, of God with us. It emphasizes God's dominion in this world. Success, progress, overcoming, and victory are highly valued.[125]

Apophatic spirituality places its emphasis on the values of self-emptying or denial—on suffering, sacrifice, and serving.[126] This sounds very much like the stories we've read of Quakers who speak of taking up the cross, of denying self, or overcoming their own will in order to be faithful, and for good reason. This is the signature Quaker spirituality. Scripture passages that illuminate this spirituality are familiar to us all: the suffering servant passage in Isaiah,[127] the humility of Christ in Philippians,[128] and those folks in Hebrews who are praised for acting in faith contrary to their own self-interest.[129]

The spirituality of subtraction, in my understanding, is a practice aimed at developing a single-pointed awareness toward God. The spirituality of subtraction makes room in our lives for the type of direct interaction with the Divine that George Fox reported and that we wait for, expectantly, in open worship. As it is hard to hear one another in a noisy room, it is hard to hear God in a noisy life. As our heart-longing for God grows, it is only natural that we should be continually simplifying our life, subtracting whatever is not God or not of God so that our awareness is single-pointed and competition for our attention is minimized. A noisy life not only competes with the divine message, it distorts what it cannot drown out completely.

[125] Andrew Pritchard, "Your Church's Personality," *Reality Magazine*, Issue 45, http://www.reality.org.nz/articles/45/45-pritchard.html.

[126] *Ibid.*

[127] Isaiah 53.

[128] Philippians 2:5–11.

[129] Hebrews 11:35–39.

This admittedly large effort is worth our while because the dialogue it readies us for is, in fact, continuous. It may wax and wane, but seasoned Friends over the centuries have reported that God's presence is an ongoing personal conversation, not the intermittent and infrequent reception of a general broadcast. It is as if whenever we stop to listen, we discover that God is already speaking with us.

Perhaps the most common practice among other Christians that is similar to Quaker spirituality is contemplative prayer. Quaker practice is very similar, yet distinct from contemplative prayer. It is not so much that we Quakers choose to contemplate the Divine as that we choose to receive—to hear and accept—what the Divine has to impart to us.

The second pillar of classic Quaker spirituality is the direct, unmediated relationship with the Divine. Christ spoke directly with George Fox, revealing truths to him that only later, with divine assistance, could he find confirmed in Scripture. Some Christian traditions emphasize the Scripture as the pre-eminent source of guidance for the believer; some emphasize the teachings or traditions of the institutional church. Christians in the Wesleyan tradition talk of a "quadrilateral" of Scripture, tradition, reasoning, and experience that interact with one another. Friends add a fifth element, and consider it more important than the others: this immediate relationship, direct communication, continuing revelation. It is this direct revelation that adds creativity and innovation to the Wesleyan quadrilateral.

In the contemporary world, many persons experience the scriptures as devaluing them as individuals, or condoning violence, or having been used as a tool to keep them "under control." Whether Scripture, properly understood, can be said to support these understandings is less important than the fact that a large number of persons are turning away from Scripture and the ways Scripture is presented as irrelevant or even inimical to their own lives. Church tradition, and the institutional church generally, no longer receive the trust of many persons. The recent problems of the Roman Catholic church are only the latest and most publicized of the many reasons individuals have become increasingly suspicious of the truths the institutional church is trying to teach them—suspicious even of the motives of their own church leaders.

Our own reason has proven us false, as well. We are the heirs of over two centuries of the great Enlightenment project. I stand before you as an example of the idea—the faith, really—that the intellect and reason of human beings could and would solve all our problems, leading humanity ever forward in a steady progress toward a better and better world. I was raised and educated in the great tradition of the modern mind; I have two degrees from MIT, and went through my college years convinced that technology, the fruit of our human reason, could and would solve all our problems in time. Nearly forty years after first setting foot on the MIT campus, I must admit technology has failed us. Our human reason alone has not enabled us even to feed, clothe, and house each other adequately.

The fourth side of the Wesleyan quadrilateral is experience. It is to experience that many persons have retreated as these other sources of truth have proven untrustworthy. "At least I can depend on my own experience," seems to be the common thought. But our personal experience is not big enough to answer the really important questions. It seems to draw us into an egocentric view of the world, where accumulating stuff—possessions, power, and prestige—provides meaning to one's life. It is a transient, hollow meaning because ultimately we all die, and our "stuff" vanishes or passes to someone else.

What Friends have to say to people who have experienced the unreliability of these other sources of truth and guidance is, "Listen." There is One who is already reaching out to you, One who is already talking to you, who yearns to be in intimate relationship with you all your life, and beyond. This One is reliable; this One is completely trustworthy, because this One loves you infinitely.

The third pillar of our common Quaker spirituality is the centrality of the faith community. We are a people, not a collection of individual worshippers. George Fox did not see a great crowd of individuals to be reached and taught individually. Fox knew that Jesus Christ had not come to teach him in isolation. His call was always to a people. He understood that Christ had come to teach his *people*—a great people yet to be gathered but whose gathering was beginning. It seems obvious in some ways: Christ was always talking about how we should relate to one another, and said that the way we treat one another is the true measure of how we feel about and treat God. Friends have been a peculiar people over the centuries as much for what we did as communities of faith as for what we have believed as individuals. There is something about the human condition, though, that keeps persuading us that we can be right with God by thinking primarily about ourselves. This is particularly seductive today, when the dominant culture all around us seeks to convince you and me that we are in fact at the center of our story—rampant individualism. Quakerism has always understood this to be untrue, and its emphasis on community is a great theme of the Quaker faith tradition.

Let's face it, claiming that one hears the voice of God whenever one stops to listen for it is more often perceived as a sign of mental illness than as a sign of a great spiritual gift. It is the stabilizing and refocusing effect of the gathered faith community that demonstrates the true nature of our witness. Our experience is that there is one truth, and that truth is discernible by each individual—especially in the context of the gathered, seeking community. The continual searching after common discernment by the faith community keeps the individual from following after a misunderstood leading or guidance very far, before the lack of unity in the community becomes a sign that one's own discernment may be incomplete.

The common commitment to the spirituality of subtraction as a means of clearing the decks for God's guidance has contributed to what Fran Taber has called a "culture of listening" among committed Friends.[130] We see how to listen more completely, and to prepare ourselves to hear more clearly, in the examples of our fellows. The supportive community also encourages us in our efforts to live focused lives, providing a counter-message to that of the dominant culture.

130 Fran Taber, plenary presentation, North Carolina Yearly Meeting (Conservative) sessions, July 17, 2004.

The faith community is also a prime location for service to one another and for witness about how the kingdom of God truly looks and feels and how it works in daily life. Here we practice (in the piano practice sense) our practice (in the sense of our daily spiritual walk and discipline). We learn to love the world by practicing on our fellow meeting members.

So the faith community, which is always at its heart a worshipping community, is a central place for the presence of Christ —divine immanence; for the communication and guidance that I like to call the divine conversation; and for the loving service to one another that is both how we exercise the gifts God has given the community and how we develop them for proper and more extensive use in the wider world.

Our common Quaker spirituality, with its three pillars of the spirituality of subtraction, the direct relationship with God, and the importance of the community of faith, should be very attractive to many spiritual seekers in the twenty-first century. For those overwhelmed by the dominant culture's acquisitiveness and materialism, we can offer a way of life whose theme is subtraction, not hoarding. For those suspicious, often with good reason, of absolute truths proclaimed by the interpreters of Scripture, church hierarchies, or other authorities, we offer the local faith community as the organ of discernment and interpretation of truth—guided, of course, by the quadrilateral I spoke of earlier, but grounded on the guidance of the Holy Spirit. As George Fox said, the Holy Spirit told him things that later he found affirmed in Scripture.

The combination of the spirituality of subtraction and the discernment of the faith community helps us focus on what is really important, and not to be distracted by the loud or flashy. Because our spiritual heritage is to remember what God is not, rather than what God is, Quakers are inclined to hesitate before embracing the latest religious fad. Paradoxically, that frees us to pay attention to that still small voice that may be directing us in an entirely new direction—so that in the really important things, Quakers may end up being leaders after all.

I spent a couple of weeks at the Earlham School of Religion last month, and while there I heard a story about the process of merging

Earlham School of Religion with Bethany Theological Seminary some years ago. The consultant retained to do a feasibility study reported one cautionary item about differences in culture. When the Brethren make a decision, the consultant reported, it is a commitment to begin action. When the Quakers make a decision, it is a commitment to begin discussion. This "slow leap forward" is very appropriate for today's world, where getting the information we need, understanding the complexities of each situation, and understanding just where God is leading us take time and quiet listening for the divine word. For those who question whether this process is compatible with the leadership role Friends would like to assume on peace and justice issues, consider the Quaker "slow leap" regarding slavery. It took 88 years to move from the Germantown Remonstrance to the Philadelphia Yearly Meeting minute regarding slave owning; but it took another 88 years for the rest of the country to realize that the North was indeed going to win the War between the States and that with that victory, chattel slavery would be ended.

It is a paradox in our dominant culture of rampant individualism that the only individual that matters is me—not you, not anyone else. I'm important—I'm central to my universe—and you're not. No wonder so many people feel alienated, unloved, and alone, no matter how many material possessions they may amass. Quaker spirituality affirms the importance of each individual in relationship with God and the faith community. The defining factor for Quakers is not how many toys each one possesses, but the loving relationship we have with one another and each has with God. George Fox said that the love Friends show for one another was a prime evangelical witness to the world,[131] and this is still true today.

In a time when many people are losing faith in institutional structures and hierarchical authorities as being able to tell the truth in any consistent or dependable way, the classic Quaker tradition embodies the local community as a dependable vehicle for discernment of the truth and of what actions the truth requires of those

---

131 Lewis Benson, "'That of God in Every Man'—What Did George Fox Mean by It?" *Quaker Religious Thought*, Vol. XII, No. 2, Spring 1970.

who hear it. In our tradition, the individual participates in the discernment of truth—or, put another way, in the discernment of the will of God for this group at this time. It is not that Friends don't have doctrines or principles of our understanding of the truth, but that these doctrines and principles have been discerned by the communities of faith, not by individuals whose ideas are then promulgated by hierarchical or authoritative means.

Now some have called this the "triumph of congregationalism;" but my sense is that in the core Friends tradition, something else is going on. Many Christian groups, of course, emphasize the church community. What is peculiar about the Quaker experience is our sense of the "gathered meeting," when the assembled worshippers become, for a brief period, a new creation: a mystical experience of participation in the body of Christ in the present moment. We have not abandoned the quadrilateral for understanding truth, but added to it. The discernment of the community and the individual must include the wisdom of Scripture, tradition, reason, and the experience of individual Friends and the faith community stretching back some 350 years.

It has been the experience and testimony of our Quaker forebears that this peculiar Christian spirituality, if pursued and practiced faithfully, will lead us to live as if the kingdom of God were already here—that the kingdom is here, in the relationships we have with one another, with other people, and with the rest of creation. I believe this is still true, and that non-Quakers can see and feel this as well. Our best hope for mending the world is to be faithful to our identity and heritage as Friends.

If this is true—if the classic Quaker spirituality we share is still authentic and powerful in the present day, if it speaks to the people of the world and empowers us to establish the kingdom of God here on earth, at least in some small measure—how do we nurture and sustain this precious heritage? It seems to me that there are at a minimum four actions we need to pursue.

First, we need to recognize that Quaker spirituality is distinctly different from the dominant culture, and in some ways strongly in tension with it. In fact, it seems to me the dominant culture understands our spirituality as a threat, and will try to undo it whenever possible. I do not intend to portray the North American culture we live in as evil or appear to be promoting a siege mentality among Friends; but we do need to keep in mind how different our way of life is from the secular culture in which we live. Our heritage is *apophatic*, unmediated, and community-oriented; the dominant culture is *kataphatic*, mediated, and highly individualistic. Friends heritage is the spirituality of subtraction; the dominant culture thrives on the practice of acquisition. Friends experience an unmediated relationship with God; the dominant culture thrives on supplying mediators of every sort, who will lead us to the promised land—whichever promised land we desire: salvation, financial independence, a new body image, a new career, or merely improved prestige among our neighbors and acquaintances.

As much as we strive to live lives consistent with our spiritual experiences and beliefs, the dominant culture is following close behind, striving to undo whatever we've accomplished, or to re-interpret whatever we've experienced. Sometimes it operates in the form of a neighbor, sometimes in that nagging notion of common sense that we just can't put aside, sometimes it comes in the next really neat commercial that almost convinces us that we need that stretch Lincoln Navigator with the built in GPS location system to take our two children to and from day care safely. We may not decide to build the same sort of hedge to separate us from the world as our spiritual ancestors did, but we have to admit that they were right about one thing—it is not at all easy to be "in the world but not of it."

The second action is that we need to help one another practice the spirituality of subtraction as individuals, families, and meeting communities. It requires of us a constant vigilance to simplify our lives—not economically, but spiritually, so there is nothing to distract us from giving our full attention to God—listening for, and participating in, the divine conversation. We can't help each other in this way unless we are active participants in each other's lives—much more than an hour on First Day morning plus the occasional committee meeting each month. If we are behaving like the church described in the second chapter of Acts, praying together, breaking bread together, visiting in one another's homes, then we will come to know one another in that which is eternal, and can support each other's spiritual practice, with encouragement and joint participation.

Third, we need to help each other hear and feel the guidance of the Holy Spirit in our hearts, and be willing to engage each other helpfully in exploring how this guidance compares and contrasts with the wisdom of Scripture, tradition, reason, and experience. This will require an improved effort at making our meetings safe places to share our deepest spiritual insights and struggles, where no one has to keep up a façade of "having it all together." We need to be able to discuss differences of understanding about the gospel message and our own leadings without becoming angry or putting other people on the defensive. Remember, our heritage is a belief that everyone can discern the will of God if we pursue that understanding corporately, diligently, and with integrity. We have nothing to lose, nothing at risk in discussing anything together.

There is a practice among a certain school of Tibetan monks of holding theological debates with everyone sitting in a circle, facing inwards and smiling. The debate is lost by the first monk who stops smiling. We need that patience and love for one another.

The fourth action is that we need to build up our meeting communities, our communities of faith, as the primary points of reference for understanding, interpreting and acting out the great query: What does it mean for us to be children of God, God's agents in the world, at this particular time, in this place, among these people? I hear many Friends complain that their meetings are not the community they hoped for; but I don't see many Friends putting in the long-term, faithful effort to be community for other people in their meeting. Community takes a long time; it means not keeping score; it means caring for the other person more than caring about how I'm getting treated. Even after all that, community is never finished. Community is the place where we're all practicing what it means to be the people of God—and we need the practice! So let's spend less time being upset at other people's mistakes and more time concentrating on how we can eliminate our own.

In healthy community, we can take risks and try new things just to see if they will work. In healthy community, our experiences with one another will guide our attitudes and practices toward the rest of creation. In healthy community, the tough questions are not accusations but opportunities for individuals and families to grow closer together and also closer to being the people God has always yearned for us to be.

If we are faithful in these actions, I believe the Religious Society of Friends will continue to be a leaven for the world, and particularly for those in the North American culture. Membership will grow, in all probability, but our influence will extend far beyond our meetinghouses, to include all those who see our example—our faith and our practice—and are inspired to live just a little bit differently because of that. Let us agree to meet here again in another hundred years, so that our grandchildren can assess our faithfulness and chart their own course for continuing the faith tradition we share.

How to be Non-Egyptian in the Land of Pharaoh

I was invited to offer the Bible study during the 1997 sessions of New York Yearly Meeting. At first I thought that I would explore a number of "mountaintop" experiences recounted in Scripture, but as the time approached, that topic was taken from me and the following presentation was given. My deep appreciation goes to Ched Myers, who opened my eyes to this Bible passage.

Monday: Let My People Go!

I am not going to give the Bible study I had planned to give here this week. In the midst of my planning and studying and writing what I would share with you all, God intervened and let me know that the divine plan was something different. I don't know the reasons for the change—to teach me humility, to reach one person in Wednesday night's audience with a single thought, or something entirely different—but here I am, being as faithful as I can figure out to be.

Instead of talking about the series of encounters with God that I originally had in mind, I am led to share with you my reflections on what seems to be the core theme of the Bible, from one end to the other—Genesis to Revelations. It seems increasingly clear to me that there is only one real story in the universe. One side of that story, as I presently perceive it, is the story of God's intervention in history to liberate us from our suffering—the Exodus story—God leading the chosen people out of Egypt. Of course, the Israelites left Egypt only to settle in the territory of one of Egypt's vassal states, Canaan, and that is the other side of the cosmic story—our fallible yet persistent efforts to learn how to be non-Egyptians in the land of pharaoh.

These two intertwined themes are present throughout the Bible and form much of the context of the Bible story. I believe they are the relevant context for us today, as we seek to understand God's will for the world we live in and our role in making that will a reality.

Although the cosmic story is present everywhere in Scripture, there are a few places where it is presented so succinctly, in such a focused fashion, that one can see all the major subthemes in one place. One such place is Jesus Christ's vision quest in the desert immediately following his baptism. No one except Jesus and the devil were present at this time. Since we can assume that the devil did not assist the gospel writers in their task by reporting his failure in such telling fashion, Jesus must have told the story of his temptation himself. This tells me the account has significance, and the details themselves were told to teach us important facts about Jesus' ministry on earth.

From the perspective of the sweep of time from creation to the end of the universe, this moment as Jesus left the Jordan was probably the last best opportunity the devil (the adversary, the tester) had to derail God's project with humanity. If Jesus could be diverted from his ministry, the kingdom of God could be deferred indefinitely—perhaps even eternally. This was the time for an attack on the very fundamentals of God's story and plan for creation. The leaping-off point for us this week, therefore, is the story of Jesus' forty days in the desert immediately following his baptism.

Luke tells the story like this:

> Filled with the Holy Spirit, Jesus left the Jordan and was led by the Spirit into the desert, for forty days being put to the test by the devil. During that time he ate nothing and at the end he was hungry. Then the devil said to him, "If you are Son of God, tell this stone to turn into a loaf." But Jesus replied, Scripture says: *"Human beings live not on bread alone."*

> Then leading him to a height, the devil showed him in a moment of time all the kingdoms of the world and said to him, "I will give you all this power and their splendour, for it has been handed over to me, for me to give it to anyone I choose. Do homage, then, to me, and it shall all be yours." But Jesus answered him, Scripture says: *"You must do homage to the Lord your God, him alone you must serve."*

Then he led him to Jerusalem and set him on the parapet of the temple. "If you are Son of God," he said to him, "Throw yourself down from here, for Scripture says: *"He has given his angels orders about you, to guard you."*

And again: *"They will carry you in their arms in case you trip over a stone."*

But Jesus answered him, Scripture says: *"Do not put the Lord your God to the test."*[132]

Today I want to look at just the first two sentences of this passage:

Filled with the Holy Spirit, Jesus left the Jordan and was led by the Spirit into the desert, for forty days being put to the test by the devil. During that time he ate nothing and at the end he was hungry.

For the Jews who formed the core of Jesus' audience, these two sentences are packed with references to Moses and the Exodus story. Jesus is fairly shouting his claim that he was part of, continuing, and extending the Exodus story. Jesus was led by the Spirit into the desert as the Israelites had been led into the wilderness; the forty days of his testing clearly refers to the forty years the Israelites wandered about, being tested by Yahweh. Moses also fasted, as Jesus did.

The Exodus story is the oldest in the Bible. It is the formational story of the Israelites, and I believe it is the formational story of our own covenant relationship with God in the present day. The heart of the story is contained in the very beginning, in the account of the encounter between the shepherd Moses and Yahweh in a burning bush. The story goes like this:

A long, long time ago, in a place very far away from Silver Bay, the children of Abraham, Isaac, and Jacob fled to Egypt as refugees from a devastating drought and the resulting famine. They were well received there, and protected from starvation. The drought eventually ended, but the Israelites stayed on in Egypt. Gradually, however, their life there worsened, until they became virtual slaves in the land, forced to the harshest labor and the worst living conditions,

---

[132] Luke 4:1–12, New Jerusalem Bible.

so that the Egyptians could live lives of relative ease. This went on for a long time, and there seemed no hope for the Israelites.

From the Book of Exodus, chapter two:

> During this long period the king of Egypt died. The Israelites, groaning in their slavery, cried out for help and from the depths of their slavery their cry came up to God. God heard their groaning; God remembered his covenant with Abraham, Isaac, and Jacob. God saw the Israelites and took note.

> Moses was looking after the flock of his father-in-law Jethro, the priest of Midian; he led it to the far side of the desert and came to Horeb, the mountain of God. The angel of Yahweh appeared to him in a flame blazing from the middle of a bush. Moses looked; there was the bush blazing, but the bush was not being burnt up. Moses said, "I must go across and see this strange sight, and why the bush is not being burnt up." When Yahweh saw him going across to look, God called to him from the middle of the bush. "Moses, Moses!" he said. "Here I am," he answered. "Come no nearer," he said. "Take off your sandals, for the place where you are standing is holy ground. I am the God of your ancestors," he said, "the God of Abraham, the God of Isaac and the God of Jacob." At this Moses covered his face, for he was afraid to look at God.

> Yahweh then said, "I have indeed seen the misery of my people in Egypt. I have heard them crying for help on account of their taskmasters. Yes, I am well aware of their sufferings. And I have come down to rescue them from the clutches of the Egyptians and bring them up out of that country, to a country rich and broad, to a country flowing with milk and honey, to the home of the Canaanites, the Hittites, the Amorites, the Perizzites, the Hivites, and the Jebusites. Yes, indeed, the Israelites' call for help has reached me, and I have also seen the cruel way in which the Egyptians are oppressing them. So now I am sending you to pharaoh, for you to bring my people the Israelites out of Egypt."

> Moses said to God, "Who am I to go to pharaoh and bring the Israelites out of Egypt?" "I shall be with you," God said, "and this is the sign by which you will know that I was the one who sent you. After you have led the people out of Egypt, you will worship God on this mountain."

Moses then said to God, "Look, if I go to the Israelites and say to them, 'The God of your ancestors has sent me to you,' and they say to me, 'What is his name?' what am I to tell them?" God said to Moses, "I am he who is." And he said, "This is what you are to say to the Israelites, 'I AM has sent me to you.'" God further said to Moses, "You are to tell the Israelites, 'Yahweh, the God of your ancestors, the God of Abraham, the God of Isaac, and the God of Jacob has sent me to you.' This is my name for all time, and thus I am to be invoked for all generations to come."[133]

This is the taproot, the solid foundation of our faith: that the God of all creation has chosen to love us and care about our circumstances and to intervene in ways that liberate us from our suffering. The Israelites were not crying to Yahweh for help—the writers of Exodus are careful to make that clear in their narrative. Yahweh heard them anyway, and chose to care that they were suffering, and chose to take up their cause, to intervene in history to end their suffering, to bring them to a land flowing with milk and honey. Yahweh did that for the Israelites because Yahweh chose to be in this special, covenant, relationship with them.

Part of Christ's mission among human beings is to reveal to us that God has chosen to be in this same relationship with every human being who is on earth—or who has been, or who will be. We all share in God's love and protection, not because of anything we have done or said, or our genetic makeup, or geography of birth but because God has chosen to love and care for all of us. Every human being is equal in the sight of God, because God loves and cares for us all equally—and that love and care set the standard for our relationships with God and one another.

Friends have been proud of their testimony of equality. We are all equal, Friends often say, because we each have a bit of God within us. We speak reverently and thankfully of our experience of the Inner Light, the Inner Christ, which guides us and heals us in daily life. I wrote in my conscientious objector application during the Vietnam War that if there is God within each one of us, as I believe, then an attack on another human being is an attack on

---

[133] Exodus 2:23–3:15, New Jerusalem Bible.

God—blasphemy and sacrilege! Each human being should be treated with the respect and dignity appropriate to the temple of God. Here in Exodus we find a different twist on the basis for our equality. We are equal because God cares for each of us equally. To jump forward about fourteen centuries, we are equal because Christ died as much for you as for me, and as much for Adolph Hitler and Timothy McVeigh as for either one of us.

It is not wrong to say that we are equal because there is that of God within each of us, but it is dangerous. It is spiritually dangerous because we live in such an individualistic culture. We talk about the "me generation" but the phenomenon is much larger than any one generation. In all of North American culture—religious, political, economic, and social—the individual is supreme. The focus is on whether I will get into heaven, whether my rights have been recognized or violated, whether I am financially secure into my retirement, and whether I am fulfilled as an individual. These concerns are not wrong in themselves, but they tempt us to substitute the good for the gospel—the most dangerous of substitutions. All of these cultural forces encourage us to put ourselves at the center of our story rather than God. When we add to that an emphasis on the God within, we must struggle fiercely against the temptation to become little gods in our own little universes, where the meaning of anything is decided by how it affects my own welfare and happiness. We have no responsibility for anyone or anything else because we did not create them and do not sustain them from moment to moment—forgetting that God created and sustains us always. At the center of our little story, the only meaning is "more for me," which ultimately is meaningless since ultimately "me" dies.

Yahweh revealed in the burning bush is not God within Moses, or God within the Israelites, but God the profoundly other—the mighty creator and sustainer of all creation. I cannot be at the center of any story that includes Yahweh as revealed in Exodus—only God can be at the center of that story. Paradoxically, it is only when I am no longer at the center of my story, and Yahweh is, that my life assumes its deepest, truest, and eternal meaning.

Please don't misunderstand me. God is both immanent and transcendent—within and without—and has been since the beginning of creation. George Fox's realization of and emphasis on the direct communion with Christ, and the expression of that realization by Friends as God within, were an important manifestation of truth. In a time and culture that debated whether women had souls, that countenanced slavery and economic oppression, that denied the value of the individual human being in so many ways, early Friends emphasis on the immanent nature of God was a blessing and sweet savor to many souls. God has not changed; the God within is still there, as much as ever.

Time and culture do change. In the present day and in the North American culture, we do not need to emphasize the worth or rights of the individual—the secular culture is doing that to excess, and much of the so-called religious culture is also. Our challenge is to re-attach the individual to the source of meaning beyond the personal pronoun, beyond "I" and "me" and "mine." Our call is to tell the old, old story in new and fresh ways, to re-acquaint souls with the Author and Perfecter of their very being—to help them hear the story with new ears and to see the world and their place in it with new eyes. Those who do will realize that the only story that is ultimately satisfying has God at the center—not them.

Every time we do this—every time we tell the big story from the heart—the one person we know will be changed is ourselves. As we say at Norfolk Quaker House, our work is to be spiritual midwives in a process of spiritual conversion in our clients—and the one person we know will be converted is the counselor. Considering the Exodus story, hearing and telling of this first encounter between Moses and Yahweh, I am transported by the transcendent God—creator and sustainer of the universe, profoundly other—not human at all—yet filled with such love and care for suffering human beings. I am inseparably caught up in the cosmic story, with God at the center. The meaning of my life is expressed in God's infinite love for me: God created me, and God sustains me from moment to moment by continuing to will my existence; and the same is true for you and for all of creation. I have meaning because God's love affirms that I am indeed, for all my warts and flaws, very good.

That is the beginning of a new understanding of how you and I are called to be in the world. When I understand the transcendent God to be at the center of the cosmic story, then God's affirming and sustaining love for me calls me to act on behalf of my fellow human beings with new strength and courage and commitment. God's love and care for those who suffer calls each of us and all of us to care equally deeply—and like God, to take up the cause of the suffering and oppressed and to intervene on their behalf.

God cares about the Israelites because they are God's chosen people and they are suffering. Whether they have an Inner Light is never mentioned; whether or not they are living righteous, holy lives is not discussed; there is no intrinsic quality in the Israelites that makes them worthy or deserving of God's care and intervention. God cares about the Israelites because God chooses to care: God chooses to love. God loves without regard to the worthiness of the individual, and intervenes to end their suffering and oppression because of God's love. So should we.

God's love and care for those who suffer makes clear why I should care about my neighbor's plight: I should care because God cares. Realizing that God is the true center of my story and every story, and experiencing God's infinite and unmerited love for all of creation, will result in a change of the central faith question for most North Americans. The central faith question for Christians in North America is usually some variation of "How can I be saved?" or "How can I be righteous enough to earn God's favor?"

That question comes from a number of sources, including our individualism, the richness of our society which gives us what the rest of the world would experience as limitless options to do or not do works of faith and religious discipline, and the desire of individuals at the center of their own story to control an uncontrollable God. "How do I get into Heaven?" is the question most of us are asking, and it also translates into "What is the minimum necessary for me to do that will force God to accept me?"

When God is at the center of the story, when my relationship to God is bound up in God's love and concern for me and my plight, and I experience that God loves and cares for every person and all of creation with the same intensity, then the central faith question is no longer "Am I saved?" or "How can I get saved?" I am justified not by my works, and not by my faith, but by God's unmerited grace. I am already saved, by God's initiative. I have only to respond to God's invitation. The central faith question then becomes "Why is the world this way, and what can I do about it?" Surely it is not God's will that there be so much suffering and oppression and grinding poverty in the world that God created and sustains from moment to moment and loves so much. What causes the suffering? Not generic suffering, but the suffering of this individual person, and that individual person: why do they suffer?

And what can I do about it? God's example in Exodus is clear—God not only hears the groans of the Israelites, God cares, God takes sides, and God intervenes in history on behalf of the poor, the oppressed, and the powerless. We are called to do the same in the present day.

In the gospel of Matthew Jesus makes the one unequivocal promise of when we will meet him in our daily life: when we give food and drink to the hungry, hospitality to the homeless, clothing to the naked, when we visit the sick and the prisoner.[134] When we do this to the least of persons, we do it to Christ. The concern of the church—particularly the church in North America—has been for the nonbeliever: who has been saved so far and how do we reach the rest? From Moses to Jesus to John Woolman to Dom Helder Camara, God has been telling us that the more important concern is for the nonperson—the one whom we discount and treat as being of no value in our society.

My wife Susan and I help out on the breakfast line with the Norfolk Catholic Worker folks one morning each week, on a side street not too far from the center of downtown. Salter Street runs between a parking lot and a cemetery. After forcing the breakfast line to move from several other locations more convenient to the people we serve, city officials have tolerated our presence on Salter Street—after all, our homeless friends observe, "No one lives there to complain!" Working from three coffee tables in good weather or out of the back and side of a van when it rains, we give grits, coffee, and a sandwich to as many as 125 homeless men, women

[134] Matthew 25:34–40.

and children. I realize that I can be present in that activity in many different ways that really center on me, not them: out of a sense of guilt and obligation, or a desire to record another good work on my spiritual ledger, or to enhance my reputation in the religious community, or other reasons you can name. And the hungry will get fed, and the institutions of power, prestige and possessions will applaud the work—see, we care about the poor—they get their meals at that breakfast line.

However, when I am feeding the hungry out of participation in God's love for them, when God is at the center of the activity, then simply feeding them soon becomes insufficient. If God loves these homeless people so much, then it cannot be God's will that they experience such poverty and pain. One has to ask the question, "Why is the world this way? Why do these people suffer?"

Asking that question "problematizes" the situation, and brings the wrath of the same institutions of power, prestige and possessions that applauded the simple act of feeding the poor. If God does not will that some people be homeless, have no job or access to health care, who does? If we agree not to blame the victim, then why is the world this way? Who put the structures together so that these people suffer? Who benefits from their being kept where they are, where they suffer so much? These are not questions that those at the top of society like to hear. As Dom Helder Camara, former Archbishop of Recife, observed, "When I give food to the poor they call me a saint. When I ask why the poor have no food, they call me a communist."

Susan tells a story of discovering a baby in the midst of a river, about to drown. Naturally, you jump in and save the baby. Before too long, you see another baby, and jump in and save that one, too. Before too long, you have organized a rescue squad to watch the river and pull the babies out, built an orphanage to take care of them once they are safe and a school for the older children who have been at the orphanage for a number of years. You develop a network of supporters whose donations help finance better rescue equipment, buy food and clothing for the babies, and so on. You've gotten really good at pulling babies out of the river. When are you going to send someone upstream to find out how and why the babies are getting into the river to begin with?

Yahweh is not content to start a soup kitchen for hungry Israelites, or to arrange for better medical care, or supply better tools to ease their workload. Yahweh goes upstream, to change the structure of Egyptian society to liberate the Israelites from their oppression. Yahweh's word to pharaoh is not "Pay my people better" or "Overtime for more than forty hours per week" or "Free straw for brick-makers;" Yahweh's word is "Let My People GO!"

If we really experience the direct communion with God proclaimed by George Fox and multitudes of other Friends for 350 years, then we can't help but share God's concern for the poor and oppressed, God's preferred location among them, and God's commitment to intervention in human history on their behalf. We're going to have to live in solidarity with the poor—not just throw money over the wall at them—and work to establish an entirely new great economy that reflects God's values and God's love for all people and all of creation. We're going to have to build an economy of grace to replace the economy of debt that encircles and enslaves us all.

The story of the burning bush calls us to live in community, tells us who is in that community, and shows how it is to be done. Our basis for being able to be in community with one another is our covenant relationship with God. In the Exodus story God demonstrates the nature of that covenant: God initiates, and we respond. God heard the groans of the Israelites, even though they were not calling to Yahweh; God cared about their plight, and intervened radically on their behalf. We are called to emulate that relationship with one another by hearing, and caring, and taking radical action.

We can be in community with God only when our community includes those people for whom God has shown a loving preference: the poor, the powerless, the oppressed people who are at the periphery of society, at the bottom of the pyramid of power, wealth, and prestige. They are not the only members of God's community, but if they are not fully part of it, God is not fully present.

To include these folks in our community forces us to step outside the social, political, religious, and economic structures that serve you and me so well. We will have to see these institutions from the perspective of the bottom, of the margins, and understand their flaws as well as their strengths. And because these structures in fact do not work for all the members of our community, we will have to re-structure ourselves in ways that more truly reflect the value God places on each human life.

I do not mean that we should dedicate our lives to opposing the structures and institutions of social and economic injustice, or political oppression. To quote Richard Rohr, the Franciscan monk:

> You cannot build on death. You can only build on life. We must be sustained by a sense of what we are for and not just what we are against.[135]

Our struggle is not against the oppressors, or the powerful, or the rich, or the institutions that serve their purposes. That struggle is just another form of domination, and our victory would only perpetuate the old injustices, with different actors in the various roles. You become what you fight against, and if we fight against the structures of oppression hard enough we will succeed in placing ourselves at the top of the pyramid instead of who is there now—another failure. Our struggle is for the oppressed, for the suffering, for the poor and powerless, to relieve their pain and create a world free of all forms of domination.

To do this we must learn to create new social and economic relationships, new circles of community that embody God's great economy, God's divine plan for all of creation. It will not be easy, and those who benefit from the present system will not come flocking to join us. Jesus' parable in Luke 19 warns us, as it warned the disciples, just how hard and painful this effort will be. Also, it will not be quick. Jesus said that if we exorcise one demon, seven more would come to confront us. If we exorcise those, forty-nine more will come, and so on—you do the math. It will be the work of a lifetime just to start the journey toward the great economy.

The Israelites came out of the desert, where they had been led by Yahweh, and crossed the river Jordan into the promised land. Jesus came out of the river Jordan and went into the desert:

135 Personal conversation, 1995.

Filled with the Holy Spirit, Jesus left the Jordan and was led by the Spirit into the desert, for forty days being put to the test by the devil. During that time he ate nothing and at the end he was hungry.[136]

With just these few words Jesus evoked the deepest cultural memories of his listeners, and raised the theme we have explored tonight: God's project to liberate creation from suffering. He claimed a place in the one big story, and declared his role to continue and extend our understanding of the relationship between Yahweh and Yahweh's creation.

Jesus' role as teacher, exemplar, and herald of the reign of God rested on three "pillar principles." Like a three-legged stool, the reign of God depends on each principle for stability. The great adversary tested Jesus on each of these principles, to see if Jesus could be subverted and Yahweh's project derailed. Over the next few days we will look at the tests which Jesus faced in the desert, and try to understand why they are crucial tests for us today as we try to live the lives God yearns for us to live, to fulfill our role in the cosmic story.

Tuesday: No Silos

Filled with the Holy Spirit, Jesus left the Jordan and was led by the Spirit into the desert, for forty days being put to the test by the devil. During that time he ate nothing and at the end he was hungry. Then the devil said to him, "If you are Son of God, tell this stone to turn into a loaf." But Jesus replied, Scripture says, *"Human beings live not on bread alone."*[137]

Jesus started his public ministry with a vision quest that emphasized the continuity between his project and the great story of the Exodus: forty days in the desert, reminding the readers of the Scripture accounts of the forty years the Israelites spent in the wilderness leaving Egypt. Furthermore, he fasts for these same forty days, bringing to mind Moses' forty-day fast recounted in Deuteronomy

[136] Luke 4:1–2, New Jerusalem Bible.
[137] Luke 4:1–4, New Jerusalem Bible.

9:18. There is no human witness to these events other than Jesus, whom we must assume was the original reporter. It follows, therefore, that these descriptions of times and events, and the others which we will explore, were chosen by Jesus for their symbolic value. Jesus wants us to make the sort of connections we will explore. It is the point of the episode.

After forty years of wandering, the Israelites came out of the desert and into Canaan—a vassal state of Egypt. Yahweh liberated them from the power of pharaoh, led them on a forty-year spiritual purification trek, and delivered them across the Jordan—through the back door, as it were—into Canaan, a nation-state that paid tribute to Egypt and was part of the Egyptian empire.[138] They were back in Egypt!

Yahweh's point, it seems, was not to help the Israelites escape bodily from Egypt, but to liberate them by teaching them how to be non-Egyptian in Egypt. This is still God's project today: to teach us how to lead a kingdom life in a non-kingdom world.

Jesus has set a most dramatic stage for his report of his experience in the desert. He did not just get sprinkled, leave the baptismal font and go to a retreat center, even though that would have made an individual story of great interest and even drama. He came up out of the River Jordan and at once went straight into the desert. Jesus is claiming his place in the big story. Jesus is saying that what happened next and what continues to happen through the gospel stories is nothing less than a continuation of the one cosmic story of the relationship between God and creation. His "vision quest" in the desert is not merely individual, but profoundly corporate.

This vision quest is both a time for solidifying Jesus' commitment to his project and a time of great vulnerability, when the magnitude of the task and its awful cost might dissuade him. The devil—the adversary—the tester—chooses this opportune moment to attempt to derail the whole deal. He will test Jesus' understanding of and commitment to the coming reign of God. The three tests attack the three "pillar principles" on which the reign of God rests—if these can be subverted, Jesus' work will be useless and the threat to the devil's domain will be averted. Furthermore,

138 See Genesis 47:14 for Joseph's policy concerning Canaan during the famine.

the tests are subtle: Jesus is not urged to turn to evil, but to accept a lesser vision: to substitute the good for the gospel, which is always the most dangerous of substitutions.

The first test, therefore, is of the utmost relevance to the inhabitants of this poor, rocky, occupied land: If you are Son of God, tell this stone to turn into a loaf of bread. Rocks are plentiful in the Holy Land, and bread is hard to come by. One who could routinely turn stones into bread would be rich and influential, indeed!

Jesus responds by quoting Scripture: Human beings live not on bread alone. He is quoting Deuteronomy 8:3, which is itself a passage recalling the Exodus experience. Verses 2 and 3 read as follows:

> Remember the long road by which Yahweh your God led you for forty years in the desert, to humble you, to test you and know your inmost heart—whether you would keep his commandments or not. He humbled you, he made you feel hunger, he fed you with manna which neither you nor your ancestors had ever known, to make you understand that human beings live not on bread alone but on every word that comes from the mouth of Yahweh.[139]

The manna experience is the key to understanding how it is that human beings live not on bread alone, and hence the key to understanding Jesus' response to this first temptation—and to understanding the temptation itself. This is recounted in Exodus chapter 16.

Yahweh said to Moses, look, I shall rain down bread for you from the heavens. Moses told the people, Yahweh commands that each of you must collect as much as he needs to eat: one *homer* per head for each person in his tent. The Israelites collected it; some more, some less. When they measured out what they had collected, no one who had collected more had too much; no one who had collected less had too little. Each had collected as much as he needed to eat.

Moses then said, no one may keep any of it for tomorrow. But some of them did not listen and tried to save for the next day: it bred maggots and smelled foul. So they could not save it, but it fell day by day, and they gathered and were full. When the full sun rose, whatever they had not collected melted away.

[139] Deuteronomy 8:2–3, New Jerusalem Bible.

On the sixth day, Moses told the people to collect twice as much as usual, and to boil whatever was left at day's end—for Yahweh wanted the seventh day to be a Sabbath, a day of complete rest. So they did, and what they collected extra on the sixth day and boiled did not spoil or smell bad on the seventh day.

Moses then told the people to save an *homer* of the manna to show to their descendants, so that they could see the bread on which Yahweh fed the Israelites when he brought them out of Egypt. Aaron did this and put it in the ark along with the tablets of the law. We all remember that the ark held the tablets of the law— we often forget that it also held a jarful of manna, equally symbolic of Yahweh's presence and covenant relationship with the chosen people.

What are we to make of this story of divine provender in the wilderness? As a child I accepted it as literal truth, meaning just what it said. As I grew older and more sophisticated, I came to understand this and many Bible stories in more sophisticated, more complex ways. I looked for scientific explanations of what manna really was (there are many), or anthropological descriptions of how an early story might have gotten changed and distorted during the many generations during which it was transmitted as an oral tradition. I wanted to be in control of the story, to set boundaries on what it might mean and what its significance to me might be. I wanted to explain it away, so it would not have power over me.

Now I have come nearly full circle, and hear these old stories with much of the awe and wonder that they elicited from me as a child. As my teacher Richard Rohr says, "All the Bible stories are true, and some of them really happened." Biblical archeology is providing more and more evidence that many of the Bible stories, including the Exodus, really happened. What is clear to me in my heart of hearts is that these stories are profoundly true. They would not otherwise have been preserved at such great personal effort from generation to generation, first by oral storytellers and later by scribes. They would not otherwise ring so true in my heart whenever I hear them.

How Yahweh fed the Israelites in the wilderness is not a scientific question that I care about. That Yahweh fed them, and that the Israelites experienced that feeding as described, and that as they told and retold the story the truth emerged as we receive the story today, seems to me self-evident. All the stories are true, and some of them really happened.

Manna is a symbol of and example of an economy of grace. Everybody gets enough manna, by the grace of God. It cannot be hoarded or stored; no matter how much you gather, there is always just enough. God provides because God loves us, not because God owes us or we have earned it.

The point of manna is to rely on God rather than our own efforts to provide our needs. We evoke the manna experience every time we pray to God to "give us this day our daily bread," but that doesn't seem to stop us from accumulating our 401(k) plans, our savings for a "rainy day," or our precious metal jewelry "as a hedge against inflation." The Israelites couldn't save up manna for a "rainy day," they had to rely on God to provide every day. The devil wanted Jesus to intervene by his own hands to make bread, but Jesus refused to stop relying on God to provide what he really needed.

Jesus returned to this theme again and again throughout his ministry. Perhaps the most dramatic example is the parable in Luke 12:

> Then he told them a parable, "There was once a rich man who, having had a good harvest from his land, thought to himself, 'What am I to do? I have not enough room to store my crops.' Then he said, 'This is what I will do: I will pull down my barns and build bigger ones, and store all my grain and my goods in them, and I will say to my soul: My soul, you have plenty of good things laid by you for many years to come; take things easy, eat, drink, have a good time.' But God said to him, 'Fool! This very night the demand will be made for your soul; and this hoard of yours, whose will it be then?' So it is when someone stores up treasure for himself instead of becoming rich in the sight of God."[140]

This is the first principle of the reign of God—the first rule of the road for learning how to be non-Egyptian in the land of Egypt: no silos.

---

[140] Luke 12:16–21, New Jerusalem Bible.

The Israelites listening to Jesus had a rich if painful shared experience which served as the context for hearing Jesus teach about not building silos: their ancestors, by forced labor imposed on them without mercy, had built not just the silos, but the "store-cities" of Pithom and Rameses for pharaoh.[141]

Jesus has set the vision of the economy of God over against the economy of empire in the starkest of terms. On the one hand there is the model of Egypt, which under the guidance of Joseph carried out the economy of empire to a state of near perfection. Under the guise of helping the people survive a famine,

> Joseph acquired all the land in Egypt for pharaoh, since one by one the Egyptians sold their fields, so hard pressed were they by the famine; and the whole country passed into pharaoh's possession, while the people he reduced to serfdom from one end of Egypt to the other. The only land he did not acquire belonged to the priests, for the priests received an allowance from pharaoh and lived on the allowance that pharaoh gave them. Hence they had no need to sell their land.[142]

Joseph, as pharaoh's agent, became the sole landlord and the only source of seed grain in the nation. The former landowners became tenant sharecroppers, and pharaoh became fabulously wealthy—so wealthy that Joseph's kinfolk were reduced to slavery building silos and silo-cities to store pharaoh's wealth. Egypt was not unique or even unusual in doing this: the Babylonians, the Greeks, the Romans all did it—even the Israelites gathered in wealth from the ends of their little empire during the days of the monarchy, and accumulated it in the center of power. Think of the description of the Temple and where the materials came from to build it. Think of the ways our own United States empire gathers material wealth from the ends of the earth and accumulates it here for our own benefit. This economy of empire accumulates wealth for some and debt for the many. In the present day, we even call the nations of the world either creditor nations or debtor nations. We might call this an economy of debt.

141 Exodus 1:12–14.
142 Genesis 47:20–22, New Jerusalem Bible.

After the parable of the silos, Jesus immediately describes a starkly different economy—one we might call an economy of grace.

> Then he said to his disciples, "That is why I am telling you not to worry about your life and what you are to eat, not about your body and how you are to clothe it. For life is more than food, and the body more than clothing. Think of the ravens. They do not sow or reap; they have no storehouses and no barns; yet God feeds them. And how much more you are worth than the birds! Can any of you, however much you worry, add a single cubit to your span of life? If a very small thing is beyond your powers, why worry about the rest? Think how the flowers grow; they never have to spin or weave; yet, I assure you, not even Solomon in all his royal robes was clothed like one of them. Now if that is how God clothes a flower which is growing wild today and is thrown into the furnace tomorrow, how much more will he look after you, who have so little faith! But you must not set your hearts on things to eat and things to drink; nor must you worry. It is the gentiles of this world who set their hearts on all these things. Your Father well knows you need them. No; set your hearts on his kingdom, and these other things will be given you as well."
>
> "There is no need to be afraid, little flock, for it has pleased your Father to give you the kingdom."[143]

The raven and the wildflower are set before us as examples of how we ought to act and feel about our needs for daily bread and adequate clothing. Rather than build bigger silos, we should be trusting that Yahweh will provide each day the food we need for that day, so that we have no need to store any for tomorrow, and that Yahweh will provide excellent clothing for us to wear, without any need for us to worry about providing it for ourselves. Each day Yahweh will provide the food we need for that day? Sound familiar? Jesus is not setting forth an unattainable ideal, or some spiritualized head-trip, telling us to act "as if." Jesus is calling up the central story of the faith: that Yahweh did indeed intervene in history on behalf of the Israelites, and in fact provided them with manna in the wilderness that each day turned out to be just enough to meet their needs.

143 Luke 12:22–32, New Jerusalem Bible.

In feeding the people with manna, Yahweh is demonstrating two important truths: God is the source of all good things, not we human beings; and the purpose of economic organization is to see that everyone has enough, not to maximize wealth—either in the aggregate or in the individual case. Each of us has food to eat and clothes to wear because Yahweh caused the rain to fall and the earth to be fruitful; to claim the fruits of the earth for our own and to charge others exorbitantly for them is contrary to God's will.

In case the Israelites—or you and I—were to think that this "everyone has enough, no one has too much" economic model were only applicable to the Exodus experience itself, Yahweh institutes a permanent Sabbath structure to the economy that begins in Exodus and is elaborated in Deuteronomy and Leviticus. The Israelites were instructed during their journey through the desert to make every seventh day "a day of complete rest, a Sabbath sacred to Yahweh."[144] Later in Exodus this is made a permanent sign of the bond between Yahweh and the Israelites,[145] and in Leviticus it is expanded to include a sabbatical year and every forty-nine years a jubilee year,[146] including the forgiveness of debts, the return of ancestral land that had been sold, and freeing slaves and indentured servants.

There is a seemingly inevitable tendency, in any economic system, for wealth to become unequally distributed: some people/ families grow more and more wealthy, and some people/families fall deeper and deeper into poverty. This seems to be true in every economic system: capitalist, socialist, communist, or whatever. The jubilee year imposed by Yahweh does not value any particular economic system over another, nor does it discriminate between wealth justly accumulated or unjustly accumulated. Every forty-nine years, says Yahweh, the debts of the poorest are to be forgiven, and their fundamental means of livelihood—their land—is to be returned to them. The wealthy will not necessarily be recompensed for their loss; the poor will be liberated from the burden of their poverty.

Now the jubilee is an example of the economy of grace. Only by grace can we wealthy folks realize that Yahweh is far more reliable

144 Exodus 16:23, New Jerusalem Bible.
145 Exodus 31:12–17.
146 Leviticus 25:1–55.

than our silos and storehouses to provide for our needs; only by grace can we bear to release our hard-won wealth without compensation—even though it clouds our vision and distances us from a close relationship with God. Only by grace can the poor receive the jubilee distribution, because they are certainly powerless to win it for themselves: that is the definition of poor—those without power, possessions, and prestige.

What we have all around us today is an economy of debt. In the economy of debt people get things because they can pay for them, or promise to pay for them in the future (i.e., go into debt). The economy of debt acts to create more and more economic stratification and hierarchy, so that "the rich get richer and the poor get poorer." Even programs that purport to serve the interest of the whole community in the face of impending disaster, like Joseph's food policy in Egypt, create ever-greater accumulations of wealth and deserts of grinding poverty. All this is explained away by saying the rich deserve their riches and the poor have earned their poverty: a theology of prosperity, a theory of social Darwinism, a culture of the Protestant ethic.

So in the economy of debt folks get what they deserve, and the language of the economy of debt reflects this. "Act deservingly, and you will be rewarded." (For you English students, that is the imperative first, then the indicative.) "Do this, then these other things will happen." A great example of the language of the economy of debt is the current Pepsi advertising campaign:

"Buy Pepsi. Get Stuff."

Also:

"Dial 1-800-COLLECT. Save 44%!"

In the economy of grace people get what they need because it is God's good pleasure to give it to them. There are no silos in the economy of grace because God is faithful and the people place their trust in God. The language of the economy of grace is just the reverse of the economy of debt: "This is how grace is at work in the world, so act accordingly." It has pleased your Father to give you the kingdom, so there is no need to be afraid.

Now before you start discounting the economy of grace as pie-in-the-sky idealism, realize that there are numerous examples of this economy in our everyday lives. The home is the most common and one of the best illustrations. We operate our homes as an economy of grace: we feed and clothe our children out of our love for them, not because they can pay for their room and board. From our sons' and daughters' perspective, the kitchen is a magic cupboard, providing enough to satisfy their hunger every day: they don't have to build a food pantry in their bedroom to store up against some future famine. When Jesus tells us that we must become like little children in order to enter the kingdom of God, or participate in the reign of God, he is saying in part that we must trust God's economy of grace to provide for us as children trust their parent's economy of grace to provide for them.

Another example of the economy of grace is the experience of the early church in the period immediately following the resurrection of Christ. Luke reports in the Acts of the Apostles that

> all who shared the faith owned everything in common; they sold their goods and possessions and distributed the proceeds among themselves according to what each one needed. Each day, with one heart, they regularly went to the Temple but met in their houses for the breaking of bread; they shared their food gladly and generously;[147]

> The whole group of believers was united, heart and soul; no one claimed private ownership of any possessions, as everything they owned was held in common. . . . None of their members was ever in want, as all those who owned land or houses would sell them, and bring the money from the sale of them, to present it to the apostles; it was then distributed to any who might be in need.[148]

Two present-day examples of the economy of grace are the many monastic communities all over the world and the Catholic Worker movement, which has its roots here in the United States. When we were first planning how to bring Norfolk Quaker House from dream to reality, Steve Baggarly of the Norfolk Catholic Worker House reminded us that we did not have to be incorporated, or gain tax-exempt status from the Internal Revenue Service, or accept

---

147 Acts 2:44–46, New Jerusalem Bible.
148 Acts 4:32,34–35, New Jerusalem Bible.

grants from foundations. We could be like Catholic Worker. "How do you get what you need?" we asked. "We beg," replied Steve.

"We beg." How simple, and how powerful a statement of faith. They depend on the economy of grace to supply their needs: and that small community of five or six people, including a very young child, not only have all they need but are able to provide hospitality to several people at a time and to serve breakfast to 100–125 homeless men, women, and children four mornings a week. They have a roof over their heads, clothes for themselves and to give away to those in need, and money to buy medicine for the poor and even to support the work of Norfolk Quaker House. "There is no need to be afraid, little flock, for it has pleased your Father to give you the kingdom."

The economy of debt is very powerful and is, in fact, trying to overwrite the economy of grace wherever it finds it. One of the most powerful tools it has for this effort is spiritualization: reinterpreting the teachings of Jesus and the rest of the story to understand rich-ness and poverty as a state of mind, rather than a physical reality. Now there is such a thing as spiritual poverty—but most of Jesus' teachings have to do with physical poverty and physical wealth—how the one offends God and the other distances us from God.

When as a child I was taught the Lord's prayer, the radical nature of the petition that God would give us this day the bread we need this day was not clear to me or my teachers. The other great petition was completely spiritualized: "Forgive us our trespasses, as we forgive those who have trespassed against us." Matthew puts it bluntly and plainly:

> And forgive us our debts, as we have forgiven those who are in debt to us.[149]

Our participation in the jubilee is directly linked to how well we allow others to participate—if we give up the accumulation of wealth, and depend solely on Yahweh to provide, there will be enough for everyone. If there are only two fish and five loaves of bread for five thousand people, everyone will have enough and no one will have too much.[150]

[149] Matthew 6:12, New Jerusalem Bible.
[150] Mark 6:30–44.

"Human beings live not on bread alone." With these seven words Jesus invokes a pillar principle of the reign of God, evoking the deepest cultural memory of all of us who trace our religious heritage back to the God of Abraham, Isaac, and Jacob. If you want to be part of Yahweh's economy of grace, Jesus says, "No silos."

Wednesday: No Kings

Filled with the Holy Spirit, Jesus left the Jordan and was led by the Spirit into the desert, for forty days being put to the test by the devil. During that time he ate nothing and at the end he was hungry. Then the devil said to him, "If you are Son of God, tell this stone to turn into a loaf." But Jesus replied, Scripture says: *"Human beings live not on bread alone."*

Then leading him to a height, the devil showed him in a moment of time all the kingdoms of the world and said to him, "I will give you all this power and their splendour, for it has been handed over to me, for me to give it to anyone I choose. Do homage, then, to me, and it shall all be yours." But Jesus answered him, Scripture says: *"You must do homage to the Lord your God, him alone you must serve."*[151]

The devil is not discouraged by Jesus' resistance to his first temptation—there are other tricks in his bag. Next he shows Jesus all the kingdoms of the world at once, and offers them to Jesus. What an opportunity! How many times has each of us thought, "If only I were president (or king, or queen)—I'd run things differently, and there would be peace in the world and people would have enough to eat and be treated fairly." Here is Jesus' chance to do just that—and with perfect knowledge and wisdom, Jesus would do it right—he would make no mistakes.

Jesus turns it down flat. Our first clue as to why comes straight from the devil's mouth: "I will give you all this power and . . . splendour, for it has been handed over to me." The kingdoms of the world belong to the devil.

Now this is a truth we embrace in part, and firmly deny in part. We are all ready to agree that that kingdom over there—the

151 Luke 4:1–8, New Jerusalem Bible.

one we are not on top of—is evil. From the perspective of the United States, the Third Reich was evil, the USSR was evil, the Sandanistas are evil, Fidel Castro is evil. It is harder to accept that our own kingdoms, the ones we participate in and benefit from, also belong to the devil.

How can this be? All the kingdoms of the world, including our own, belong to the devil because they concentrate power: first to do what is properly God's work, and eventually they accumulate power for power's sake. As Lord Acton observed, "Power corrupts, and absolute power corrupts absolutely."

The preamble to the constitution of the United States gives the following reasons for a centralized national government:

> We the people of the United States, in order to form a more perfect union, establish justice, insure domestic tranquility, provide for the common defence, promote the general welfare, and secure the blessings of liberty to ourselves and our posterity, do ordain and establish this constitution for the United States of America.

To establish justice, ensure domestic tranquility, provide for the common defense, promote the general welfare, and secure the blessings of liberty: Yahweh's work. The reason that the kingdoms of the world belong to the devil is that their best and highest purpose is to do work that is properly left to Yahweh—they are evidence that the people no longer place their faith in Yahweh. Over time, they gather more and more power to themselves and build an ever-higher, ever-steeper pyramid, all in the name of doing work best left to Yahweh. When asked how much money was enough, Nelson Rockefeller is reported to have said, "Just a little more." When confronted with the question of how much power is enough, the kingdoms of the world respond, "Just a little more."

So Jesus responds to the offer of becoming king of the world with a quote from Deuteronomy, this time from chapter 6:

> Be careful you do not forget Yahweh who has brought you out of Egypt, out of the place of slave-labour. Yahweh your God is the one you must fear, him alone you must serve, his is the name by which you must swear.[152]

[152] Deuteronomy 6:12–13, New Jerusalem Bible.

The experience of the Israelites is that the premier kingdom of the known world—Egypt—was for them a place of slave labor. Yahweh extracted them from this kingdom and established them as a chosen people, a loose confederation of tribes with primary loyalty to Yahweh. Their struggle has been to resist the temptation to install their own king, to become just like all the other peoples around them. They have given in to this temptation, and the results have been disastrous. Now the devil offers one last chance to get it right.

When Yahweh leads the people out of Egypt, they are leaving the model of centralized power: pharaoh is both god and king, the supreme authority. In contrast, Yahweh tells the people they are to have no king, and symbolizes this by the ark of the covenant—in which the judgment seat is empty! There is no one on the throne, no human king, because their total allegiance is to be given to Yahweh.

The decentralization of the Israelite government is symbolized by the account of the crossing of the River Jordan recorded in the book of Joshua, chapter 3. The priests carried the ark of the covenant ahead of the people, and as soon as their feet touched the waters, the river separated. The upstream water stood still and the downstream water flowed on its way, leaving a dry path for the people all the way across. When the people were all across, Yahweh told Joshua to choose one man from each tribe to go to the place in mid-river where the priests were now standing with the ark, and to have each one take a stone from mid-river and carry it to the camp. These stones are to be a reminder of the way that Yahweh separated the river and allowed the Israelites to pass—as this whole episode is a reminder of the parting of the Red Sea as they left Egypt. Furthermore, the twelve stones are a symbol that they are the twelve tribes of Israel—not a centralized government but a decentralized people. They will be guided by judges, not kings, until the people can no longer bear being different.

The first major Israelite flirtation with monarchy is reported in the book of Judges—and that experience alone should have been enough to warn them away from kings. After Gideon's great victories in the territories beyond the Jordan River, the Israelites wanted him to rule them and to establish a royal house. Gideon refused, saying, "I will not rule you, neither will my son. Yahweh will rule you."153

Gideon's son Abimelech could not resist the temptation to make himself king, and after murdering seventy of his brothers, seized power—for about three years. Abimelech's youngest brother Jotham hid himself and escaped from the massacre. Going to the top of Mount Carmel, Jotham tells the gathered people a fable about a time when the trees decided to select a king to rule over them:

> Hear me, leaders of Shechem so that God may also hear you!
>
> One day the trees went out
> to anoint a king to rule them.
> They said to the olive tree, "Be our king!"
>
> The olive tree replied
> "Must I forgo my oil
> which gives honor to gods and men,
> to stand and sway over the trees?"
>
> Then the trees said to the fig tree,
> "You come and be our king!"
>
> The fig tree replied,
> "Must I forgo my sweetness,
> forgo my excellent fruit,
> to go and sway over the trees?"
>
> Then the trees said to the vine,
> "You come and be our king!"
>
> The vine replied,
> Must I forgo my wine
> which cheers gods and men,
> to go and sway over the trees?"
>
> Then the trees all said to the thorn bush,
> You come and be our king!"
>
> And the thorn bush replied to the trees,
> "If you are anointing me in good faith to be your king,
> come and shelter in my shade
>
> But, if not, fire will come out of the thorn bush
> and devour the cedars of Lebanon."154

153 Judges 8:23, New Jerusalem Bible.
154 *Ibid.*, 9:7–15.

This is apparently the oldest parable in the Bible that uses plants or animals to make a moral point about human behavior in the style of the Aesop's fables. The olive and fig trees, along with the grape vine, are the basis of life and culture in the Biblical culture. The story is telling us that the worthy, valuable trees all have their own role in the order of things—in the gospel order, we might say—and being king is not part of that role. The only one willing to be king is the thorn bush, who plays no positive role in the culture—and even the thorn bush warns that choosing him to be king could be very dangerous, indeed.

The monarchy of Abimelech was dangerous and bloody for the Israelites, and not just for his close relations—you can read the gory details in Judges. After this brief interlude, however, the Israelites went back to the system of judges—including, among others, Samson and eventually Samuel.

Samuel was a prophet[155] and a judge over Israel[156] throughout his life. When he grew old, however, the people of Israel asked for a king to rule over them, "like other nations."[157] Despite his personal reservations about this, Samuel prayed to Yahweh, who responded:

> Obey the voice of the people in all that they say to you: it is not you they have rejected, but me, not wishing me to reign over them any more. They are now doing to you exactly what they have done to me since the day I brought them out of Egypt until now, deserting me and serving other gods. So, do what they ask; only, you must give them a solemn warning, and must tell them what the king who is to reign over them will do.

> Everything that Yahweh had said, Samuel then repeated to the people who were asking him for a king. He said, "This is what the king who is to reign over you will do. He will take your sons and direct them to his chariotry and cavalry, and they will run in front of his chariot. He will use them as leaders of a thousand and leaders of fifty; he will make them plough his fields and gather in his harvest and make his weapons of war and the gear for his chariots. He will take your daughters as perfumers, cooks and bakers. He will take the best of your fields, your vineyards

155 I Samuel 3:20.
156 *Ibid.*, 7:15.
157 *Ibid.*, 8.

and your olive groves and give them to his officials. He will take the best of your servants, men and women, of your oxen and your donkeys, and make them work for him. He will tithe your flocks, and you yourselves will become his slaves. When that day comes, you will cry aloud because of the king you have chosen for yourselves, but on that day Yahweh will not hear you.

The people, however, refused to listen to Samuel. They said, "No! We are determined to have a king, so that we can be like the other nations, with our own king to rule us and lead us and fight our battles."[158]

Samuel speaks very clearly about two consequences of choosing to have a national government—a monarchy rather than a theocracy. The first consequence is that the people will suffer. The king will take away the sons of families and put them in his military; he will put the young men of the nations to work increasing his own wealth and his power to protect that wealth from anyone who threatens it. The king will take away the daughters of families and put them to work making his own life more luxurious. He will take the harvests and the livestock and the very fields and vineyards away from the people until they become his slaves. The king will become richer and richer, more and more powerful; and the people will pay the price. The Israelites have personal experience confirming these predictions: Samuel could easily be describing their history in Egypt and the effects of Joseph's work on pharaoh's behalf.

A king does not do this because he is a bad person, but because he is a king. Solomon is the prime example of a good and great king; when he died, the whole assembly of Israel spoke to his son of the "cruel yoke" Solomon had laid on them, a heavy yoke of cruel slavery[159] imposed on them. In spite of Samuel's warnings, which were to come tragically true, the people insist: they want a king.

A kingship is a power system: an institutionalized hierarchy of power. Samuel is not engaging in a comparative political science lecture—he is talking of the consequences of instituting any power system—any institutionalized hierarchy of power—whether it be an absolute monarchy, a republic, or a representative democracy/federal

[158] I Samuel 8:7–22, New Jerusalem Bible.
[159] I Kings 12:4, New Jerusalem Bible.

government of the type we have in the United States. Samuel is not differentiating between those governments which are established for "good" reasons and those which are established as the result of raw power grabs.

The reason Samuel does not make these distinctions is that they are not very important. No matter how or why a power system is established, or what form it takes outwardly, a power system imposes its will on people in order to attain certain objectives. Having chosen to attain its objectives through the use of power, a power system will always determine that it could do a better job if it had a little more power. As it accumulates power in order to accomplish its objectives, the institution perceives real or imagined threats to its existence, and accumulates more power in order to protect itself. Eventually its own protection comes to replace the original objectives as the primary activity of the power system, and it accumulates more and more resources in order to protect itself better and better.

The second consequence of choosing to have a king is Yahweh's reaction to the choice. Yahweh tells Samuel exactly what the Israelites are doing by choosing to be ruled by a king:

> They are now doing . . . exactly what they have done to me since
> the day I brought them out of Egypt until now, deserting me
> and serving other gods.

This is how seriously Yahweh takes this business of kings and power systems: choosing them is the same as deserting Yahweh to serve other gods. If that is not clear enough, Yahweh says exactly what will happen as a result of choosing to have a king:

> You will cry aloud because of the king you have chosen for your-
> selves, but on that day Yahweh will not hear you.

You will cry aloud, but Yahweh will not hear you. Wait a minute—this is Yahweh who heard the Israelites in Egypt when they weren't even crying to Yahweh, and who cared for them so greatly that nothing less than liberating them from their oppression would do. Now Yahweh tells these same folks that if they go choose a king instead of depending on Yahweh, even if they cry directly to Yahweh about the consequences of their choice, Yahweh will not hear them. Yahweh will deliberately not be listening on that day.

To choose a human king, to give power and allegiance to human systems of power rather than to Yahweh, is so destructive of the covenant relationship between Yahweh and human beings that Yahweh will not listen to our complaints about how badly our choice has turned out. Isaiah also speaks of Yahweh's refusal to listen to the prayers of those whose hands are dirtied with social injustice. The prophet Micah catalogs the many sins of the princes of the house of Israel against the people—actual sins, not just anticipated ones—and then says this:

> Then they will call to Yahweh,
> but he will not answer them.
> When the time comes he will hide his face from them
> because of the crimes they have committed.[160]

The royalty have inflicted dire suffering on the people, as Micah has just cataloged; and Yahweh will hide his face from them because of their crimes. Samuel says that kingship is itself a social injustice, and that the sin does not belong to the rulers alone: the people share in that sin by choosing to be ruled by a king rather than Yahweh.

Samuel is saying that the Israelites have chosen to forget how to be non-Egyptian: they want to be just like all the other nations, participating in the systems of hierarchy. They have chosen a human king, a human power system, in place of Yahweh. They just couldn't bear to let the judgment seat on the ark to stay empty; they had to put somebody in it.

Jesus' teaching and example continued and confirmed Yahweh's condemnation of systems and institutions of power. The early church understood this, suffering persecution and even death rather than support the imperial government by participating in its armies, until 313 AD. Then the church made a deal with Emperor Constantine, and the church itself became part of the imperial hierarchy—with disastrous results for the ministry of the church.

The only sign of hope in all this is that Yahweh does not refuse to listen forever, but only "on that day." My sense of the meaning of this limitation is that as we understand how much we have erred by participating in the power system, and begin to extract ourselves

160 Micah 3:4, New Jerusalem Bible.

from that system, Yahweh will again listen and be reconciled to us, and intervene to help us. Isaiah reports that this is indeed Yahweh's desire and intent, in a passage spanning parts of chapters 57 and 58:

> For I do not want to be forever accusing
> nor always to be angry,
> or the spirit would fail under my onslaught,
> the souls that I myself have made.[161]

> I saw how he behaved, but I shall heal him,
> I shall lead him, fill him with consolation,
> him and those who mourn for him,
> bringing praise to their lips.
> Peace, peace to far and near, Yahweh says,
> and I shall heal him.[162]

A few verses later, Yahweh tells us what will restore the covenant, what it will take for Yahweh to listen to us again:

> Is this not the sort of fast that pleases me:
> to break unjust fetters,
> to undo the thongs of the yoke,
> to let the oppressed go free,
> and to break all yokes?
> Is it not sharing your food with the hungry,
> and sheltering the homeless poor;
> if you see someone lacking clothes, to clothe him,
> and not to turn away from your own kin?
> Then your light will blaze out like the dawn
> and your wound be quickly healed over.
> Saving justice for you will go ahead
> and Yahweh's glory will come behind you.
> Then you will call for help and Yahweh will answer;
> you will call and he will say, "I am here."[163]

Jesus rejects power for himself in the desert, and teaches his disciples to pray for Yahweh's kingdom, not a human one. Repeatedly, Jesus talks about the kingdom of God,[164] and contrasts

161 Isaiah 57:16, New Jerusalem Bible.
162 *Ibid.*, 57:18–19.
163 *Ibid.*, 58:6–9.
164 Luke 4:43; 10:9.

that kingdom with the flawed, imperfect nature of even the best of human kingships.[165]

It is the nature of kings that I can be the servant of only one. The authorities who brought Jesus to Pilate understood that, because they began their accusation by saying that they had found Jesus claiming to be a king.[166] Pontius Pilate understood that, because he put the question to Jesus directly: "Are you the king of the Jews?"[167] The chief priests understood that, because they said, "We have no king except Caesar."[168] Jesus' claims for the reign of God were sufficient to get him executed. You and I have largely forgotten this, or we spiritualize God's kingdom, and pretend we can serve both Yahweh and the kingdoms of this world. No one can have two masters.

Yahweh did not give Israel a thorn bush to be their king. In David and Solomon the Israelites got just about the best father-son royal succession one could hope for. Yet in spite of a brief flurry of glory, the long-term legacy of the house of David was disastrous for Israel. If these two couldn't get it right, who could? Perhaps the Christ, God incarnate—but Jesus turns the job down flat. It is not that the people who have been king were flawed (though they all have been, on every throne in every nation)—it is that the kingship itself, the system of hierarchy and accumulation of power, is no more a part of the reign of God than the silo. No silos, and no kings in the reign of God.

Thursday: No Idolatry

Filled with the Holy Spirit, Jesus left the Jordan and was led by the Spirit into the desert, for forty days being put to the test by the devil. During that time he ate nothing and at the end he was hungry. Then the devil said to him, "If you are Son of God, tell this stone to turn into a loaf." But Jesus replied, Scripture says: *"Human beings live not on bread alone."*

Then leading him to a height, the devil showed him in a moment of time all the kingdoms of the world and said to him, "I will give you all this power and their splendour, for it has been

[165] Luke 11:31 and 12:27 re Solomon, 20:41–44 re David.
[166] *Ibid.*, 23:1–2.
[167] *Ibid.*, 23:3.
[168] John 19:15, New Jerusalem Bible.

handed over to me, for me to give it to anyone I choose. Do homage, then, to me, and it shall all be yours." But Jesus answered him, Scripture says: *"You must do homage to the Lord your God, him alone you must serve."*

Then he led him to Jerusalem and set him on the parapet of the temple. "If you are Son of God," he said to him, "Throw yourself down from here, for Scripture says: *"He has given his angels orders about you, to guard you."*

And again: *"They will carry you in their arms in case you trip over a stone."*

But Jesus answered him, Scripture says: *"Do not put the Lord your God to the test."*[169]

The devil has one last test for Jesus, one last attempt to derail the coming kingdom of God. 'Jump from the highest point in Jerusalem, the pinnacle of the cult of Yahweh, and force God's hand to save you!' The devil takes Jesus to the holiest place in the Holy City, the Sanctum Sanctorum, and quotes Scripture—Psalm 91—to persuade Jesus to make the apparent "leap of faith." Jesus resists, and one last time quotes Deuteronomy as his reason:

Do not put Yahweh your God to the test as you did at Massah.[170]

What happened at Massah? We have two accounts: one in Exodus chapter 17, and one in Numbers chapter 20. The Exodus account runs like this:

The whole community of Israelites left the desert of Sin, travelling by stages as Yahweh ordered. They pitched camp at Rephidim where there was no water for the people to drink. The people took issue with Moses for this and said, "Give us water to drink." Moses replied, "Why take issue with me? Why do you put Yahweh to the test?" But tormented by thirst, the people complained to Moses, "Why did you bring us out of Egypt," they said, "Only to make us, our children and our livestock, die of thirst?" Moses appealed to Yahweh for help. "How am I to deal with this people?" he said. "Any moment now they will stone me!" Yahweh then said to Moses, "Go on ahead of the

169 Luke 4:1–12, New Jerusalem Bible.
170 Deuteronomy 6:16, New Jerusalem Bible.

people, taking some of the elders of Israel with you; in your hand take the staff with which you struck the river, and go. I shall be waiting for you there on the rock (at Horeb). Strike the rock, and water will come out for the people to drink." This was what Moses did, with the elders of Israel looking on. He gave the place the names Massah and Meribah (Trial and Contention) because of the Israelites' contentiousness and because they put Yahweh to the test by saying, "Is Yahweh with us, or not?"[171]

Is Yahweh with us, or not? Show me proof! Because if Yahweh can't produce, I'm going to make a golden calf, or some serpents, or a mansion, or a flag, or a nuclear warhead—something I can see— and put my faith in that! When we put God to the test we are already idolaters, because we have already put ourselves at the center of our story, rather than God.

This is Jesus' test: whether or not he will put himself at the center of his story by jumping, and thereby put God in a subordinate role—God on Jesus' side. The same temptation confronts every one of us every day of our lives: the temptation to put our own projects first, relegating God to a supporting role.

Psalm 91, from which the devil quotes, locates the temptation for us neatly. When it is read from the margins of society, from the bottom of the pyramid, Psalm 91 reminds the reader that we are all under God's protection, and need not fear. Read from the top of society, from the pinnacle of power and wealth, the psalm begins to sound like confirmation of our entitlement to all good things, to our manifest destiny of victory and empire. And in fact, the psalm was read just that way in imperial Israel (short-lived as that was), and in every so-called Christian empire since. God is on our side.

Satan also locates the temptation by his choice of site: the parapet of Herod's Second Temple, the pinnacle of the religious, political, and economic pyramid of Israelite society. In our projects of aggrandizing wealth, power, and influence we are continually putting ourselves at the center of our story, claiming God's approval, blessing and important role in assisting the success of our own projects. God gets the Oscar for "Best Supporting Actor."

171 Exodus 17:1–7, New Jerusalem Bible.

"Not so!" says Jesus, "You shall not put the Lord your God to the test."

The third "pillar principle" of the reign of God is "no idolatry." If it is to be really the reign of God rather than the reign of the Golden Calf or the almighty dollar or the nuclear umbrella, then God must be at the center, not anyone or anything else. We must cultivate single-pointed awareness, centering wholly on Yahweh. Putting our faith anywhere but with Yahweh is idolatry. Yahweh cannot be fully and completely our God if we will not be fully and completely Yahweh's people.

As I prepared for this Bible study several months ago, my friend Steve Baggarly and the rest of the Prince of Peace Plowshares activists were being tried and convicted in federal court for their prophetic actions at the Bath shipyard in Maine. By hammering on the *USS Sullivans* and pouring their blood on the ship, the Plowshares activists were undertaking symbolic action to remind us all of the idolatry of placing our faith in weapons of mass destruction rather than on the guidance and protection of God. Steve and his wife Kim are founders of the Norfolk Catholic Worker House, and as such have undertaken voluntary poverty: they are without possessions of their own, depending on the generosity of others for their very survival. They are to my best perception the embodiment of a life without silos, kings, or idolatry—not the only life that embraces those principles, but surely a true life in the reign of God. Their life is not only one of service to those on the periphery of society, but a life of prophecy to those of us nearer the center of the circles of power, possessions, and prestige. The truth they speak, by daily service, public demonstration, and civil disobedience is that our national love affair with weapons of mass destruction is idolatry. Pharaoh loves his chariots, but to non-Egyptians they are nothing more than idols, unable to protect us any more than a figurine carved of stone or wood. Yahweh demands our full commitment, loyalty, and trust; the reign of God won't work any other way.

Some 550 years after the Exodus, around 850 BC,[172] another prophet without possessions or property confronted his national

[172] *The Interpreter's Bible*, Vol. I, p. 146.

government about its idolatry, and received no warmer welcome than the Prince of Peace Plowshares. Elijah did not wait to be arrested and tried, but fled for his very life—after a most remarkable and dramatic showdown on Mount Carmel. Elijah's story dramatizes the exclusive relationship Yahweh wishes to have with each of us, and the divine power that such a covenant releases for our good.

Elijah's name means "Yah is El"—El being the general Semitic name for the high God. Hence Elijah's very name declares his mission: to declare that Yahweh is the one and only God.

Elijah's story is told in I Kings 18—but the story actually begins in chapter 16, when King Ahab succeeds his father Omri and begins a reign of twenty-two years in Israel. At this time Asa, a devoted follower of Yahweh (for whom my son is named), was king in Judah. In contrast to Asa, Ahab is unfaithful to Yahweh, worshipping Baal and erecting a temple dedicated to him. I Kings records the story this way:

> Ahab son of Omri became king of Israel in the thirty-eighth year of Asa king of Judah, and reigned over Israel for twenty-two years in Samaria. Ahab son of Omri did what is displeasing to Yahweh, and was worse than all his predecessors. The least that he did was to follow the sinful example of Jeroboam son of Nebat: he married Jezebel daughter of Ethbaal, king of the Sidonians, and then proceeded to serve Baal and worship him. He erected an altar to him in the temple of Baal which he built in Samaria. Ahab also put up a sacred pole and committed other crimes as well, provoking the anger of Yahweh, God of Israel, more than all the kings of Israel his predecessors.[173]

> Elijah the Tishbite, of Tishbe in Gilead, said to Ahab, "By the life of Yahweh, God of Israel, whom I serve, there will be neither dew nor rain these coming years unless I give the word."[174]

> A long time went by, and the word of Yahweh came to Elijah in the third year, "Go, present yourself to Ahab, and I will send rain on the country." So Elijah set off to present himself to Ahab.[175]

---

[173] I Kings 16:29–33, New Jerusalem Bible.
[174] I Kings 17:1, New Jerusalem Bible.
[175] I Kings 18:1, New Jerusalem Bible.

Obadiah went to find Ahab and tell him the news, and Ahab then went to find Elijah. When he saw Elijah, Ahab said, "There you are, you scourge of Israel!" "Not I," he replied, "I am not the scourge of Israel, you and your family are; because you have deserted Yahweh and followed Baal. Now give orders for all Israel to gather round me on Mount Carmel, and also the four hundred prophets of Baal who eat at Jezebel's table.

Ahab called all Israel together and assembled the prophets on Mount Carmel. Elijah stepped out in front of all the people. "How long," he said, "do you mean to hobble first on one leg and then on the other? If Yahweh is God, follow him; if Baal, follow him." But the people had nothing to say. Elijah then said to them, "I, I alone, am left as a prophet of Yahweh, while the prophets of Baal are four hundred and fifty. Let two bulls be given us; let them choose one for themselves, dismember it but not set fire to it. I in my turn shall prepare the other bull, but not set fire to it. You must call on the name of your god, and I shall call on the name of Yahweh; the god who answers with fire, is God indeed." The people all answered, "Agreed!" Elijah then said to the prophets of Baal, "Choose one bull and begin, for there are more of you. Call on the name of your god but light no fire." They took the bull and prepared it, and from morning to midday they called on the name of Baal. "O, Baal, answer us!" they cried, but there was no voice, no answer, as they prepared their hobbling dance round the altar which they had made. Midday came, and Elijah mocked them. "Call louder," he said, "for he is a god: he is preoccupied or he is busy, or he has gone on a journey; perhaps he is asleep and needs to be woken up!" So they shouted louder and gashed themselves, as their custom was, with swords and spears until the blood flowed down them. Midday passed, and they ranted on until the time when the offering is presented; but there was no voice, no answer, no sign of attention.

Then Elijah said to all the people, "Come over to me," and all the people came over to him. He repaired Yahweh's altar which had been torn down. Elijah took twelve stones, corresponding to the number of tribes of the sons of Jacob, to whom the word of Yahweh had come, "Israel is to be your name," and built an altar in the name of Yahweh. Round the altar he dug a trench of a size to hold two measures of seed. He then arranged the wood, dismembered the bull, and laid it on the wood. Then he said, "Fill four jars with water and pour it on the burnt offering and on the wood." They did this. He said, "Do it a second time;" they did it a second time. He said, "Do it a third time;" they did it a third time. The water flowed round the altar until even the trench itself was full of water. At the time when the offering is presented, Elijah the prophet stepped forward. "Yahweh, God of Abraham, Isaac and Israel," he said, "Let them know today that you are God in Israel, and that I am your servant, that I have done all these things at your command. Answer me, Yahweh, answer me, so that this people may know that you, Yahweh, are God and are winning back their hearts."

Then Yahweh's fire fell and consumed the burnt offering and the wood and licked up the water in the trench. When all the people saw this they fell on their faces. "Yahweh is God," they cried, "Yahweh is God!" Elijah said, "Seize the prophets of Baal: do not let one of them escape." They seized them, and Elijah took them down to the Kishon, and there he slaughtered them.

Elijah said to Ahab, "Go back now, eat and drink; for I hear the approaching sound of rain." While Ahab went back to eat and drink, Elijah climbed to the top of Carmel and bowed down to the ground, putting his face between his knees. "Now go up," he told his servant, "and look out to sea." He went up and looked. "There is nothing at all," he said. Seven times Elijah told him to go back. The seventh time, the servant said, "Now there is a cloud, small as a man's hand, rising from the sea." Elijah said, "Go and say to Ahab, "Harness the chariot and go down before the rain stops you." And with that the sky grew dark with cloud and storm, and rain fell in torrents. Ahab mounted his chariot and made for Jezreel. But the hand of Yahweh had come on Elijah and, hitching up his clothes, ran ahead of Ahab all the way to Jezreel.[176]

What has happened here? Yahweh sends a severe drought upon Israel, proclaimed by Elijah the Tishbite, who announces in the name of Yahweh that neither rain nor dew will fall in Israel until he gives the word. (That this drought actually occurred is confirmed by the Greek historian Menander of Ephesus, who records a great

[176] I Kings 18:16–46, New Jerusalem Bible.

drought during the reign of Eithobaal, father of Ahab's wife Jezebel.)[177] Ahab had probably married Jezebel to seal a trade agreement with her father; it is this connection with the Phoenicians, personified in Jezebel, that is blamed for the introduction of Baal-worship to the royal house and Israel at large. Jezebel thus seems to have gotten an unfair rap—she did nothing wrong, other than to continue to be faithful to the religious traditions in which she was raised and taught.

The Baals are local fertility gods, worshipped at every village shrine. They are all local manifestations of the great sky-god Baal, who controlled the weather and therefore gave or withheld fertility. Baal gets all the advantages in this contest: 450 prophets to one, hours of incantation to one short petition, and the location is on the border of Baal's native land and far from Mt. Sinai. Even the context of the challenge is Baal's specialty: the drought which has plagued Israel for three years is the result of dry weather, which should be Baal's forte.[178]

The point of the contest is that the god who answers the call, by bringing fire down on the sacrifice, is the real God, who will then be expected to end the drought by bringing rain. Surely this was right up Baal's alley—but in spite of the impressive display of the 450 priests of Baal, "there was no voice; no one answered, no one heeded."

Elijah seems to have presented a very calm, confident demeanor as he went about rebuilding the altar that had been thrown down. Pouring water on the altar seems to our ears to be showmanship, but in Elijah's time it was a form of sympathetic magic: make rain fall on the land as we have poured water on the sacrifice. Repeating the action three times helped ensure the magical effect. Elijah is making a symbolic statement that the old ways of Yahweh, the desert God of Israel, are effective, while the more spectacular show of Baal's prophets is not.

Yahweh's fire falls on Elijah's sacrifice in impressive fashion. Vindication for the persecuted righteous prophet and spectacular

177 Colin Alves, *The Covenant*, Cambridge University Press, London, 1957, p. 66.

178 The four hundred prophets of Ashe'rah, who were subsidized by Queen Jezebel, are invited to the spectacle but play no active part.

punishment for the wrongdoers! Elijah metes out the punishment of the times for losing such a contest by murdering all the opposing prophets of Baal—although considering the logistics of the situation, this may be hyperbole on the part of the storytellers. Finally, Yahweh intervenes to end the drought, using divine power to create rain out of nothing to ease the suffering of the Israelites, who have once again acknowledged that Yah is El—Yahweh is God.

The principle of non-idolatry means God first, foremost, and only. Elijah's story dramatizes that following God requires total commitment—no divided loyalties or hearts. This is not a contest to see who is lord of the mountain, or who is stronger, Yahweh or Baal: it is a test to see who is God. Monotheism is Elijah's claim. There is no God but Yahweh.

Elijah reproaches Ahab (and through him, the people of Israel): How long will you hobble between two opinions? If the Lord is God, follow him: but if Baal, then follow him. And the people answered not a word. We are faced with the same situation, and must wrestle with the same question—how long will we hobble between two opinions? The writers of I Kings had one great theme—monotheism. The point of the Elijah cycle is to teach the benefits of belief in only one God, Yahweh, and the costs of any other belief. A divided loyalty costs us double, as our attentions and energies are split into different, and often conflicting, camps. Our own life reflects the image Elijah presents of hobbling first on one foot, then the other—a sort of hopping made even more difficult by the hobble that keeps our feet unnaturally close together. We may not have been present on Mt. Carmel for Elijah's rather dramatic demonstration, but equally convincing demonstrations—because more personal—surround us every day. "Had we but the eye of faith," as Bill Taber has written, we would see these examples all around us.

There is a fear expressed among many liberal persons that single-pointed devotion to God (as God is experienced by Christians) means that one cannot recognize or honor the truth in other religions, or respect their adherents. Over the centuries, many Christians have behaved as if this were true, with lamentable results. This does not have to be the case; and if we are truly worshipping God, rather than our conception of God, it will *never* be the case.

I cannot know what it is to love and be loved truly and completely until I commit my love to a single person over an extended period of time. Those of us who have been blessed in marriage can testify positively to the truth of this statement. If, like me before I married Susan, you have tried to find this deep love outside of an extended, faithful, monogamous commitment, you can join me in testifying negatively: it can't be done. The love of God is parallel to our love for that one special human being: we have to make that total, unreserved, and undivided commitment to one revelation of God before we can learn and experience the divine love in all its fullness.

After I learned what true love is, then I could look around and see it everywhere. My ability to see and honor love everywhere in the world was enhanced, not diminished, by my undivided love for my wife Susan. Our experience of God is like that. When we have made the unreserved plunge into a covenant relationship with God, when we have experienced God directly and personally through that relationship—why then we look up and see God everywhere. My own ability to see and honor and be thankful for the way God is revealed to the followers of all the great religions— Islam, Hinduism, Buddhism, Judaism, Taoism and the rest—is enhanced as my own relationship to God as encountered in my own faith tradition is deepened and strengthened.

The salad bar approach to spirituality—I'll have a little chanting from here, a little dietary advice from here, an icon from there and some moral teaching from over there—paradoxically does not deepen our ecumenical awareness or enhance our true spiritual growth. What happens is one ends up giving away a little of oneself at each station, never staying long enough or being present fully enough to enter into that great love relationship which is waiting only for our unguarded acceptance. Being human, one tends not to choose those salad bar items that might offer the greatest chance for true spiritual growth because they look distasteful, old-fashioned, or hard to swallow.

Elijah's image of hobbling, first on one foot and then another, is a wonderful description of the effect of divided loyalties. We can't step forward fully on either foot, because we are tied to the other which is walking a different path. Thousands of years have passed, but human nature is unchanged and Elijah's message is as valid and pertinent today as when he confronted Ahab. If we are to walk into the reign of God, then God must be at the center of our life and our story, with no competing idols.

Monday night I spoke of encountering Yahweh in the burning bush as the profoundly "other." We can keep God at the center of our story and resist the temptations to put idols there instead only to the extent that we remember that God is Yahweh—a power, not only a presence, a light, or a guide. Elijah's story reminds us forcefully of just that: God is the ultimate power—creator of the universe, willing and able to intervene in human affairs for the sake of the people of the creation. That we are made in the image of God reminds us at the same time that God also has the attributes of person, which enables us to enter into the deep personal relationship with God that seems so clearly to be the divine desire.

We who live on the verge of the twenty-first century have the advantage, to paraphrase Isaac Newton, of being able to stand on the shoulders of giants. Thanks to those who have gone before us and who have shared their learnings and experiences, we know—far better than the people of Old Testament times—that God is both immanent and transcendent. The common expression among Friends about "that of God in every one" would have been blasphemy to Elijah; but we know it to be blessed truth. I feel the touch of God within, and know it to be undeserved mercy, unmerited grace—and I expect I am not alone in this experience among those gathered here tonight.

However grateful we may be for this new truth, it does not nullify older truth, but expands and fulfills it. God did not give up divine transcendence when we discovered a divine guide within. Unfortunately, there is a modern tendency to fall into thinking that God is only interior to myself—a sort of personal guidebook that will help me make good choices, but powerless to affect the physical world. We are reluctant to pray for specific physical events in part because we are afraid that God can't really bring them about. Elijah's demonstration on Mount Carmel is a resounding rebuttal to that pattern of thought. Elijah is direct and dramatic in his action. "Here is Yahweh, God who is real and God who can do dramatic acts that no pretend-gods can. Believe in the real God, the true Power!" It is Baal who proves to be powerless to intervene in the physical world, and Yahweh who hears the call of one solitary prophet and displays divine power in the most dramatic of fashions. Finally it is Yahweh who produces a cloud out of nothing and ends the drought by bringing the rain down in torrents.

Yahweh, the God of all creation, of limitless power and infinite love, is pleased to give us the kingdom: to introduce us to the joys of the divine economy, to the peace of the peaceable kingdom, to the perfect life of the new Jerusalem, to the new heaven and new earth. The catch is that there is no catch: simply live in a way that allows Yahweh to provide. That means to live without silos, without kings, and with no idols to compete for the loyalty and faith that rightfully belong to Yahweh alone.

Friday: Continuing the Story

Filled with the Holy Spirit, Jesus left the Jordan and was led by the Spirit into the desert, for forty days being put to the test by the devil. During that time he ate nothing and at the end he was hungry. Then the devil said to him, "If you are Son of God, tell this stone to turn into a loaf." But Jesus replied, Scripture says: *"Human beings live not on bread alone."*

Then leading him to a height, the devil showed him in a moment of time all the kingdoms of the world and said to him, "I will give you all this power and their splendour, for it has been handed over to me, for me to give it to anyone I choose. Do homage, then, to me, and it shall all be yours." But Jesus answered him, Scripture says: *"You must do homage to the Lord your God, him alone you must serve."*

Then he led him to Jerusalem and set him on the parapet of the temple. "If you are Son of God," he said to him, "Throw yourself down from here, for Scripture says: *"He has given his angels orders about you, to guard you."*

And again: *"They will carry you in their arms in case you trip over a stone."*

But Jesus answered him, Scripture says: *"Do not put the Lord your God to the test."*

Having exhausted every way of putting him to the test, the devil left him, until the opportune moment.[179]

In his life and teachings Jesus chose to continue the big story, to live into the reign of God. He paid a series of escalating prices for this decision: misunderstanding of family and friends, disapproval and rejection from many whom he wished deeply to reach with his message, betrayal from those closest to him, and ultimately death by grisly execution on the part of those in power in the promised land. We, too, are called to continue the big story, to live into the reign of God. Repeatedly Jesus warns us that the cost to us will be no less than the cost to him: the price of discipleship is everything. Lest we think that we can slip into the reign of God like slipping on a bathrobe, or sweep out our old life and habits like cleaning a house, Jesus told a parable:

> When an unclean spirit goes out of someone it wanders through waterless country looking for a place to rest, and not finding one it says, "I will go back to the home I came from." But on arrival, finding it swept and tidied, it then goes off and brings seven other spirits more wicked than itself, and they go in and set up house there, and so that person ends up worse off than before.[180]

This is how it will be with us: the more we clean our lens of discernment and clean up our practice, the more stuff we will dredge up from within that must be dealt with, and the more our outward practice must be cleaned up. In fact, Jesus is saying it will get harder and harder as we go along, not easier and easier! When I exorcise one demon from my life, seven more will assault me. If I succeed in overcoming them, forty-nine more will come! And if by great effort I drive them out of my life—well, you do the math.

Jesus is not painting a picture of instant victory, of being born again in a moment of time and forever after free to live wholly in the reign of God. His imagery seems much closer to Friends understanding of the "conversion of manners:" the life-long effort to

179 Luke 4:1–12, New Jerusalem Bible.
180 Luke 11:24–26, New Jerusalem Bible.

bring one's inner and outer life—one's manners—into conformity with one's vision of the divine will, or the gospel order.

Jesus warns us again about how hard it will be to be non-Egyptian in the land of pharaoh later on in Luke's gospel, in the parable of the talents, or the parable of the pounds, as the New Jerusalem Bible calls it. Not only will our inner work be fierce and life-long, the world around us will actively oppose our efforts, even if all we are trying to do is to be neutral, like the third servant in this passage from Luke chapter 19:

> While the people were listening to this he went on to tell a parable, because he was near Jerusalem and they thought that the kingdom of God was going to show itself then and there. Accordingly he said, "A man of noble birth went to a distant country to be appointed king and then to return. He summoned ten of his servants and gave them ten pounds, telling them, "Trade with these, until I get back." But his compatriots detested him and sent a delegation to follow him with this message, "We do not want this man to be our king."
>
> Now it happened that on his return, having received his appointment as king, he sent for those servants to whom he had given the money, to find out what profit each had made by trading. The first came in, "Sir," he said, "your one pound has brought in ten." He replied, "Well done, my good servant! Since you have proved yourself trustworthy in a very small thing, you shall have the government of ten cities." Then came the second, "Sir," he said, "Your one pound has made five." To this one also he said, "And you shall be in charge of five cities." Next came the other, "Sir," he said, "Here is your pound. I put it away safely wrapped up in a cloth because I was afraid of you; for you are an exacting man: you gather in what you have not laid out and reap what you have not sown." He said to him, "You wicked servant! Out of your own mouth I condemn you. So you knew that I was an exacting man, gathering in what I have not laid out and reaping what I have not sown? Then why did you not put my money in the bank? On my return I could have drawn it out with interest." And he said to those standing by, "Take the pound from him and give it to the man who has ten pounds." And they said to him, "But, sir, he has ten pounds. . . ." "I tell you, to

everyone who has will be given more; but anyone who has not will be deprived even of what he has."

"As for my enemies who did not want me for their king, bring them here and execute them in my presence."[181]

Now I grew up thinking—and being taught—that this parable was about making the best use of the gifts or talents that God had given me. God is the king, right? And I'm supposed to be like the first servant, and do great things with my talents, earning a rich reward from God. If I can't do that, I should at least be like the second servant and do good things and get a good reward. At all costs I should avoid being like the third servant, who didn't use his talents at all, and was punished. And that model was confirmed in the life that went on around me: straight-A students and basketball stars got rewarded, poor students and clumsy folks got punished and harassed.

That's the North American reading of this parable—the reading from the perspective of the dominant culture—and I bought into it completely, along with my schoolteachers and parents and pastor and fellow Methodist Youth Fellowship members. We silently agreed, along with the rest of the dominant culture, to ignore the real difficulties this reading of the text produces. If God is the king, why did he have to get appointed by someone else? Who are the folks who followed after him to lobby against his appointment? Does God really gather in what he has not laid out and reap what he has not sown? Does God really take up the cause of the rich against that of the poor, to the extent of robbing the poor to give to the rich? How does this king's execution of his enemies match up with what Jesus taught about loving our enemies and praying for them that persecute us? This is a very difficult parable, indeed, but we ignored it for the easy interpretation that God wants us to make a profit and God will reward us even more for making a big profit: a theology of prosperity.

It took poor people, people at the bottom of the social pyramid, to tell us what this parable is really about. In the base communities of Latin America, the peasants read this passage without the benefit

181 Luke 19:11–27, New Jerusalem Bible.

of "educated" persons to tell them what it meant. Free from that distortion, they saw clearly that God was not the king in this parable. The king was the local strong man, the one with the power and the money and the prestige to control the community. The first two servants were the people who go along with the system, collaborating with the strong man and supporting the existing structure of society. The third servant is the one who tries to live a kingdom life; in fact, all he is doing here is trying to be neutral. He is not opposing the strong man, simply trying not to participate in the unjust economic system. Even that is unacceptable, and he is robbed of what little he had. As for those who dared to make a political protest, even their lives are taken from them.

This reading turns the parable upside down. The king is not God; he is God's adversary. Instead of striving to be like the first two servants and different from the third servant, we should strive to be like the third servant and unlike the first two! The deep message here is that trying to live like non-Egyptians in the land of pharaoh will draw the active opposition and persecution of the existing economic, political, and religious power systems. They cannot bear to allow the reign of God to coexist with them.

Now when this reading of the parable made it back to the seminaries in the large cities of South America, and eventually to the seminaries of North America and Europe, theologians saw immediately that now every sentence of the parable made sense, and the problems of the former reading were all dissolved. A little historical research revealed that a man named Archelaus had indeed gone from Jerusalem to Rome in 4 BCE, to have the will of Herod the Great confirmed in his name. A deputation of Jews in fact followed him to Rome to lobby against him, but failed to defeat his nomination. When Jesus said, "A man of noble birth went to a distant country to be appointed king and then return," his audience knew immediately he was referring to Archelaus, not God. The rural peasants of Latin America had gotten the parable right.

From either perspective, the effort to live in the reign of God looks to be a lifelong struggle, full of pain and discouragement. Our inner work will be an experience of driving out demon after demon, never seeming to get ahead no matter how hard we try, how disciplined we become. Our efforts to establish the reign of God in our outward lives will meet with the active opposition and outright persecution of all the structures and institutions of society, much more powerful than we and able to constantly overwrite all our efforts.

So all our efforts appear to be doomed to failure. The whole Gospel of Mark can be seen in this context: in Mark's story Jesus' project to teach his disciples collapses, he regroups and tries again, and the project collapses again. The reader of Mark's gospel knows, however, that somehow the story continues, somehow the project has not failed—because we are reading the story, we ourselves are caught up in the effort to live discipleship lives.

So we have on the one hand the doctrine of perfection: "Be ye therefore perfect, even as your father which is in heaven is perfect."[182] a principle long affirmed by Friends[183] and Scripture. On the other hand we have Jesus apparently teaching that the forces in opposition to our discipleship are so strong that we will never wholly reside in the reign of God. We live in that in-between place, caught between the now and the not yet: never allowed by the doctrine of perfection to rest short of the reign of God, yet never arriving in the promised land—wandering painfully and with great effort in the desert.

Yet we follow the pillar of fire and the column of smoke: there is a pattern to our lives of effort that we only rarely, briefly, and incompletely glimpse. And always there is Emmanuel, God-with-us, infusing and redeeming the present moment with infinite, unmerited grace.

How do we live in that in-between place, how do we carry on the big story, how do we live as non-Egyptians in the land of pharaoh? I would like to suggest some rules of the road, some directions for the journey.

First, living as non-Egyptians will require a **change in perspective** to the view from the bottom. We need to see the world from

---

182 Matthew 5:48, King James Version.

183 e.g., Barclay's *Apology* and more recently, *A Brief Synopsis of the Principles and Testimonies of the Religious Society of Friends*, approved by the seven Conservative yearly meetings in 1912.

the perspective of those with no silos, no kings, and no idols: the poor, the powerless, and the peripheral. When Jesus said we could not enter the kingdom of heaven unless we became as little children, he was holding up as example those who are least powerful, who have the least possessions and options of their own, who are most dependent on an economy of grace for their very survival. We must learn to see the world from that perspective. As the example of the parable of Luke 19 so clearly shows, everything looks very different from this new perspective, and much that was unclear or confusing becomes crystal clear in its meaning.

This is not a virtual reality experience. This can't be done with mirrors or visits to the Head Start center. To begin to shift from our perspective as part of the dominant class to a God's "preferential option for the poor," we will have to be with the poor ourselves: not merely doing good things for them, but standing with them in their pain and vulnerability and their poverty.

Standing with the poor, we will realize God's preferential option throughout history, from Exodus onward: God as liberator—caring, choosing sides, and intervening in human history. From that perspective it becomes clear that Scripture is written by and for the underclass.

Living in the big story requires a **change in questions**. The dominant question in North American religious circles today is "How do I succeed religiously?" That is, "How do I get to heaven?" or "How can I be saved?" When we begin to see the world from a different perspective, the question becomes "Why is the world this way?" followed by "What can I do about it?" To live as non-Egyptians we must move beyond the personal pronoun, get ourselves out of the center of our story and put Yahweh at the center. We must look at the world with Yahweh's eyes and act accordingly.

Asking a different question results in a **change in goal**. Our project in North America has been building up the church; God's project as lived out in the Scripture stories has been and is beginning the reign of God. Our culture sees a full church as a sign of a successful ministry. It can be—but it often is just as much an idol in itself, because we put our faith in church membership to do

Yahweh's work. Jesus Christ, God's beloved son, seems to have gotten his ministry cracking only when he stopped attending formal worship services, because he was no longer wanted there. When our goal is the reign of God, church membership figures and Sabbath worship attendance are peripheral, not central, measures of our work. The institutional church is no longer the only way station to heaven.

A change in goal requires a **change in means**. Our hierarchical society follows what may be called the "banking theory" in many different fields, from education to salvation to national development to cultural growth. In the banking theory, there are two parties: party A, who has a large bank account full of stuff, and party B, who doesn't have any stuff at all. Party A opens an account for party B and deposits a certain amount of stuff in party B's account. After this happens, party B is educated, or saved, or culturally developed, or whatever. Ever have a schoolteacher like that? I have.

The banking theory is a great model for hierarchical societies. In the reign of God, we need to use a different means. The leading contender seems to be what Paulo Freire calls conscientization—a word difficult to pronounce in every language. If there is no dominant institution to do good things to the poor, then we poor will have to do good with each other: self-liberation (by grace). From learning to read to Bible exegesis to economic development to political organization, this self-help process of conscientization has proven to be the one effective means of truly liberating people from their dependence on (read bondage to) dominant institutions—even benevolent institutions.

As we begin to see, perhaps still far off in the distance, the coming reign of God we will begin to experience a **change in issues**. Issues of race, gender, religious denomination, sexual orientation, or ethnic background that now seem so divisive will not seem so important. In fact, they are often merely tools used by those who benefit from the dominant culture to protect their position. The real issues will be the three P's: power, possessions, and prestige. In analyzing any situation, in attempting to understand our circumstances and what we should to try to move closer to the reign of God, our questions become: Who has the power? Prestige?

Possessions? Where are the silos? Who wields the authority? Who receives the worship that is rightfully Yahweh's?

Understanding God's project among humans as we have explored it this week leads to a **change in sin**. North American culture has overemphasized individual wrongdoing and virtually ignored structural, corporate evil. This focus on personal righteousness keeps most of us too preoccupied with our own holiness to pay any attention to institutional evil, and too worried that our own sinfulness will be revealed to speak up about what we do see. Let us have less emphasis on who I go to bed with tonight and more on how I may abuse the power, prestige, and possessions that are under my influence. This is not to say that "anything goes" when it comes to personal morality—that is simply not so. However, let us not allow Egypt to divert all our attention from the principles of the reign of God to personal righteousness: that only allows them to proceed unopposed.

We've been talking a lot this week about how to live, and not very much at all about what to believe. Living as non-Egyptians in the land of pharaoh will involve for most of us a change in emphasis from **orthodoxy to orthopraxy**. Our emphasis in the North American church as been on right belief: doctrine shaped by the Bible as read through the filter of Paul's epistles. We argue whether or not Paul was sexist, or this-ist, or that-ist; but right doctrine, or right belief, seems less than central to Jesus' project, to say the least. Our emphasis must instead be on right action: individual and group practice shaped by the Bible as read through the filter of Jesus' gospel and life. Theology is the second step, as a reflection on *praxis* in the light of faith—*praxis* comes first.

Most Christian theology has been the result of what is called *a priori* thinking: from first principles. In *a priori* theology one considers first what God must be like, and from that what Jesus and the Holy Spirit must be like, and from that what creation and the fellowship of believers must be like, and from that one concludes what is moral and what is not: how one should behave. That sort of thinking has run us way up some box canyons over the centuries, and seems on its face unsuited to what we've been saying about the perspective of the poor and marginalized.

Our emphasis needs to be on right action—*orthopraxy*—rather than on right belief—*orthodoxy*. The model for doing that thoughtfully is *praxis*: the cycle of action and reflection. First comes action: encountering the world in what seems like right action. Then comes reflection: contemplating one's actions and their consequences to learn what one can about how the world really is and what one's experience tells one about God and how God must want us to behave. From these insights one then chooses a next action, and the cycle continues. Is this theology? Absolutely! But it is theology based on our experience, not on our imagination of what God must be like. Our imagination and our experience are always finite and incomplete, while God is infinite beyond comprehension; but experience always shakes us out of our boundaries and opens us up to more potentials.

All these changes both reflect and help bring about a **change in scope** for our spiritual work, from individual spiritual salvation to creation-wide integral liberation. Every part of every individual must be free from involuntary poverty and oppression to achieve God's plan for creation. There are no throwaway people, no human beings outside God's good news, and no part of creation that is disposable or for which God has no regard.

The Buddhist tradition speaks of the Bodhisattva, who achieves Buddhahood but rejects it in order to go back into the world to help any and every soul who has not yet achieved enlightenment. When as Christians we glimpse the big story in all its glory, then we can no longer strive for our individual salvation irrespective of the rest of creation. Instead we must commit ourselves to God's project to liberate each and every soul and every part of this creation which God created and sustains from moment to moment and loves so much. By "liberate" I don't mean some sort of escapist, spaceship theology that tells the suffering and oppressed person to ignore their pain and think about the great time they're going to have in heaven after they die. I mean that we must commit ourselves to hearing the cry of the oppressed and suffering, as Yahweh heard the Israelites; we must truly and deeply care for their plight, and we must commit ourselves wholeheartedly to intervene in the very structure of human society to end their suffering. Only then do we have any right to talk to anyone about spiritual salvation.

It is an impossible task, as we have discussed; it is the only meaningful role we have in creation. It has never been achieved, yet it is always just around the corner, just beginning to become reality, all around us and yet nowhere. We are caught between the now and the not-yet, as Paul writes in 2 Corinthians:

> In everything we prove ourselves authentic servants of God; by resolute perseverance in times of hardships, difficulties and distress; when we are flogged or sent to prison or mobbed; labouring, sleepless, starving, in purity, in knowledge, in patience, in kindness; in the Holy Spirit, in a love free of affectation; in the word of truth and in the power of God; by using the weapons of uprightness for attack and for defence: in times of honor or disgrace, blame or praise, taken for imposters and yet we are genuine; unknown and yet we are acknowledged; dying, and yet here we are, alive; scourged but not executed; in pain yet always full of joy; poor and yet making many people rich; having nothing, and yet owning everything.[184]

We have the assurance of things unseen, setting out by faith from this kingdom to the next, living ever as strangers in our own land, as non-Egyptians in the land of pharaoh, living in the promise of the new heaven and new earth foreseen in John's vision. O come, Emmanuel.

---

[184] 2 Corinthians 6:4–10, New Jerusalem Bible.

About the Author

Lloyd Lee Wilson was born in 1947 on the Eastern Shore of Maryland and raised in the Methodist Church. He became a certified lay speaker in his early teenage years, and served as a replacement preacher for several area churches.

While attending college at MIT, Lloyd Lee became estranged from the Methodist Church and began to doubt his Christian faith. A period of spiritual seeking which lasted several years ended when he was invited to attend a Quaker meeting in Cambridge, Massachusetts, where he had a deep spiritual experience including the reassurance that he had found his permanent spiritual home.

Convinced of the correctness of the Friends spiritual path, Lloyd Lee joined the Religious Society of Friends at Friends Meeting of Cambridge and resigned his reserve commission in the air force on the grounds of conscientious objection. He was eventually discharged "at the convenience of the government" and began a career of service in the management of nonprofit and charitable organizations.

Lloyd Lee has been active in Quaker institutions since he became a convinced Friend. His service has included the Permanent Board of New England Yearly Meeting, the board of managers of the Bible Association of Friends in America, the board of directors of the American Friends Service Committee, and various committees in Baltimore Yearly Meeting and North Carolina Yearly Meeting (Conservative). He has served as General Secretary of Friends General Conference, clerk of North Carolina Yearly Meeting (Conservative) and of the Meeting of Ministers, Elders and Overseers of that yearly meeting, and as assistant clerk of the Communications Commission of Friends United Meeting. In 1989 Virginia Beach Friends Meeting, where Lloyd Lee was then a member, acknowledged him as a minister of the gospel.

Lloyd Lee's previous publications include *Essays on the Quaker Vision of Gospel Order*, a contribution to *Walk Worthy of Your Calling*, and numerous pamphlets and articles in Quaker publications. He is a frequent speaker among Friends groups and to other audiences.

In 2000 Lloyd Lee and his family transferred their membership to Rich Square Monthly Meeting in Woodland, North Carolina, following a leading that they should help nurture and sustain that faith community, the "mother meeting" of Conservative Friends in North Carolina. Rich Square Monthly Meeting has also acknowledged him as a minister of the gospel.

Lloyd Lee's work career has been dedicated to using his management skills and training to help nonprofit and charitable organizations in fields such as housing for low-income persons, affordable health care, and services to victims of domestic violence. He presently serves as Registrar, Assistant Professor of Accounting, and Director of Institutional Research at Chowan College in Murfreesboro, North Carolina 27855. He can be contacted via email at llwilson@alum.mit.edu.